Contents

Contributors

Professor Paul W MacAvoy is Williams Brothers Professor of Management Studies, Yale School of Management, New Haven, Connecticut.

William J Baumol is Director of the C V Starr Center for Applied Economics, Professor of Economics, New York University, and Professor Emeritus, Princeton University.

J Gregory Sidak holds the F K Weyerhaeuser Chair in Law and Economics at the American Enterprise Institute for Public Policy Research, Washington DC.

Michael J Doane is a Principal, Analysis Group Inc, San Francisco, California.

Michael A Williams is Vice President, Analysis Group Inc, San Francisco, California.

Adam B Jaffe is Associate Professor of Economics at Brandeis University and a Principal of the Economics Resource Group, Cambridge, Mass.

Stephen D Makowka is a Consultant with the Economics Resource Group, Cambridge, Massachusetts.

Todd Strauss is Assistant Professor of Public Policy and Management Science at the Yale School of Management, New Haven, Connecticut.

Dennis E Logue is Steven Roth Professor of Management, Amos Tuck School of Business Administration, Dartmouth College, Hanover, New Hampshire.

Sharon M Oster is Frederic D Wolfe Professor of Management and Entrepreneurship at the Yale School of Management, New Haven, Connecticut.

George S McIsaac is AT&T Resident Management Fellow and Executive Professor, Business and Publiic Administration, at the William E Simon Graduate School of Business Administration, University of Rochester, Rochester, New York.

John Burton is Professor of Business Administration at the Birmingham Business School, University of Birmingham, Birmingham, England.

THE DAVID HUME INSTITUTE

Hume Papers on Public Policy
Volume 3 No 3 Autumn 1995

DEREGULATION AND PRIVATIZATION IN THE UNITED STATES

Edited by
Paul W MacAvoy

EDINBURGH UNIVERSITY PRESS

Edinburgh University Press
22 George Square, Edinburgh
Transferred to digital print 2008
Typeset in Times New Roman by WestKey Limited, Falmouth,
Cornwall and printed and bound in Great Britain by
CPI Antony Rowe, Eastbourne

A CIP record for this book is available from the British Library

ISBN 0 7486 0738 2

Foreword

On 5 and 6 May 1995 there took place at the Yale School of Management a conference on the theme of deregulation and privatization in the United States. The conference was organised by Paul W MacAvoy, Williams Brothers Professor of Management Studies in the School, and a member of both the Advisory Council of The David Hume Institute and the Editorial Board of *Hume Papers on Public Policy*. Over two stimulating days, conference attendees presented and discussed the papers final versions of which are now published in this issue of *Hume Papers on Public Policy*. The David Hume Institute is delighted to be able to bring these papers before a wider audience, and is grateful to Professor MacAvoy for the initiative which has enabled this publication to occur, although as usual it will leave the authors with the entire responsibility for their various statements, arguments and conclusions. The collection was designed to inform readers of *Hume Papers on Public Policy* worldwide about the US experience on deregulation and privatization to date. The collection is thus essentially and naturally concerned with the US experience of deregulation and privatization. But there are lessons to be learned in Britain (and perhaps Europe as well), where the future of privatization and regulation of enterprises formerly owned by the State is very much on the agenda.

In the opening paper, MacAvoy surveys twenty years of deregulation, noting that industries labouring under, first, price-control regulation and then, more recently, health and safety regulation, have performed poorly; and forecasts substantial deregulation of the whole American economy by the end of the century. Baumol and Sidak provide a fascinating analysis of the regulatory problems posed for network industries such as telecommunications by technological change facilitating "interconnection pricing", where competitors are buying services from the incumbent against whom they sell in the market, e.g., local distribution of electricity, natural gas, or telephone calls.

Doane and Williams explore the problem of "stranded costs" for incumbent utilities, which arises when costs, having been incurred through past investments and contractual arrangements, cannot be fully recovered owing to regulatory changes that affect the pricing regime. Jaffe and Makowka examine in detail the regulatory developments in natural gas transportation, and argue for a combination of further deregulation and, where regulation continues, flexibility in relation to what has been perceived as the natural monopoly of gas pipeline transportation. Strauss examines environmental regulation, and concludes that where "the market has been tried, it works better than command-and-control" in reducing sulphur emissions, but where the market has not been tried, as in reducing nitrogen emissions, there have been extremely limited results.

The thrust of all these papers is the success and widespread effects of deregulation in the United States; this may be contrasted with the disappointing experience of privatization. Logue puts forward a political explanation for this phenomenon, the vested interests of politicians and officials in state-owned enterprises. Oster focuses on the US mail service, arguing that it is run more as a welfare program than as a commercial enterprise, and putting the case for more deregulation and privatization. MacAvoy and McIsaac wrap up the American contribution by pointing out that the prices charged by public sector enterprises in the United States have increased more rapidly than those of comparable private sector companies, while they also show a relative decline in productivity. It is argued that the case for further privatization seems strong.

This American picture may be contrasted with that of Britain and Europe, which has seen extensive privatization but far less deregulation; indeed, arguably, regulation has increased and continues to grow. The David Hume Institute is grateful to Professor John Burton for agreeing to provide the commentary on the papers summarised above, considering the issues raised from a British perspective. The growth of regulation is contrasted with the original spirit of the privatization movement in the UK which, under the influence of Professor Littlechild, was one of increased competition in the medium term, albeit after an initial period of regulation. Burton finds the contrasting experience to lie far back in the respective histories of the two countries. But this does not mean that Britain has nothing to learn from the American experience. The form of regulation established in Britain in the 1980s was deliberately different from that in the USA, although the promotion of competition where hitherto there had been none was seen as the central task of the regulatory agencies, rather than price capping. But in fact price capping has been the most significant element in the practice of regulation, and competition has been slow to arrive. This has led to debate about regulation in the future. Burton suggests that the lesson of these essays may be, not more regulation, but liberalization: 'competition where feasible, regulation only where not', and even then, to be based upon the relevant principles of economics. With the initial momentum of the privatization movement faltering in the UK, the essays presented below offer a valuable US perspective on an alternative regulatory regime that is itself in a state of flux.

Hector L MacQueen and Brian G M Main
Directors
The David Hume Institute

Twenty Years of Deregulation

Paul W. MacAvoy

Synopsis

The Gerald Ford Administration experiment in deregulation of the price-controlled industries generated in successive administrations a broadly-based reduction in the percentage of gross domestic product in the regulated sector. At the same time, expansion of health and safety enhancement policies put in place another regulatory system in much of manufacturing. However, the continued poor performance of the regulated industries under both regimes has ensured that deregulation will continue at a significant rate. By the end of the century the United States economy should be substantially deregulated.

*   *   *   *

Although the American experience with governmental control of industry dates from state-mandated road tolls and grain storage charges in the 1820s, specific federal regulation by an agency operating under a Congressional statute began little more than one hundred years ago. The Act to Regulate Commerce (1887) marked this beginning by establishing the Interstate Commerce Commission to set railroad rates and (later) prices for telephone service. Many state governments, following the lead of Massachusetts, set up agencies before the turn of the century to control prices of transportation companies and electric and gas utilities within their borders.

After a second surge of legislative activity to extend controls of prices in the economically depressed 1930s, federal and state regulation encompassed the utility energy (electric and gas), transportation (railroad, truck, and airline) and communications (telephone and telegraph) industries. The Federal Food, Drug and Cosmetic Act of 1938 rewrote a 1906 Act to extend authority to a federal agency to eliminate products from markets that did not meet safety and effectiveness standards. Federal/state agencies and bureaus controlled entry and some prices of banking and financial institutions, and controlled entry but not pricing in radio and (later) television broadcasting.[1] A third broad-based wave of new regulatory policy "deregulation" in the 1970s, this time of "deregulation", pushed back these agencies so that they no longer had jurisdiction in more than half of these industries. Yet, at the same time, the scope of regulation

---

[1] Last of all, the Congress in successive statutes regulated entry and pricing, then deregulated, and then reregulated cable television. Cf. Hazlett, T.W. & Spitzer, M., *Cable Television: Competition, Regulation, and the First Amendment*, AEI Press, Washington, D.C., 1995.

was extended – to enhance product safety and the quality of the environment – to establish jurisdiction over most, if not all, of manufacturing.

Important questions for the performance of the economy are prompted by this movement of government in and out of business. How widespread has regulation become, and does it result in lower prices, increased production, and increased quality of products and the environment? Has deregulation in the last twenty years then succeeded in finding the efficiency boundaries on the use of the regulatory process?

To answer these questions there should be agreement first on what constitutes "regulation". The agencies define it in terms of procedures they have developed to implement statute requirements – procedures quite different from those used in other governmental organizations. First and foremost they determine whether companies in a statute-defined jurisdiction are to be allowed to provide service in the process of granting them a certificate of "necessity and convenience". As a condition of operating the franchise, they have approved "just and reasonable" prices. For fifty years the procedure for doing so has centered on company submissions calling for prices or rates that would generate revenue just sufficient to cover operating and capital costs inclusive of "reasonable" returns to stockholders.

Even though setting the tariff has been the focal point in regulation, there have been substantial differences in methods for doing so across agencies and their jurisdictions. In transportation and banking, the regulatory agencies have had to deal with too many companies to set individual tariffs and instead have resorted to capping prices across companies at levels consistent with their average costs of service. In the 1960s and 1970s, this price cap system was extended first to natural gas and then to crude-oil production, as Congress tried to hold down prices during periods of shortages. Both established and newly-created agencies put in place price ceilings in designated field areas that had the tendency to enlarge and prolong the shortages. The airline regulatory agency allowed any airline serving a city-pair to charge up to a maximum set by industry-wide cost index numbers. This again caused the high-cost suppliers to reduce their services or exit from city-pair markets with higher than average operating costs.

The regulation of savings and loan institutions centered on ceilings on the rates they could offer for deposits. The late 1960s saw a burst of inflation, and the oil crisis of the early 1970s fueled further inflation that coincided with the end of the post WWII housing boom. However, regulators did not allow rates to change until March 1980, when interest rate controls were phased out and savings and loan institutions were allowed to invest in and sell adjustable rate products that could adapt to changing conditions. But bank and brokerage competition forced thrifts to pay up to eighteen percent to depositors, while maintaining mortgage portfolios financed by deposits at six percent. Price ceilings were raised too late, and without authorization to improve or diversify financial product offerings, so that these institutions were forced to speculate on potential high return investments with low probabilities of returns, setting the stage for the 1980s bankruptcies.

But these procedures do not constitute a description of "health and safety" regulation. The statutes calling for this new type of regulation certainly did not specify the use of the orthodox tariff system to develop health, safety, and environmental improvements. Rather than focusing on pricing, the relevant agencies require that companies install equipment or processes to reduce specified harmful or dangerous conditions. This "command and control" method was developed in meat packing and pharmaceuticals in the first half of the century and extended in the 1970s to chemicals, paper, automobile and other manufacturing industries.

The second step in answering the basic questions is to assess the changes that have taken place in the last two decades in the boundaries between regulated and unregulated industry. The system of price controls has greatly contracted in its coverage of industry. Public antagonism to energy shortages, and to declining quality of service in transportation, both attributable to price controls in the 1970s, moved Congress to reduce federal regulation in these industries. This policy shift did not occur all at once nor was it entirely consistent over time. But it went beyond making mid-course corrections in the process to curtailing agency coverage and even to eliminating one of the key agencies.

The Ford Administration in the mid-1970s began deregulation by proposing to end federal control of airlines, trucking companies, natural gas producers, and, spaced over five years, crude-oil and petroleum products producers. With one exception, that for petroleum products, President Ford and his White House staff were not able to convince Congress to pass the necessary legislation. But the Carter Administration, by the end of the 1970s, had successfully sponsored legislation to abolish regulation of the airlines and also to phase out federal controls over interstate railroads and trucking. In setting out energy policy, President Carter and his staff initiated legislation that would end price controls on natural gas at the wellhead by the mid-1980s.

The Reagan Administration made deregulation (or "Regulatory Relief") one of the four foundations of its New Economic Program for the 1980s. Price controls of petroleum products, which were being phased out according to the Ford initiative, were eliminated entirely by an early Reagan Administration Executive Order. More sweeping was the Reagan Order that required any agency promulgating a new regulation to undertake the burden of proving that it would improve the performance of the economy. The agencies' response has taken decades. Indeed, it remains to be determined whether such "benefit" analyses are required in most cases, such as for existing regulations and for health or safety regulation. The 1995 Congressional "Contract with America" calls for finally making that requirement universal and immediate. Even so, regulation was greatly reduced in the 1980s by rulemaking in the agencies themselves, as undertaken by Reagan and Bush Administration appointees to chair positions. Barriers to competition were lowered in telephone, gas and electric service markets and prices were allowed to fall, even below levels determined as "reasonable" in the tariffs.

This patchwork of reductions in controls resulted from numerous, uncoordinated initiatives by the Executive Office, Congress and the regulatory commissions themselves. The common driving force, however, was a new political consensus on where to set more restrictive limits on regulatory activity in the domestic economy.

The justification since the Act to Regulate Commerce had been that regulation was necessary for firms with market power to hold prices down and thereby increase supply of goods and services to consumers. But such public justification was never enough to put in place a full system of controls. In establishing regulation of railroad rates in the 1880s, Congress was responding to shippers' antagonism toward discriminatory pricing by the rail cartels, which had those shipping goods longer distances paying less, or paying half during periods of competitive discounting of the cartel tariff. But in addition, the railroads in the cartels anticipated that their long-distance rates would increase and discounts would be made illegal so that they stood to gain.[2] Both trucking and airline regulation were based on rationale that included potential gains for producers similar to those in railroad regulation. While the Motor Carrier Act of 1935 sought to "promote adequate, economical, and efficient service," it also had as its goal that regulation "develop and preserve a transportation system adapted to the needs of commerce," which was to be achieved by controlling competition. The House Report accompanying the Civil Aeronautics Act of 1938 set out that the purpose of regulation was to prevent high passenger fares but also to prevent "competing carriers from engaging in rate wars which would be disastrous to all concerned." Regulation was to bring an end to "this chaotic situation of the air carriers which has shaken the faith of the investing public in the financial stability and prevented the flow of funds into the industry."

Regulation of natural gas, electricity, and telephone companies was put in place by both federal and state legislators not only to set prices based on costs of service but also to extend more service to favored classes of consumers. In the Communications Act of 1934, the Federal Communications Commission was to "make available so far as possible to all people of the United States a rapid, efficient, nationwide and worldwide wire and cable service with adequate facilities at reasonable charges." This was taken by that agency to be a requirement that prices to consumers on the high-cost fringe of the market had to be below the costs required to sustain their services, and prices elsewhere in the system had to be set above costs to cover resulting losses.

Regulation was intended further to have stabilizing effects on the economy. No matter in which infrastructure industry, once established, the tariff setting process was supposed to prevent sharp increases in prices at any point in time but to allow price levels that generated sufficient revenues to cover costs over the lifetime of plant and equipment. Such rate averaging, over long periods of time, and over classes of service, was intended to have dampening effects on inflation. Unregulated commodity prices could increase rapidly, responding to sharp increases in current marginal costs, but regulated utility prices stayed constant according to average historical costs.

Thus the regulatory agency had to manage a complex combination of non-competitive, service-oriented and artificially stabilized prices. They were

2 MacAvoy, P. W., *The Economic Effects of Regulation: The Trunkline Railroad Cartels and the Interstate Commerce Commission 1870 – 1900* (MIT Press, 1965).

non-competitive given that the regulated firm had market power. But if the firm did not then subsidize service in some markets the agency had to restrict competing services to raise prices in other markets. This was done by holding supply at monopolistic levels to the extent necessary to generate enough excess profits to provide the required subsidies. There had to be cash flow from high-priced services to extend supply to fringe consumers, to have "available so far as possible to all people of the United Sates a rapid, efficient, nationwide service." But during periods of high inflation, these same prices had to be held stable (not to just cover current costs of services). Achieving that combination required elaborate systems of management; and where that system broke down, due to politics, markets, and technology, so did regulation.

The new consensus was to the effect that, given the experience of the 1960s and 1970s, prices could not be reduced or stabilized by regulation. Further, while cross-subsidization was to be achieved, it could not be contained, as more groups sought to be the subsidized and not the subsidizer. The limit was the monopoly price, with maximum transfer payments to impacted classes of customers, fixed over decades without response to new products or services waiting on the fringe of the market.

The Current Extent of Regulation

What then is regulated in the mid-1990s in the United States? The important sectors subject to regulation are shown in Table One, in terms of their contributions to total gross domestic product (GDP).

TABLE 1   PERCENT OF GROSS DOMESTIC PRODUCT IN
THE REGULATED SECTOR OF THE ECONOMY[a]

Category	1970	1980	1990	1992
Price Regulation [b]	12.1	11.6	5.1	5.1
Financial Market Regulation [c]	3.5	3.4	6.1	6.8
Food and Drug Regulation [d]	2.6	1.9	1.8	1.7
Health and Safety Regulation [e]	–	12.0	10.2	9.4
Total	18.2	28.9	23.2	23.3

Source: National income and product accounts, Survey of Current Business (US Dept. of Commerce) for 1990 through 1992 see p. 31, Gross Domestic Product by Industry, Oct. 1994.

[a] The calculations are industry-group gross product originating as a percentage of all-industry gross product originating. Industries are defined as including those companies or activities accounted for in the Department of Commerce's standard industrial classification.
[b] Includes railroads; trucking and warehousing; air transportation; telephone and telegraph; electric, gas, and sanitary services; and oil and gas extraction.
[c] Includes finance and insurance.
[d] Includes all food product classes regulated by the U.S. Food and Drug Administration; pharmaceutical products included in chemicals below.
[e] Includes metal mining; coal mining; construction; paper and allied products; chemical and allied products; petroleum and related industries; stone, clay, and glass products; primary metal industries; and motor vehicles and equipment.

The telephone, electricity, and gas transportation companies still under the jurisdiction of price-regulating commissions have accounted for slightly more than five percent of GDP throughout the last three decades. While they now constitute all that there is in the regulated utility sector, previously there were many more firms in other industries; the airlines, railroad, and trucking companies were regulated, as were gas production, crude-oil and petroleum products companies, accounting for six to seven percent of GDP in the 1960s.[3] Thus the share of GDP from companies under price regulation decreased from twelve to five percent due to deregulation.

Financial regulation, accounting for approximately three percent of GDP, continues to exert controls on entry, service offerings, and interest rates at both the national and state levels. The relative growth of the financial sector caused regulated financial institutions to account for only three percent in the 1970s, but for six percent of GDP in the latter part of the 1980s and the 1990s. Here "deregulation" was by control process rather than firm or market; controls over interest rates were eliminated in 1982, but not control of entry, and monitoring of operations for "fairness" in lending increased. Lowered capital requirements and higher federal deposit insurance effectively loosened rate controls on savings and loans and, in 1982, the Garn-St. Germain Bill allowed savings and loan institutions to expand beyond the home-building loan business into other loan markets including the higher-risk junk bond market.

The monopoly case for regulation fit financial services awkwardly. Restrictions on interest rates paid on deposits, on branch locations, and on permissible activities all restrict supply. However, in practice the rules created supported a large number of small-scale or marginal banks. With large numbers of small suppliers, insofar as financial services benefit from economies of scale, the oversupply costs consumers in higher loan rates. And although the case for financial services deregulation was significantly weakened by the savings and loan failures, that case could be viewed as an argument for less, but better, regulation. Deregulation would eliminate incentives for irresponsible behavior inherent in flawed federal deposit insurance and inadequate private capitalization. Deregulation of savings and loan institutions and commercial banks in the early 1980s could have had the same beneficial consequences and outcomes as that of airline and trucking; its failure was not a statement on the deregulation initiative *per se*, but on its form.

This decline in the scope of regulatory practice was due not only to deregulation, but to the decline of these industries relative to the rest of the economy. The Carter and Reagan Administrations in succession stripped away part of the controls in railroad, trucking, and airline passenger service so that by the middle 1980s they operated without price controls. Oil and gas extraction moved out from under regulation through "phased decontrol" in the late 1970s that eliminated price caps and allocation of the resulting shortages. These reform initiatives came late, given that productivity growth decreased by fifty percent or more during the last stages of regulation. Rail transportation GDP

---

[3] The last vestiges of trucking regulation disappeared in January, 1995 when the Federal Congress exercised its power under the Commerce Clause of the Constitution to bring an end to state regulation of rates and service offerings.

decreased by 0.5 percent, airline passenger service increased only by 2.4 percent, and electric/gas only by 3.6 percent in the 1970s. This continued the decline of the railroads, and began the decline of the energy utilities and airlines, given that airline and electric/gas growth were half as large per annum as in the previous decade.[4]

The deregulation initiative made sense. The anti-monopoly rationale for controls made at inception in airline and trucking was weakened by findings that regulated prices were higher than those in unregulated markets for the same services. Subsidies to rural traffic and feeder services had increased the supply of productivity activities. As markets for surface transport increased in scale and breadth, there were many more transporters servicing a city pair outside the jurisdiction of the agencies. The extreme cases were in oil and gas production where field markets contained so many suppliers that price regulation only held down competitive prices. That had to result in deteriorating service quality, and did result in shortages, which in turn provided the case for deregulation put forward by both producers and (deprived) groups of consumers.

The second track taken by regulatory policy was initiated with controls over the products of the drug industry in the early part of this century. The system of controls is centered on certifying the legality of production and distribution of pharmaceuticals and medical devices by the Food and Drug Administration. The process is that of screening new therapies and devices before release to the market, only allowing those to go forward if found by testing to be "safe" and "effective" on standards of the FDA. It was fully established by the 1962 Kefauver-Harris Amendments to the 1938 Food, Drug and Cosmetic Act; since then there have been significant declines in the number of important new therapies, and in new therapies put in the market in the United States relative to European countries. This has been reflected in the decline in that regulated sector, from 2.6 percent in 1970 to 1.7 percent in 1992, due only to decline in market size and not to the extent of regulation. The figures (Table One) reflect all food product classes regulated by the FDA, but do not include pharmaceuticals which are already accounted for as part of the chemical industry under health and safety regulation.

The regulation of product quality at the FDA, which extended to specifications of pharmaceutical manufacturing processes, was replicated in design and focus in new agencies established in the 1970s. This regulation newly initiated to increase workers' safety and enhance the environment added almost fifteen percent of GDP to the regulated sector of the economy. The Clean Air Act Amendments of 1970 put the process most firmly in place; the newly created Environmental Protection Agency set out national air quality standards to be implemented by state agencies that required companies to install pollution control technologies. The mining, petroleum refining, and chemical industries were most affected by this regulation; substantial percentages of their investment outlays in the late 1970s and 1980s were for such equipment to meet

---

[4] MacAvoy, P.W., *Industry Regulation and the Performance of the American Economy* (1992), Table 3:10 Real GNP Growth Rates, 1969–1987, p. 59.

scheduled state implementation plans. The paper, metals, automobile, and glass industries were required to make extensive investments in plant and equipment, as well. These controls on the processes of companies in these industries were important enough to affect price levels. Thus the new regulatory process gained jurisdiction over at least twelve percent of GDP by 1980 (Table One).

Price and health/safety regulation together covered twenty-nine percent of GDP in 1980. The decline in GDP share in industries under health/safety controls, along with the elimination of price regulation, caused the percent of GDP under regulation to be reduced to slightly more than twenty-three percent by 1990-1992. The reduction of GDP in the regulated industries was half as much the result of declines in production in those industries as it was deregulation. That decline, particularly in automobile and chemicals production rates, relative to the economy as a whole, was large enough to raise the question as to whether there have been significant adverse effects on direct production from the regulatory process itself.

The Effects of Regulation on the Performance of the Economy

Over the last two decades, as the share of the regulated sector has grown and then declined, the concern at any point in time has been with how well this sector has performed. In general, the price-regulated industries have not performed well, while the health-and-safety-regulated industries have done even worse, in comparison to other industries in the economy.

There are numerous reasons for relatively poor performance. Business cycle conditions in the 1970s and early 1980s were marked by high levels of inflation. The regulators, when reviewing rate increase requests during that period, made decisions that kept prices below levels necessary to cover increases in fuel, labor, and interest costs. Resulting stringencies in cash flow kept the regulated companies from generating internally or acquiring externally the capital for capacity expansion. At the same time, their relatively low prices fostered growth in demands for service that could be satisfied only so long as there was substantial expansion of capacity. The performance of these firms was necessarily marked by excess demands for service, manifest in declining quality of service in elasticity supply and in shortages in gas deliveries.

By the middle of the 1980s, the economy had moved to much lower inflation and higher GDP growth rates, allowing the regulated firms to catch up on expansion even with limited price increases. Further in that direction, gains from technology in power generation and gas transmission extended the lifetimes of installed systems and reduced the capital costs of new systems.

Even so, the contrast in performance by then between regulated and deregulated sectors was striking. The four deregulated industries – rail, trucking, airline and petroleum products – experienced price declines of the order of twenty-six percent to fifty percent after controls were ended.[5] The three

---

[5] MacAvoy, P.W., "Prices After Deregulation: The United States Experience," *Hume Papers on Public Policy*, Vol. 1, No. 3, p. 45 (1994).

regulated industries – natural gas, electricity, and telephone – continued to experience price increases except in markets specifically subject to decontrol. Consumers with access to gas supplies in deregulated field markets paid twenty percent less; the difference became so apparent that the regulatory agency had to make it possible for wellhead purchases to be made by retailers previously buying a package of both gas and transportation from the regulated pipelines.[6] Electric utilities with access to power generated by new unregulated dual-purpose steam and electric producers paid approximately ten percent less than from sources subject to regulation on "cost of service".[7] Only the third major regulated industry – telecommunications – failed to realize some lower prices from partial deregulation. The long-distance telephone service providers were decontrolled by the Federal Communications Commission, except for AT&T which in the late 1980s and early 1990s was still subject to both regulated caps and floors on its prices. Long-distance rates declined but not because of competition from the unregulated specialized carriers, but because the FCC shifted the local service subsidy from long-distance rates to local access charges.[8] Because of continuing federal control of entry into long-distance markets, there has yet to be enough deregulation to develop competition that generates price reductions.

The economic performance of companies subject to the second track of regulation was relatively as poor. Those most subject to health, safety, and environmental controls experienced larger price and smaller output increases than others in manufacturing. It was as if regulation had made production relatively more costly. And such a result was adverse to the growth of the economy because it was not beneficial in reducing "bads" such as pollution and workplace accidents. There is no evidence that in general controls operated to significantly improve the quality of working conditions or of the environment.[9] The price increases in the most affected industries were large, and benefits were not of comparable scale, so that the extension of new regulation had similar effects on the economy as those from price regulation.

[6] MacAvoy, P.W., Doane, M.J., and Williams, M.A., "Federal Energy Regulatory Commission Order No. 636 as the Penultimate Regulatory Reform of the Gas Industry," *Yale School of Management, Working Paper No. 38*, April, 1995.
[7] MacAvoy, P.W., "Prices After Deregulation: The United States Experience," *Hume Papers on Public Policy*, Vol. 1, No. 3, p. 52, fn. 10 (1994).
[8] As Lee Selwyn indicates (in Cole, B.G., *After the Breakup: Assessing the New Post-AT&T Divestiture Era* (1991) at p. 157), "The forty percent reduction in interstate message toll service rates is not attributable either to divestiture or to the entry of competition per se; it is instead the direct result of shifting [access line charges to local subscribers] and of the Commission's requirement that AT&T pass through all reductions in such access charges to end users of its toll services." Crandall (in Crandall, R.W. (1991) *After the Breakup: U.S. Telecommunications in a More Competitive Era*) credits part of the reductions in long-distance rates for larger business users to the divestiture of AT&T from the seven regional Bell operating companies by antitrust court decree in 1984. His position is that "competition", the repricing of access, and technological progress provide impetus for lower real interstate telephone rates" (p.59). But reductions in long-distance rates were exceeded by increases in local rates in the post-divestiture period (p. 59). Local rates rose by seventeen percent in 1984 and nine percent in 1985, as indicated by Roger G. Noll and Susan R. Smart's "Pricing of Telephone Services" (Cole, p. 190).
[9] MacAvoy, P.W., *The Regulated Industries and the Economy*, W.W. Norton 1979, pp. 90–105.

The Next Twenty Years of Industry Deregulation

An initial impression might well be that deregulation has run its course. Those industries that would experience the largest price reductions, and thereby produce the greatest gains consequent from deregulation have already been subject to that process. The "bad" agencies have been decommissioned, or at least cut back in their authority to control entry, require service, and authorize prices. The contrary view is that there are still substantial targets for decontrol. Pipeline rates for transmitting gas interstate would fall at least twenty percent – the difference currently between tariff rates and emerging spot prices for pipeline space between market links – if the Federal Energy Regulatory Commission were prevented from imposing cost of service rate schedules.[10] Electricity prices for kilowatts transmitted into California and the Northeast would be sufficiently lower than current regulated prices to reduce the national average price by two percent; that would require decontrol of entry into use of the transmission grid at the commission.[11] Elimination of controls on entry into long distance telephone services by basic exchange and foreign companies should reduce rates now set non-competitively by three large carriers by thirty-five to forty percent.[12] While the gains each year to consumers in gross domestic product from these price reductions would only be 0.6 percent from electricity, and 0.20 percent from gas transmission, they would be 1.24 percent from opening up long-distance telecommunications to market pricing. Almost 1.5 percent of GDP adds up – gains could be in the range of $64 billion per annum. Extrapolation of this recent experience allows us to anticipate more deregulation in the near and perhaps the far future. The continuation of "reform", with the much more activist current Congress, likely will result in *three major steps* to reduce regulation in the American economy. Each would build on techniques for achieving major legislative change developed in the first half of the 1990s. When they have been completed, then regulation as we knew it at mid-century will have essentially disappeared from the American economy.

The first step will be to extend the deregulation actions taken at the federal level to eliminate state agencies and their control activities. The strategy will be to assert federal jurisdiction, and then deregulate, since the relevant activities are essentially "interstate" in nature. This was done during the last stages of the 1994 Democratic Congress when legislation was passed and signed by President Clinton to eliminate state controls of entry and rates in the trucking

---

10 MacAvoy, P.W., Doane, M.J., and Williams, M.A., "Federal Energy Regulatory Commission Order No. 636 as the Penultimate Regulatory Reform of the Gas Industry," *Yale School of Management, Working Paper No. 38*, April, 1995.

11 Cf. *Promoting Wholesale Competition Through Open Access Transmission Services*, 70 FERC, ¶61,357 (1995), cf., Appendix A for electric utility average revenue per kwh by state; on reasonable assumption on transmission costs these revenues equalize at levels in exporting states.

12 MacAvoy, P.W., "Tacit Collusion Under Regulation in the Pricing of Interstate Long-Distance Telephone Services", *Journal of Economics and Management Strategy*, Vol. 4, No. 2, Summer (1995).

industry.[13] And, while little noticed, controls disappeared on the first of January, 1995 in many major transportation markets, including those between the largest cities in Texas and in California. Similar incursion into state agency authority will take place in gas and electricity distribution. Using the existing network of transportation lines in these industries, suppliers other than the regulated transporter will be allowed access to retailers and final consumers.[14] Their bypass activities will open up to competitive forces gas and electricity supply now available only from the transporter that has had a (regulated) franchise monopoly.

The second step will be to require by legislation the "unbundling" of levels of service where competitive forces can prevail. Pressures for entry into franchised and tariffed markets are now present where prices are high. Entrants and shippers that demand access to "unbundled" service will open up either the transport or the exchange levels of the industry separate from other "utility" levels. Federal Communications Commission limitations on entry of the regional operating companies into long-distance services will break down when unbundling legislation passes Congress. This will open up long-distance to competitive pricing so as to leave only local exchange under public utility controls.[15]

Unbundling has begun in the Federal Energy Regulatory Commission (FERC) with its rulemaking decision No. 636 that, in 1992, required the regulated pipelines to divest their contract ownership of wellhead gas and instead provide common carrier services for gas owned by brokers, dealers, producers, and local distributing companies.[16] This was the "penultimate" step, given that the last stage of gas deregulation will consist of decontrol of transport rates between field and resale pipeline hubs. Only the retail distributing companies will then remain under local controls on rates for delivery to household and small businesses. FERC replicated the gas unbundling order with a 1995 Notice of Rulemaking to separate electricity generation from transmission and distribution;[17] when this is complete, prices for electricity will

[13] Cf. *Economic Report of the President Transmitted to the Congress* (Washington: U.S. Government Printing Office, 1995). Intrastate Trucking Deregulation enacted in 1994 eliminates "inefficient business practices predicated on state regulation" and replaces it with "Competition [that] implies that much of the savings from deregulation will be passed through to consumers", pp. 140–141.

[14] MacAvoy, P.W., Doane, M.J., and Williams, M.A., "Federal Energy Regulatory Commission Order No. 636 as the Penultimate Regulatory Reform of the Gas Industry," *Yale School of Management Working Paper No. 38*, April, 1995.

[15] Cf. *The Telecommunications and Competition Deregulation Act of 1995* as reported to the U.S. Senate Commission on Commerce, Science and Transportation, March 23, 1995 which calls for eliminating limitations on the entry of local exchange carriers into providing long-distance services based on complicated and difficult criteria for first establishing "competitiveness" in access services to local exchange. This is subject to revision in joint House/Senate Committees and may not pass this session. However, it sets the pattern for future deregulation.

[16] MacAvoy, P.W., Doane, M.J., and Williams, M.A., "Federal Energy Regulatory Commission Order No. 636 as the Penultimate Regulatory Reform of the Gas Industry", *Yale School of Management Working Paper No. 38*, April, 1995.

[17] Cf. *Promoting Wholesale Competition through Open Access Non-Discriminatory Transmission Services by Public Utilities*, Notice of Proposed Rulemaking (Federal Energy Regulatory Commission, Docket No. RM 95-8-0000, March 29, 1995).

be set in spot markets, while transmission and distribution rates will be set by FERC and the state commissions. With transportation eventually deregulated, electricity will eventually be less costly as well.

Then what will there be left for the regulatory authorities? They will set "value added" margins for so-called natural monopoly transmission and distribution services, but even then not for long as technical changes provide ever more effective substitutes for these services over time. Gas and electric transmission will continue to be unique "utility" type services, but even in these services technology will reduce costs sufficient to make the "value added" that is regulated a small part of price to the individual household. Regulation will disappear because the regulated services will become insignificant as a part of the whole.

The third step to reduce regulation as part of the economic scene will take place by replacement of the current control systems seeking to provide more health and safety and increase the quality of the environment. Rather than regulation fading away, as in gas distribution, it will give way to other types of public management of industry activities. The pattern has already been established by the Clean Air Act Amendments of 1990. New procedures for achieving reductions in sulfur emissions from power plants have been put in place to substitute for equipment requirements. These new procedures require limits on emissions by individual plant. If a plant reduces emissions further below the limit, then that difference is tradeable for increased emissions at another plant. In effect, this process replaces agency regulation with a market for emissions rights.

Such market rights can be devised for automotive safety, plant working conditions, as well as for product quality. The dividing line between command and control regulation and markets in performance is now quite ill-defined. But command regulation has not been effective, and has been costly, and as results are achieved through performance in tradeable rights then it will be replaced. The first indications from the Clean Air Act experiment are promising (as related by Todd Strauss, in this volume). Those targeted power plants in the Eastern half of the United States have made significant strides towards achieving strict limits on emissions by trading rights and substituting low sulfur fuels, neither of which would have been options under command and control regulation.[18]

As for regulation of food and drugs, there is growing pressure for reforms of the product approval procedures of the FDA. Leading the movement is House of Representatives Speaker Gingrich who has denounced the FDA as "killing jobs and slowing down the introduction of new drugs".[19] The Clinton Administration responded by announcing on March 16, 1995 a series of

[18] Strauss, T., "Cheaper SO$_x$, Same Old No$_x$: A Look at Implementation of Title IV of the Clean Air Act Amendments of 1990", *Hume Papers on Public Policy (1995)*.

[19] Quoted in *White House Briefing*, Federal News Service, February 7, 1995. FDA reform proposals by Progress and Freedom Foundation (in Thomas Lenard, *The Future of Medical Innovation: A New Approach for Bringing Medical Products to Market*, Progress and Freedom Foundation Report, forthcoming 1995) include increased role for private sector organizations in drugs and device approval process.

measures aimed at making "high quality drugs and medical devices available to consumers more quickly and more cheaply".[20] The latest proposals to make the drug approval process more cost effective, designed by Senator Ron Wyden, encourage the FDA to use independent panels to approve and oversee early stage trials and gives the agency authority to grant conditional approvals for promising drugs and devices. Shifting the burden of proof to the FDA by allowing time-certain but provisional acceptance of promising new drugs is a limited step in regulatory reform. It would result in a more flexible system of limited drugs so that there would be more choices available to physicians and their patients in the long run.

For all intents and purposes, the twenty year process of deregulation has arrived at a point part way to a regulation-free economy in the United States. And the remaining distance may not be all that substantial – the twenty percent of GDP still regulated can be reduced to five percent. Intrastate deregulation, unbundling and rights markets are likely to reduce regulation to the extent that the affected sectors of the economy operate efficiently and flexibly for the first time. That would leave only the public enterprises and public management as in health care, as sectors in which government set the terms and conditions of individual transactions.[21]

Bibliography

Cole, B.G., *After the Breakup: Assessing the New Post-AT&T Divestiture Era* (Columbia University Press, 1991).

Economic Report of the President Transmitted to the Congress (Washington: U.S. Government Printing Office, 1995).

Hazlett, T.W. & Spitzer, M., *Cable Television: Competition, Regulation, and the First Amendment,*
AEI Press, Washington, D.C., forthcoming 1995.

Lenard, T., *The Future of Medical Innovation: A New Approach for Bringing Medical Products to Market, Progress and Freedom Foundation Report,* forthcoming 1995.

MacAvoy, P.W., *The Economic Effects of Regulation: The Trunkline Railroad Cartels and the Interstate Commerce Commission 1870 – 1900* (MIT Press, 1965).

[20] *Remarks on Regulatory Reform in Arlington, Virginia,* Public Papers of the President, March 16, 1995. According to the Administration, the following reforms would save industry and consumers $500 million a year:

"(1) FDA will stop using a full-blown review every time a biotech drug company makes a minor and risk-free manufacturing change in an established drug;

(2) FDA will stop requiring costly assessments on drugs that obviously have no significant impact on the environment;

(3) FDA will eliminate 600 pages of regulations controlling the production of antibiotics and other drugs;

(4) 140 categories of medical devices that pose low risk to patients will no longer need preapproval of the FDA to be put on the market."

[21] This paper is a project of the John M. Olin Foundation Research Program for the Study of Markets and Regulatory Behavior at the Yale School of Management. Comments and suggestions of Adam Jaffe and Michael Williams are gratefully acknowledged, as is the analytical support of Paul Coggin, Thanak DeLopez, Lisa Hartmann, Eugenio Vega, John Wakiumu, and Sharon Winer.

MacAvoy, P.W., *Industry Regulation and the Performance of the American Economy* (W. W. Norton, 1992).

MacAvoy, P.W., "Prices After Deregulation: The United States Experience", *Hume Papers on Public Policy, Vol. 1, Nos. 3 (1994)*.

MacAvoy, P.W., "Tacit Collusion Under Regulation in the Pricing of Interstate Long-Distance Telephone Services", *Journal of Economics and Management Strategy*, Vol. 4, No. 2, Summer (1995).

MacAvoy, P.W., Doane, M.J., and Williams, M.A., "Federal Energy Regulatory Commission Order No. 636 as the Penultimate Regulatory Reform of the Gas Industry", *Yale School of Management, Working Paper No. 38,* April, 1995.

Promoting Wholesale Competition through Open Access Non-Discriminatory Transmission Services by Public Utilities, Notice of Proposed Rulemaking (Federal Energy Regulatory Commission, Docket No. RM 95–8–0000, March 29, 1995).

Strauss, T., "Cheaper SO_x, Same Old No_x: A Look at Implementation of Title IV of the Clean Air Act Amendments of 1990", *Hume Papers on Public Policy (1995)*.

The Telecommunications and Competition Deregulation Act of 1995 as reported by the U.S. Senate Commission on Commerce, Science and Transportation (March 23, 1995).

U.S. Department of Commerce, Survey of Current Business, 1990–1992 (Washington: U.S. Government Printing Office, 1994).

Pricing of Services Provided to Competitors by the Regulated Firm

William J Baumol
J Gregory Sidak

Synopsis

Local telephone companies have long been regulated as natural monopolies. However, technological innovation and the prospect of falling regulatory barriers to entry now expose some portions of the local exchange to competition from cable television systems, wireless telephony, and rival wireline systems. Nevertheless, it is probable that certain parts of local telephony will remain naturally monopolistic. In these cases the local exchange carrier must be permitted to sell necessary inputs to its competitors in the market for final telecommunications products at a price that reflects all its costs, including opportunity costs. The authors' analysis applies to any network industry. Thus, it is useful in antitrust analysis of essential facilities and in regulatory analysis of transportation, energy transmission, pipelines, and mail delivery. The authors conclude by responding to comments on their work and to the reaction of the Privy Council.

*   *   *   *

The Nature of the Problem

Technological change and regulatory reform are transforming network industries, permitting competition to occur in portions of the market where it had previously been considered infeasible. In one network industry after another, this competitive transformation raises a recurrent question: How shall the regulated firm price its sale of services to competitors? The question arises whenever a firm, X, is the only supplier of an input used both by itself and by a rival to provide some final product. If X charges its rival more for the input than it implicitly charges itself, it will have handicapped that rival's ability to compete with X, perhaps seriously. The reverse will be true if regulation forces X to charge the rival less for the input than X charges itself.

The modern analysis of "interconnection pricing" arose with the purchase of trackage rights by one railroad from another. Soon, the problem manifested itself in telecommunications regulation. One of the most vexing issues facing the regulator of local telephone service in the United States is the pricing of access to the local loop when that service is supplied by the local exchange carrier (LEC) to interexchange carriers (IXCs) with which the LEC competes in toll services within a local access and transport area (LATA). Access has two significant and pertinent attributes. First, access is an intermediate good– an input used in the supply of a final product, intraLATA toll service and other final products as well. Second, this input is produced by the LEC and used not only by itself, but also by its rivals in the market for the final product. An analogous pricing problem arises with respect to network interconnection by competitive access providers (CAPs), which compete against the LEC in providing the local transport required for a long-distance call.

The electric power industry is another example of a network industry in which vertically integrated monopolists face the current or imminent obligation to sell inputs to competitors. The Energy Policy Act of 1992[1] amended section 211 of the Federal Power Act (FPA)[2] to empower the Federal Energy Regulatory Commission to order vertically integrated electric utilities to deliver competitively generated power over their transmission lines.[3] Perhaps more important, the 1992 legislation amended section 212 of the FPA to require that rates charged for mandatory wholesale wheeling "shall promote the economically efficient transmission and generation of electricity."[4] Those rates shall be high enough to "permit the recovery by such utility of *all* the costs incurred in connection with the transmission services and necessary associated services, including, but not limited to, an appropriate share, if any, of legitimate, verifiable and economic costs."[5]

The pricing of inputs sold to competitors is a problem that may arise in still other contexts, such as the potential sale of unbundled access to the local delivery network of the United States Postal Service, or the program-access provisions of the Cable Television Consumer Protection and Competition Act of 1992, which require vertically integrated cable operators to make programming available on a nondiscriminatory basis to other multichannel video distributors.[6] Finally, courts may recognize the clear relevance of interconnection pricing to the growing number of antitrust cases in which plaintiffs seek access to the essential facilities of vertically integrated monopolists that are not formally regulated by any government agency. The importance of such cases can be expected to grow as networks and information services of all sorts become more prominent features of the American economy.

The Efficient Component-Pricing Rule

The solution that we have provided to the recurrent interconnection-pricing problem described above is the efficient component-pricing rule. A critical

---

[1] Pub. L. No. 102–486, 106 Stat. 2776 (1992).
[2] 1 U.S.C. § 824 *et seq.*
[3] *Id.* at § 824j(a).
[4] *Id.* § 824k(a).
[5] *Id.* (emphasis added).
[6] Pub. L. No. 102–385, § 19, 106 Stat. 1460, 1494–97 (1992) (codified at 47 U.S.C. § 548).

requirement for economic efficiency is that the price of any product be no lower than that product's marginal cost or its average-incremental cost. Economic analysis emphasizes that the pertinent marginal cost as well as the average-incremental cost must include all *opportunity costs* incurred by the supplier in providing the product. Here opportunity cost refers to all potential earnings that the supplying firm forgoes, either by providing inputs of its own rather than purchasing them, or by offering services to competitors that force it to relinquish business to those rivals, and thus to forgo the profits on that lost business. In a competitive market, price always includes compensation for such opportunity costs–for example, for the interest forgone by the firm when it supplies funds from retained earnings rather than borrowing them from a bank. The efficient component-pricing rule states simply that the price of an input should equal its average-incremental cost, *including all pertinent incremental opportunity costs*. That is:

efficient component price = the input's direct per unit incremental cost + the opportunity cost to the input supplier of the sale of a unit of input.

We examine now the logic and consequences of that rule. In the following discussion, the term "direct costs" will refer to all costs that, from the point of view of the supplier firm, are not opportunity costs.

The literature on the economics of price regulation indicates that the pricing principle just described can guide the choice of efficient access charges. This pricing principle–variously known as the *efficient component-pricing rule*, the *imputation requirement*, the *principle of competitive equality*, or the *parity principle*–is merely a variant of the elementary principles for efficiency in pricing that have been discussed already. This rule applies to the sale of an input–a component K of the final product–by a supplier X of both the component and the final product. The purchasing firm Y uses the component to produce the same final product as X and sells that final product in competition with X. Here Y is itself assumed to make the remaining components (other than K) of the final product. If X sells component K to Y, then Y is enabled to compete with X in selling the final product. When X sells component K to Y, either voluntarily or pursuant to regulatory mandate, what price should X charge for component K?

To answer this question, we will use an example from rail transportation. Consider two railroads, X and Y, that operate along parallel routes from an

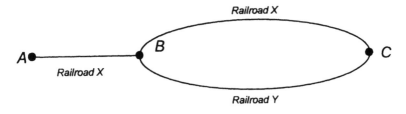

FIGURE 1   THE TRACKAGE RIGHTS-PRICING PROBLEM

intermediate point B to a destination point C, as illustrated in Figure 1. Railroad X owns the only tracks extending from the origin point A to the intermediate point B. In this case, the final product is transportation all the way from A to C. Competing railroad Y, also a proprietor of tracks from B to C, can be expected in these circumstances to apply to railroad X for "interconnection" from A to B, seeking to rent trackage rights along that route from its rival. If the transaction is completed, Y (like X) will be able to ship all the way from A to C; in regulatory parlance, X then is called the landlord railroad and Y is called the tenant. Regulators commonly have been requested by prospective tenants to force a landlord to grant them trackage rights. For obvious reasons, the regulatory agency usually has been asked to set the rental fee as well.

The sale of access by a LEC to an IXC that is a horizontal competitor of the LEC in the market for intraLATA toll services is precisely analogous to the grant of trackage rights by the landlord to the tenant railroad. Access is an input to the final product, interexchange telecommunication, and is not essentially different from the purchase of any other intermediate input. Setting a price for access to the local loop in telecommunications is, therefore, precisely analogous to setting of the rental fee for trackage rights. More generally, the pricing of access is analogous to pricing any product component in comparable circumstances, such as an electric utility's sale of transmission to a competitive generator of electricity.

The efficient component-pricing rule has already advanced from theory to practice in the United States and abroad. The Interstate Commerce Commission (ICC) has applied the rule in several railroad rate cases.[7] In 1989 the California Public Utilities Commission embraced the rule in its reform of regulation of local telephone exchange carriers.[8] In 1994 the Maryland Public Service Commission adopted a variation on the rule for pricing access to the local exchange by competitive access providers seeking to offer local telephone service.[9]

In 1992 New Zealand's High Court adopted, and in 1993 its Court of Appeal rejected, the rule (but not its logic) in antitrust litigation between Clear Communications, Ltd., and the former government telephone monopoly, Telecom Corporation of New Zealand, Ltd.[10] As we shall explain in greater

---

[7] For example, see the quartet of cases known as *Compensation I* through *IV*, St. Louis S.W. Ry.–Trackage Rights over Missouri Pac. R.R.–Kansas City to St. Louis, 1 I.C.C.2d 776 (1984), 4 I.C.C.2d 668 (1987), 5 I.C.C.2d 525 (1989), 8 I.C.C.2d 80 (1991).

[8] Alternative Regulatory Framework for Local Exchange Carriers, Invest. No. 87–11–033, 33 C.P.U.C.2d 43, 107 P.U.R.4th 1 (Cal. Pub. Util. Comm'n 1989).

[9] MFS Intelenet of Md., Inc., Case No. 8584, Order No. 71155, 152 P.U.R.4th 102 (Md. Pub. Serv. Comm'n 1994).

[10] Clear Communications, Ltd. *v.* Telecom Corp. of New Zealand, Ltd., slip op. (H.C. Dec. 22, 1992), *rev'd*, slip op. (C.A. Dec. 28, 1993). For discussions of the case, see James Farmer, *Transition from Protected Monopoly to Competition: The New Zealand Experiment*, 1 COMPETITION & CONSUMER L.J. 1 (1993); William J. Baumol & J. Gregory Sidak, *The Pricing of Inputs Sold to Competitors*, 11 YALE J. ON REG. 171, 189–94 (1994); Alfred E. Kahn & William Taylor, *The Pricing of Inputs Sold to Competitors: A Comment*, 11 YALE J. ON REG. 225, 229 n.10 (1994). The rule was rejected because the Court of Appeal held that under New Zealand law no agency has the power to prevent inclusion of monopoly profit in the opportunity cost component of the input price, a conclusion subsequently rejected by the Privy Council.

detail below, in October 1994 the Judicial Committee of the Privy Council of the House of Lords reversed in relevant part the decision of the Court of Appeal and, citing the recent economic literature on the efficient component-pricing rule, held that the rule is compatible with New Zealand antitrust principles governing the pricing of inputs sold to competitors.[11]

The Traditional Regulatory Approach to Rental Fee Determination

Until recently, regulators often have approached the rental-fee decision in the manner suggested by the following example. Let the direct average-incremental cost incurred by landlord X as a result of Y's use of its track be AIC dollars per train. This is the additional cost per train incurred by the landlord railroad–including track wear and tear, additional planning, and administrative cost–as a result of the tenant's use of the landlord's tracks.

Suppose that because of economies of scale, total revenues must exceed the sum of the incremental costs of the two types of traffic if X is to break even. Suppose further that, in the absence of trackage rights, the traffic from A to C had yielded X a net contribution toward the shortfall (that is, total incremental revenue minus incremental cost) of T, and assume that contribution T equals \$90 million per year. Finally, suppose that, after granting trackage rights, X is expected to retain two-thirds of the traffic from A to C, with the remaining traffic going to Y.

Assuming freight rates for shipments from A to C to be fixed, regulators generally have determined the proper rental fee for the trackage rights to consist of (1) a charge per train of railroad Y set equal to the (direct) average-incremental cost to X of handling Y's train, and (2) a supplement designed to leave X with exactly two-thirds of the \$90 million contribution that the traffic formerly provided. Under this regulatory rule, in other words, the landlord is granted its pro rata share of the contribution, in this case corresponding to its two-thirds expected share of the total traffic.

This regulatory rule, however, violates economic efficiency. As we shall now show, it fails to compensate railroad X adequately for its common fixed costs; thus the rule distorts the efficient division of responsibilities between X and Y in supplying transport over the competitive segment BC.

The Efficient Component-Pricing Principle as a Requirement of Economic Efficiency: What Is the Efficiency Issue?

The efficient pricing principle for product components is required not only by the competitive-market standard for defensible behavior by an allegedly dominant firm. It is also a necessary condition for economic efficiency, and

---

11 Telecom Corp. of New Zealand Ltd. *v.* Clear Communications Ltd., slip op. at 23–24, Privy Council Appeal No. 21 of 1994 (Oct. 19, 1994, Judgment of the Lords of the Judicial Committee of the Privy Council) (citing Baumol & Sidak, *supra* note 10; Kahn & Taylor, *supra* note 10).

hence for promoting the public interest. That is, product-component prices that do not follow this principle constitute an incentive for inefficiency whose costs consumers will have to pay.

Another example shows the nature of the efficiency issue. Consider a pharmaceutical manufacturer X that is the sole supplier of a medical ingredient A on which it holds a patent. The final product may require other medical ingredients, capsule cases, packaging, and marketing services, all of which firm X also can provide, although it is not the only enterprise that can do so. Economic efficiency requires that capsule cases, packaging, retail marketing services, and so on each be supplied by those firms that can do the job most efficiently–that is, by means that minimize the costs of the labor, fuel, raw materials, and other inputs used in producing the components. The choice is often interpreted as a make-or-buy decision on the part of firm X, the supplier of patent-protected component A. Firm X should make the capsule cases, the packaging, and so on only if it is the most efficient supplier of these items. Otherwise, the public interest dictates that firm X buy those components from a rival supplier who can provide them more efficiently.

Whether firm X will make the efficient choice voluntarily depends on the relative price of the competing suppliers of the capsule cases (and the other product inputs). If their price when offered by a rival supplier is lower than the cost at which firm X can make capsule cases for itself, then X will be motivated to buy the cases rather than make them. Efficiency in pricing requires the capsules to be priced so that X will find it profitable to select the more efficient provider to manufacture the capsules–supplying the capsules itself if and only if it is the more efficient supplier. In telecommunications services, the analogous problem is to price access so that the job of carrying intraLATA traffic goes to the more efficient of the competing carriers.

Efficiency of the Component-Pricing Rule and the Competitive Market Model

In brief, the optimal component-pricing rule asserts that the rent that tenant railroad Y should pay per train is the entire average-incremental cost incurred by each train traversing landlord railroad X's route AB, *including any incremental opportunity cost* that the passage of Y's train imposes on X. Expressed in this way, the rule is entirely familiar to economists, and its logic will be virtually self-evident to them, except for its focus on average-incremental cost rather than marginal cost.

The efficiency of this optimal component-pricing rule is confirmed indirectly by the fact that it yields a price level set in precisely the same way it would be in a perfectly competitive or a perfectly contestable market. To see this, imagine a set of landlords competing to rent retail space to tenants. Suppose further, as is often true, that if no suitable tenant can be found, the space can be used for the landlord's own profitable retailing establishment. No landlord who can use the property in this way will rent it to anyone for less than the direct incremental cost of the tenant's occupation of the property *plus the opportunity cost to the landlord* of the rental arrangement. If the landlord can earn $90,000 by using the property, the tenant will be required to make good the $90,000 that is forgone by renting the property. The same argument applies whether the opportunity cost is incurred because landlord and tenant compete for space or because they compete for customers.

Consequently, even in the most competitive of markets, no landlord will rent for a fee less than that given by the efficient component-pricing rule. Moreover, if competition abounds–that is, if a profusion of alternative properties are available to the tenant on comparable terms–the tenant will pay no more than that. (In practice, of course, the tenant can be expected to spend a small amount more than that, in order to induce the landlord to rent rather than use the property.)

Since, in the absence of externalities, we expect competitive prices to be consistent with economic efficiency, the preceding argument establishes a presumption that the component-pricing rule is indeed optimal. This is also made clear by our railroad example, which will now be used to show how the optimal input price is calculated.

Recall from Figure 1 that in our illustration only railroad X offers transportation from A to B (route AB) and then to C (route BXC). Its competitor, railroad Y, also offers transportation from B to C (route BYC), and it wishes to serve shippers from A as well by renting trackage rights along X's route AB. By obtaining interconnection over route AB, railroad Y will be able to offer shippers seamless transportation service from A to C, which is our illustrative final product. Suppose the competitive price to shippers for transport from A to C is $10 per ton, and X's incremental cost along each of its two route segments, AB and BXC, is $3 per ton. Thus, on its carriage of shipments from A to C, landlord X earns a net contribution toward its common fixed costs equal to the final-product price minus its two incremental costs–that is, X's earned contribution = $10 – $3 – $3 = $4 for every ton of freight X carries over the full route from A to C.

In a competitive market, what will railroad X charge railroad Y for permitting the latter to haul a ton of freight over X's route AB? Assume for simpler exposition that each ton of freight carried from B to C by Y means that one less ton is transported by X. Then, even if there are other railroads in a position similar to X's, none will rent Y their tracks unless Y pays them enough to compensate for the cost of the lost profit that Y's interconnection will impose on them. This cost includes the direct incremental cost–wear and tear of X's tracks, fuel if X is required to supply the engine, and so on–a sum that we take to be $3 in our example. But full compensation for interconnection also requires that Y pay for the incremental *opportunity cost* its traffic imposes upon X–that is, the loss of $4 of net contribution toward common fixed costs that X incurs for every ton of business that Y diverts from X by using X's tracks. Thus, the competitive-market standard requires that the price of trackage rights (or, more generally, of interconnection) must also satisfy the efficient component-pricing rule. In our example, the direct per-unit incremental cost to railroad X of permitting use of its route AB is $3 per ton. Railroad X's per-unit opportunity cost is its loss of $4 per ton of net contribution toward its common fixed costs. Thus, the efficient component price for granting railroad Y interconnection over route AB is \$7 per ton–the price that would emerge in a competitive market.

Direct Discussion of the Role of Component Pricing in Promoting Efficiency

We come now to the critical role that the component-pricing principle has in promoting economic efficiency. Continuing with our railroad example, we will show now that if the price of the component provided by landlord railroad X is set in accord with this pricing rule, then the two participating railroads will face incentives that automatically assign the business over route AB to the supplier who can provide it with the least use of fuel, labor, and other valuable inputs. But if the rental payment for the landlord's component–in this case, X's tracks over route AB–is set at a price below that required by the efficient component-pricing principle, the requirements of economic efficiency will be violated.

Economic efficiency requires that the competitive segment of the service be performed only by efficient suppliers–that is, by those suppliers whose incremental costs incurred to supply the service are the lowest available. For this goal to be realized, it must be possible for the more efficient suppliers to make a net profit when they offer the final product for a price that yields no such gain to less efficient suppliers. This condition must hold whether the more efficient supplier happens to be the landlord or the tenant.

We first will demonstrate the basic efficiency result using our hypothetical numerical example, and then we will show how to generalize it, indicating that the result is valid always, not just when the pertinent numbers happen in reality to match those in our illustration.

First, however, we must recall that even if every one of a firm's services is sold at a price equal to its average-incremental cost, the firm's total revenues may not cover its total costs. Consequently, it is normal and not anticompetitive for a firm to price some or all of its products to provide not only the required profit component of incremental cost, but also some contribution toward recovery of common fixed costs that do not enter the incremental costs of the individual products. The appropriate and viable size of the contribution of a particular product depends in part upon demand conditions for that product; it does not follow any standard markup rule or any arbitrary cost-allocation procedure. Any service whose price exceeds its per-unit incremental cost provides such a contribution in addition to the profit required on the incremental investment contained in the incremental cost.

With all this in mind, consider again our numerical example encompassing railroads X and Y. Suppose that the final product in question (transport from A to C) is sold to shippers at a price of \$10 per ton–a price deemed competitive and thus above the incremental-cost floor. We have already assumed that landlord railroad X incurs an incremental cost for transport from A to B (which we will call IC_{AB}) that equals \$3 per ton, and an incremental cost for transport from B to C (which we will call IC_{BXC}) that also equals \$3 per ton. We saw that these incremental costs leave a net contribution toward common fixed costs of \$4 per ton (that is, \$10 – \$3 – \$3) from each unit of final product sold. And we saw that the efficient component-pricing principle requires that the landlord railroad X offer interconnection over route AB to tenant railroad Y at a price equal to IC_{AB} plus X's opportunity cost (that is, \$3 + \$4 = \$7). At that price, the tenant's gross earnings per unit of final product amount to \$3. This represents the \$10 final-product price minus the \$7 fee that the tenant pays to the landlord for interconnection over route AB. But to determine Y's *net* earnings we must also subtract from this sum the incremental cost tenant railroad Y incurs when it transports a ton of freight over its own route segment to complete the trip from A to C. There are three possibilities:

Case I: If tenant railroad Y is the less efficient supplier of the remainder of the final product (transport from B to C), so that its incremental cost (say, \$4) exceeds the \$3 incremental cost of landlord railroad X for transport from B to C, then Y will lose money if it attempts to provide the final product. Here, the \$10 price for the final product must be exceeded by the \$11 sum of the efficient component price (\$7) plus Y's incremental cost of completing the final product, \$4. So, Y will be kept out–not by an improper price, but because of its own inefficiency. That is the outcome required by the public interest.

Case II: If the incremental cost of providing transport from B to C is the same for both railroads (\$3), then the two firms are equally efficient suppliers of transport from B to C. It does not matter to society which railroad provides the service. Moreover, the tenant will experience no gain and no loss by providing the service, since its profit in excess of incremental capital cost = price trackage fee Y's incremental cost over route BC = \$10 – \$7 – \$3 = \$0, so that the tenant, offered only a return equal to its capital cost, will be indifferent between entering and staying out.

Case III: In the third case, the tenant is the more efficient supplier of transport from B to C with an incremental cost of, say, \$2. Y can then undercut slightly X's final-product price (\$10) and make an additional profit for itself while still covering both the efficient component price that it must pay to X (\$7) and its own incremental cost of completing the final product (which is less than \$3). For example, Y can sell the final product for \$9.75 per unit, making a profit of \$0.75 per unit over the cost of capital (that is, \$9.75 – \$7 – \$2). The landlord will have no incentive to retain for itself the transportation business from B to C. It could do so only by matching the tenant's \$9.75 price. But at any price below \$10 the landlord would be accepting a contribution less than the contribution (\$4) that it can obtain through the efficient component prices it charges Y for Y's provision of transport from B to C.

In Case III above, the landlord is said to have chosen to "buy" rather than "make" the B-to-C transportation component of the final product. This result shows how the efficient component-pricing rule achieves the principle of indifference. That is, the rule sets the landlord's component price to include all its costs, so that the landlord is indifferent whether that particular transportation service is provided by itself or a rival, since all the landlord's costs are covered one way or the other. The rule thus ensures that the task of providing transport from B to C is performed by the firm that can do it more efficiently.

Matters work out differently if regulation forces the landlord to offer transport from A to B at a price *below* the efficient component price. If regulation permitted X, for example, to charge at most $5.50 for transport from A to B (rather than the $7 price permitted under the efficient component-pricing rule), then the tenant's gross earnings–that is, its final product price ($10) minus the rental price ($5.50)–would be $4.50, or $1.50 above X's incremental cost of providing transport from B to C. Even if Y's incremental cost of providing transport from B to C were $4, making it a *less* efficient supplier of the competitive transportation service than X, Y could still enter the arena and earn a contribution from its inefficient activity, for its per unit profit would then be $10 $5.50 $4 = $0.50. This profit to the less efficient supplier is made possible because the imposition of the $5.50 price offers the tenant a *subsidy* from the landlord of $1.50 for every unit of service the tenant elects to provide. Moreover, that subsidy is, in effect, obtainable by the tenant on demand, because the $5.50 price is imposed by the regulatory authority.

The connection between the efficient component-pricing rule and allocative efficiency should now be clear: the rule ensures proper pricing and efficiency in the competitive segment of the rail route, just as it will ensure this outcome in the local telecommunications loop. It only remains to be shown that the efficiency result is not unique to the numbers we happened to select for our illustration, but rather has general applicability. To show this, we now substitute algebraic symbols for the preceding numbers.

Formal Discussion of the Rule's Efficiency

A formal discussion enables us to prove the general efficiency of the component-pricing rule directly and offers some additional insights on its workings. Switching to the example of access to the local loop in telecommunications, we will prove that the parity price for access is both necessary and sufficient for the maximum difference in the remunerative prices of the final-product (toll) of the two firms, the access provider A and its competitor C to be exactly equal to the difference in the revenues that they require from consumers for the non-access portion of their final-product services. Let us use the following notation:

P_A	=	the access supplier's price of final product (say, per message minute)
P_C	=	the competitor's price of final product
P_{access}	=	access price per message minute
C_A	=	the cost to the access provider of supplying access for a message minute
contribution$_A$	=	the contribution the access supplier receives from a minute of access
revenue$_{NA}$	=	revenue the access supplier needs to provide a unit of non-access service
revenue$_{NC}$	=	the corresponding figure for the competitor.

Then, by definition,

$$P_A = C_A + \text{contribution}_A + \text{revenue}_{NA} \tag{1}$$

$$P_C = P_{access} + \text{revenue}_{NC} \tag{2}$$

so

$$P_A - P_C = \text{revenue}_{NA} - \text{revenue}_{NC} + (C_A + \text{contribution}_A - P_{access}). \tag{3}$$

Therefore,

$$P_A - P_C = \text{revenue}_{NA} - \text{revenue}_{NC}, \tag{4}$$

which ensures the existence of the so-called level playing field if and only if

$$P_{access} = C_A + \text{contribution}_A, \tag{5}$$

which, by equation (1), implies that

$$P_{access} = P_A - \text{revenue}_{NA}. \tag{6}$$

This last equation, however, is the parity pricing formula: the access price equals the access supplier's final-product price minus the cost (revenue requirement) of the non-access input. QED.

The Privy Council's Endorsement of the Efficient Component-Pricing Rule

Several months after the publication in the *Yale Journal on Regulation* of three essays on the efficient component-pricing rule,[12] the highest court in the British Commonwealth embraced the rule, citing two of the essays. The Privy Council of the House of Lords held in *Telecom Corporation of New Zealand Limited* v. *Clear Communications Limited* that the efficient component-pricing rule is compatible with New Zealand antitrust principles governing the pricing of inputs sold to competitors.[13]

As a result of its policies promoting competition in telecommunications, New Zealand had precipitated by 1991 the first modern litigation over the pricing of interconnection among rival local telephone companies. New Zealand's lower court, known as the High Court, ruled that the incumbent local exchange carrier, Telecom, did not abuse a dominant position in the market (in violation of New Zealand's antitrust statute, section 36 of the Commerce Act[14]) when Telecom demanded that the entrant, Clear, pay an

---

[12] Baumol & Sidak, *supra*, note 10; Kahn & Taylor, *supra* note 10; William B. Tye, *The Pricing of Inputs Sold to Competitors: A Response*, 11 YALE J. ON REG. 203 (1994).

[13] Slip op. at 23–24, Privy Council Appeal No. 21 of 1994 (Oct. 19, 1994, Judgment of the Lords of the Judicial Committee of the Privy Council) (citing Baumol & Sidak, *supra* note 10; Kahn & Taylor, *supra* note 10).

[14] Commerce Act, 1986, No. 5, § 36, 1986 N.Z. Stat. 71, 95. Section 36(1) states: "No person who has a dominant position in a market shall use that position for the purpose of (a) Restricting the entry of any person into that or any other market; or (b) Preventing or deterring any person from engaging in competitive conduct in that or in any other market; or (c) Eliminating any person from that or any other market." *Id.*

interconnection price derived from the efficient component-pricing rule.[15] New Zealand's Court of Appeal, however, reversed on the grounds that it would violate section 36 for Telecom to include any monopoly profit that it might forgo in the opportunity-cost component of the access charge paid by Clear under the efficient component-pricing rule.[16] Telecom appealed that decision (and Clear cross-appealed other aspects of the decision not discussed here) to the Privy Council of the House of Lords in London.

On October 19, 1994, the Privy Council reversed in relevant part the decision of the Court of Appeal. Writing for their Lordships, Lord Browne-Wilkinson considered the efficient component-pricing rule to have the following relevance to interpreting section 36's concept of "use of a dominant position":

> As to what constitutes "use of a dominant position", although their Lordships agree with Gault J. [of the Court of Appeal] that ultimately the question depends upon the true effect of the statutory words used in section 36 and not on any economic model, the statutory words provide no explanation as to the distinction between conduct which does, and conduct which does not, constitute such use. Both the High Court and the Court of Appeal proceeded on the basis, with which their Lordships agree, that if the terms Telecom were seeking to extract were no higher than those which a hypothetical firm would seek in a perfectly contestable market, Telecom was not using its dominant position. In order to discover what such hypothetical terms might be it is inevitable that the parties and the court must have recourse to expert economic advice. The Baumol-Willig Rule is a closely reasoned economic model which seeks to show how the hypothetical firm would conduct itself.[17]

The Privy Council then considered whether the efficient component-pricing rule would violate section 36 by allowing Telecom to recover monopoly rents in the opportunity-cost component of the access price that it proposed to charge Clear.

Their Lordships emphasized that courts applying section 36 "are not acting as regulators" and that "section 36 is only one of the remedies provided by the Commerce Act for the purpose of combatting over-pricing due to monopolistic behavior."[18] Other sections of the Commerce Act, Lord Browne-Wilkinson observed, are available to perform this role:

> Part IV [of the Commerce Act] deals separately with control of prices. Under section 53 the Governor-General, on the recommendation of the Minister, may declare that the prices for goods or services of any description supplied to or for the use of different persons are controlled. Under section 53(2)(a) a Minister cannot make such a recommendation unless he is satisfied the goods or services are supplied in a market "in which competition is limited or is likely to be lessened". Under section 70 the Commission may authorise a price to be charged for

---

[15] CP590/91, slip op. (H.C. Dec. 22, 1992).

[16] Clear Communications, Ltd. v. Telecom Corp. of New Zealand, C.A. 25–93, slip op. at 42 (C.A. Dec. 17, 1993) (Gault, J.).

[17] Slip op. at 21, Privy Council Appeal No. 21 of 1994 (Oct. 19, 1994, Judgment of the Lords of the Judicial Committee of the Privy Council). The "Baumol-Willig Rule" is another name given the efficient component-pricing rule because it was presented in the New Zealand litigation in the testimony of Professor Robert D. Willig and one of the present authors.

[18] Id. at 22.

controlled services. Therefore section 36 is only part of an overall statutory machinery for dealing with trade practices which operate to the detriment of consumers. Another part of such machinery (Part IV) is specifically directed to the regulation of prices in markets which are not fully competitive.[19]

In an earlier essay, we may have been taken to suggest that the Commerce Act provides no power to regulate prices. More precisely, we should have noted that such price regulation, while possible, was not in effect during the interconnection litigation between Telecom and Clear.

Perhaps as a consequence of our exiguous summary of New Zealand law on price regulation, counsel for Clear argued to the Privy Council that–as their Lordships restated the argument–our previous essay in the *Yale Journal on Regulation* "amounted to a recantation by Professor Baumol . . . of the evidence [he] gave in this case."[20] The controversy centered on two passages from the essay in which we discussed the possible persistence of monopoly rents in the efficient component price if no regulation existed to constrain monopoly pricing by Telecom. Quoting our essay at length, Lord Browne-Wilkinson wrote:

> . . . Professor Baumol after referring to the judgment of the Court of Appeal in the present case said (at page 195):–

> "Given these circumstances, we must sympathise with the reasoning of the Court of Appeal. As we explain elsewhere, the efficient component-pricing rule plays its full beneficial role only when adopted as part of a set of complementary rules designed to promote consumer welfare. One such rule is that a monopolist should not be permitted to charge a price for a final product sold to consumers that is higher than the price that would attract an efficient entrant into the market–a price equal to the stand-alone cost of producing that final product. But, as Justice Cooke [of the High Court] noted, no such price ceiling exists under the current laws and regulations of New Zealand. It is therefore understandable that the Court of Appeal ordered Clear and Telecom to renew negotiations to set an access price that excluded any monopoly profit foregone by Telecom."

> Later, after referring to the possible perpetuation of monopoly rents if opportunity costs are charged to an entrant, Professor Baumol said (at page 196):–

> "All this is true, but the villain is not the efficient component-pricing rule. The real problem is that the landlord has been permitted to charge monopoly prices for the final product in the first place. Had the ceiling upon final-product prices been based on stand-alone cost, which as we explain elsewhere it should be, the landlord could never have earned a monopoly profit in this regulatory scenario. The error, therefore, is the failure to impose the stand-alone cost ceiling on the final-product price, not the use of the efficient component-pricing rule."[21]

The Privy Council recognized that, contrary to the assertion of Clear's counsel, our discussion of the Court of Appeal's ruling was entirely consistent with

---

[19] *Id.*
[20] *Id.* at 23 (citing Baumol & Sidak, *supra* note 10).
[21] *Id.* (citing Baumol & Sidak, *supra* note 10, at 195, 196).

Baumol's original testimony to the High Court. With respect to the preceding statements contained in our essay in the *Yale Journal on Regulation*, Lord Browne-Wilkinson wrote:

> In their Lordships' view, the statements by Professor Baumol are not a recantation by him of his evidence given in this case. Throughout, he has accepted that the Rule will initially perpetuate monopoly rents until either (a) they are competed out by Clear's competition in the contested area or (b) they are removed by regulatory action. He is not apparently aware that Part IV of the Commerce Act does in fact provide for a regulatory machinery which could be, but has not been, brought into operation.[22]

The Privy Council similarly saw no inconsistency between Professor Kahn's testimony to the High Court and his subsequent article in this *Journal* with Dr. Taylor.[23] Their Lordships found "nothing in these articles which alters the substance of the evidence considered by the High Court and the Court of Appeal."[24] "The principal question remains, as it always was," wrote Lord Browne-Wilkinson, "whether the actual or potential presence of monopoly rents vitiates the validity of the Baumol-Willig model for purposes of section 36."[25]

The Privy Council answered that question in the negative. Lord Browne-Wilkinson wrote that "the risk of monopoly rents has no bearing upon the question whether the application of the Baumol-Willig Rule prevents competition in the contested area."[26] "If *both* Telecom and Clear are charging their customers the same amount in the area in which they are not competitors," their Lordships reasoned, "this does not have any effect on their relative competitiveness in the area in which they compete."[27] The Privy Council stated that "the underlying object of section 36 will be achieved if the Rule is applied."[28]

The Privy Council thus concluded that the Court of Appeal had erred when it "took the view that section 36 had the wider purpose, beyond producing fair competition, of eliminating monopoly profits currently obtained by the person in the dominant market position."[29] Part IV of the Commerce Act already authorized the government to impose explicit price regulation. It would misconstrue section 36, their Lordships concluded, "to extend its scope to produce a quasi-regulatory system that the Act expressly provides for, with all the necessary powers and safeguards, in another part of the Act."[30] "The

---

[22] *Id.*

[23] "Dr. Kahn also accepted throughout his evidence that, in the absence of regulatory control, his theory of competitive parity led to the possible continuance of monopoly rents. In the second article [on the efficient component-pricing rule in the Winter 1994 issue of the *Yale Journal on Regulation*] (at page 231–2) he persists in that view, although he too is under the misapprehension that no machinery exists in New Zealand to regulate the prices charged by Telecom to Clear." *Id.* at 24.

[24] *Id.*

[25] *Id.*

[26] *Id.* at 27.

[27] *Id.* (emphasis in original).

[28] *Id.*

[29] *Id.*

[30] *Id.* at 28.

consequences of so doing could be unjust and would be impracticable."[31] Moreover, their Lordships seemed to consider it beyond the authority and competence of a court to undertake, in the absence of explicit legislation, the regulation of reasonable prices:

> If, as their Lordships consider, on the true construction of the Commerce Act, section 36 does not operate to exclude Telecom from initially charging monopoly rents (if any) and the elimination of such monopoly rents is (otherwise than by competition) within the province of Part IV of the Act, it is irrelevant to the court's function to take into account Government policy. The Government can either adopt the policy of leaving Clear's competition to compete out Telecom's monopoly rents (if any) or activate the Part IV machinery which is available . . . . But what policy the Government adopts is no concern of the courts.[32]

Having so construed section 36 and the appropriate judicial function in resolving interconnection disputes, the Privy Council concluded that "the final position adopted by Telecom at trial based on the Baumol-Willig Rule did not breach section 36 since it did not involve the use by Telecom of its dominant position."[33]

The Privy Council's decision also suggests how Telecom, despite its ostensible freedom from price regulation, may be subjected to what may be termed "virtual regulation." After noting that "at the end of argument before their Lordships, the parties indicated that their negotiating positions are coming close together," Lord Browne-Wilkinson wrote that "Telecom accepts that it should not seek to recover any element of monopoly rents from Clear since, if necessary, such monopoly rents could be stripped out by the activation of Part IV of the Commerce Act."[34] Thus, the mere threat that the government may commence regulation of the price of the final product of the vertically integrated monopolist may suffice to excise some or all of its monopoly rents from the opportunity-cost portion of the efficient component price. Stated differently, the incumbent's *expected* opportunity cost of providing interconnection to a competitor would exclude the monopoly rent over the final product.

Theoretical Critiques of the Efficient Component-Pricing Rule

The efficient component-pricing rule began influencing actual regulatory policy before the rule had received extensive discussion in the academic journals. However, since courts began issuing decisions in the New Zealand interconnection litigation, thoughtful papers have been written about the rule by Jean-Jacques Laffont and Jean Tirole, by Mark Armstrong and John Vickers, and by Nicholas Economides and Lawrence White.[35]

---

[31]   *Id.*
[32]   *Id.* at 29.
[33]   *Id.*
[34]   *Id.*
[35]   Jean-Jacques Laffont & Jean Tirole, *Access Pricing and Competition*, 38 EURO. ECON. REV. 1673 (1994); Mark Armstrong & John Vickers, The Predatory Access Pricing Problem (mimeo 1994); Nicholas Economides & Lawrence J. White, Access and Interconnection Pricing: How Efficient is the "Efficient Component Pricing Rule"? (mimeo Mar. 1995).

While all three sets of authors discuss limitations of the efficient component-pricing rule, and in one case (Laffont and Tirole) propose an alternative regulatory approach, we do not believe that there is any fundamental disagreement among us. The Armstrong-Vickers paper devotes itself to the ways in which the calculations of opportunity cost must be modified in different circumstances to adapt it to the requirements of optimality. Economides and White, in effect, stress the dangers inherent in the rule when the opportunity cost includes monopoly profit–a limitation that we have repeatedly stressed ourselves, though we have also suggested complementary safeguards designed to reduce or even eliminate the problem. We conclude that these two papers make related points and points that are consistent with the *caveats* we have consistently emphasized.

Professors Laffont and Tirole, in contrast, offer an alternative approach to the prevention of overpricing and the attendant peril of monopoly pricing. They call the procedure a "global price cap," defining it as a ceiling constraint upon a weighted average of the prices charged by the bottleneck proprietor, with the prices of that firm's intermediate-good outputs included in the average, and with the weights exogenously determined. Laffont and Tirole argue that such a cap gives firms the incentive to behave in a manner consistent with the requirements of efficiency, and that the efficient component-pricing rule may then be redundant and may even, possibly, impede efficiency, though they are prepared to consider the rule's desirability as a supplement to a global price cap in practice.

On this, we have only two comments to offer. First, one of the present authors has also argued that in certain circumstances voluntary negotiation between the seller and the buyer of access services will indeed lead to appropriate pricing, because in such cases the parties will have the incentive to do so. Second, we submit that any regulatory regime that does not result in prices that satisfy the parity principle of the efficient component-pricing rule is *not* generally consistent with efficiency because, as we have proven here and elsewhere, any such prices will permit the less efficient of two suppliers of a final product to underprice its more efficient rival. Thus, any regulatory regime that does not lead to parity pricing in one way or another cannot satisfy the requirements for economic efficiency.

Conclusion

Public utility commissions and courts in the United States are likely to pay close attention to the Privy Council's decision in *Telecom* v. *Clear* because of its thorough discussion of how the efficient component-pricing rule can be applied to local telecommunications markets. For the foreseeable future, the central controversy addressed in the appellate phase of the New Zealand litigation–namely, the permissibility of allowing the incumbent firm to recover monopoly rents in the opportunity-cost component of its interconnection charge–will be a lesser concern in American regulatory proceedings than it was in New Zealand simply because virtually all state and federal regulatory jurisdictions in the United States currently regulate the prices that consumers are charged by monopolists for their end products.

Thus, the efficient component-pricing rule should be even more readily adopted in the United States than in countries with New Zealand's form of "light-handed" regulation of telecommunications. Furthermore, the regulatory changes promoting the growth of wholesale and retail wheeling of electric power in the United States will require both state and federal regulators to address interconnection pricing in the near future, if they have not already done so. These developments suggest that over the next five years a rich body of regulatory law will emerge on the price that the regulated firm should charge for its sale of services to competitors.

Bibliography

Armstrong, Mark, and John Vickers, "The Predatory Access Pricing Problem," (mimeo 1994).

Baumol, William J., and J. Gregory Sidak, "The Pricing of Inputs Sold to Competitors," 11 *Yale Journal on Regulation* 171, 189–94 (1994).

Economides, Nicholas, and Lawrence J. White, "Access and Interconnection Pricing: How Efficient is the 'Efficient Component Pricing Rule'?," (mimeo Mar. 1995).

Farmer, James, "Transition from Protected Monopoly to Competition: The New Zealand Experiment," 1 *Competition and Consumer Law Journal* 1 (1993).

Kahn, Alfred E., and William Taylor, "The Pricing of Inputs Sold to Competitors: A Comment," 11 *Yale Journal on Regulation* 225, 229 (1994).

Laffont, Jean-Jacques, and Jean Tirole, "Access Pricing and Competition," 38 *European Economic Review* 1673 (1994).

Tye, William B., "The Pricing of Inputs Sold to Competitors: A Response," 11 *Yale Journal on Regulation* 203 (1994).

Competitive Entry into Regulated Monopoly Services and the Resulting Problem of Stranded Costs

Michael J. Doane
Michael A. Williams

Synopsis

Recent attempts to achieve regulatory reform in the public utility industries have focused on separating out the potentially competitive activities of firms and deregulating these activities. This reform by vertical divestiture has raised the possibility that incumbent firms will be left with large unrecoverable costs in markets for the deregulated services. Both the incumbent firms and the regulatory agencies have proposed that stranded costs be treated as a transition payment incurred in introducing competition into a previously regulated industry. This essay reviews the Federal Energy Regulatory Commissions stranded cost experience in the natural gas industry and the events which gave rise to FERCs rationale for stranded cost recovery in the electric industry. The Commissions mechanism for stranded cost recovery in wholesale power markets is assessed based on economic efficiency criteria. We show that the Commissions proposal can fail to meet efficiency criteria, but a modification of the recovery mechanism offers improved economic performance.

*　　*　　*　　*

Introduction

"And now our case was very dismal indeed. . . ."
Robinson Crusoe

A coming storm of wholesale and retail competition threatens to sink large parts of the U.S. electric utility industry, stranding $300 billion of embedded generating costs. Utility investors financed the construction of these facilities on the basis of a "regulatory compact" in which they agreed to forgo monopoly rents in exchange for a guarantee that utility franchises had an exclusive right to serve final customers. Now the compact threatens to run aground, stranding investors.

We analyze the origins of stranded cost problems in regulated industries by examining the development and treatment of stranded costs in the natural gas industry. The Federal Energy Regulatory Commission ("FERC" or "Commission") recently restructured that industry by divesting pipelines of their merchant sales service. In the process, FERC confronted the issue of stranded costs, assessed the need for stranded cost compensation, and developed recovery mechanisms. We then discuss the evolution of the stranded cost problem in the electric industry and the likely consequences of ignoring stranded costs. Finally, we analyze whether the FERC's recent proposal for preventing stranded costs in wholesale power markets meets established economic efficiency criteria.[1] We show that the FERC's proposal can fail to meet efficiency criteria, but a simple modification of the recovery mechanism offers improved economic performance.

Vertical Divestiture of the Natural Gas and Electric Industries and the Creation of Stranded Costs

> "I cast my eyes to the stranded vessel, when, the breach and froth of the sea being so big, I could hardly see it, it lay so far off, and consider, Lord! how was it possible I could get on shore!"
> Robinson Crusoe

In the past decade, the FERC put in place rulemakings and orders designed to achieve reform of the natural gas and electric industries through vertical divestiture. In the early stages of these reforms, the FERC failed to consider the economic consequences reform would have on the obligations and costs of incumbent monopoly providers. In particular, the FERC's efforts to promote competition in the natural gas industry were hindered when the Commission refused to take action to alleviate the burden that uneconomic take-or-pay contracts placed on pipelines. FERC's unwillingness to take action caused large take-or-pay liabilities to accrue and, more importantly, delayed the introduction of competition into the natural gas industry. The lesson, however, was well learned, as more recent attempts to achieve reform through vertical divestiture have addressed the possibility that incumbent firms will be left with large unrecoverable costs. In this context, stranded costs can best be understood as a transition payment incurred in introducing competition into a previously regulated industry.[2]

---

[1] FERC (March 29, 1995), NOTICE OF PROPOSED RULEMAKING AND SUPPLEMENTAL NOTICE OF PROPOSED RULEMAKING, RECOVERY OF STRANDED COSTS BY PUBLIC UTILITIES AND TRANSMITTING UTILITIES, DOCKET NO. RM94–7–001, 70 FERC ¶ 61,357 (hereinafter "Notice"). The Notice deals only with stranded cost caused by wholesale wheeling, but the FERC notes that 85 percent of stranded costs likely will be due to retail wheeling.

[2] Seen in this way, the transition of regulated industries to more competitive structures parellels the efforts of Eastern European countries to introduce competition into their previously command-oriented economies. Not suprisingly, massive capital investments undertaken by prior regimes are now essentially worthless, the stranded costs having been paid for by wage earners. See Blanchard, O., Froot, K., and Sachs, J. (eds.) (1994), THE TRANSITION IN EASTERN EUROPE: VOLUME 1, COUNTRY STUDIES; VOLUME 2, RESTRUCTURING, Chicago and London: University of Chicago Press.

In this section, we review the Commission's stranded cost experience in the natural gas industry. We investigate the conditions that gave rise to stranded costs and the FERC's rationale for cost recovery. We then explore conditions in the electric industry that have given rise to even larger stranded costs.

The Natural Gas Experience

Since its inception, traditional buyer and seller relationships in the natural gas industry hinged on the activities of pipeline companies. Pipelines purchased for resale almost all the gas they transported, supplying marketing and transportation services as a single, bundled product. As marketers they entered into long-term contracts with field producers; as transporters they resold the gas, also under long-term contracts to local retail distributors and large industrial buyers.

The Saga of Wellhead Price Controls and the NGPA Response

The *Natural Gas Act of 1938* authorized the Commissions predecessor, the Federal Power Commission ("FPC"), to regulate pipeline rates for gas and transportation services provided to retail customers in interstate commerce according to the "just and reasonable" standard.[3] Following the Supreme Court's 1954 ruling in *Philips Petroleum Co. v. Wisconsin*, FPC jurisdiction was extended to producers selling gas in interstate commerce.[4] The *Phillips* decision resulted in a long period of wellhead price regulation that was, by all standards, a dismal failure.[5] The Commission's approach was to treat producers as individual public utilities and set prices on the basis of individual costs of service. However, there were more than 5,000 producers, and by 1960 more than 2,900 applications for increased rates awaited FPC action. To cope with the intractable problems involved in estimating gas development costs from combined oil and gas operations, and its enormous backlog of rate cases, the Commission in 1965 set regional ceiling prices in broadly defined producing regions. Price ceilings throughout the 1960s were based on drilling and development costs established in the prior decade. By the mid-1970s, these price controls caused a widespread and significant shortage of gas.[6]

The *Natural Gas Policy Act of 1978* ("NGPA") was, in part, a response to the gas shortage.[7] The plan was to deregulate marginal supplies of gas at some future date and to increase prices for gas supplies at a rapid rate in the interim. Implementation involved an elaborate plan that specified price categories on the basis of production methods; whether the gas was sold under prior interstate contracts; and many other factors. Since the NGPA maintained

---

[3] 15 U.S.C § 717–717w (1988).
[4] *Philips Petroleum Co. v. Wisconsin*, 347 U.S. 672 (1954).
[5] See Breyer, S. and MacAvoy, P. (1974), ENERGY REGULATION BY THE FEDERAL POWER COMMISSION, Washington, D.C.: The Brookings Institution.
[6] See MacAvoy, P. and Pindyck, R. (1975), THE ECONOMICS OF THE NATURAL GAS SHORTAGE (1960–1980), New York, NY: North Holland Publishing Company.
[7] 15 U.S.C. § 3301–3432 (1988).

TABLE 1   SELECTED GAS PRICES, 1982–1988
(1988 DOLLARS PER THOUSAND CUBIC FEET)

Year	Spot Gas	WACOG[1]	Long-Term Contract
1982	NA	3.73	NA
1983	NA	3.85	NA
1984	3.33	3.57	3.36
1985	2.64	3.32	3.02
1986	1.72	2.78	2.05
1987	1.50	2.41	2.06
1988[1]	1.60	2.19	2.68

Notes:
[1] Pipeline weighted average cost of gas.
[2] Third quarter (September) of 1988.
Source: Energy Information Administration (1989), GROWTH IN UNBUNDLED NATURAL GAS TRANSPORTATION SERVICES, Table 15.

strict controls on old gas, and relaxed controls on new gas and deregulated "deep" gas, pipelines seeking to contract for additional supplies (in anticipation of future shortages in the 1980s) bid up the prices of new and deep gas substantially above market-clearing levels. These price distortions were the direct result of the FERC's average cost price regulation of the pipelines merchant service. Merchant gas was priced to consumers on the basis of pipelines weighted average cost of gas ("WACOG"). Since high-cost gas and low-cost gas were "rolled-in" to the WACOG, pipelines purchased expensive new and deep gas.

Eventually pipelines with smaller "cushions" of old gas faced higher average gas purchase costs. This led to many contract disputes as pipelines sought to avoid losses from take-or-pay obligations. These losses were either in the form of payments for gas not taken; above-market payments for gas that was taken; or payments to settle contract disputes. Gas not taken reverted back to producers and was instrumental in establishing the "spot" market.[8] As shown in Table One, by 1984 pipeline merchant gas priced on the basis of the WACOG exceeded the price of gas in spot and long-term markets.

The Commission's open-access policies (Order Nos. 436 and 500) of the mid-1980s enabled local distributors to bypass pipeline merchant gas and acquire gas from wellhead suppliers at lower prices. Not surprisingly, the growth of gas purchased from parties other than pipelines increased dramatically. In 1982, pipelines owned almost all the gas they transported, but by 1991, pipelines owned less than one-fifth of the gas transported in interstate commerce. Divestiture of pipeline merchant service had, in effect, occurred without a formal ruling.

Continuing its efforts to establish unbundled, open-access pipeline transportation services, the Commission in April 1992 established a detailed plan

[8]   *See* Doane, M. and Spulber, D. (1994), *Open Access and The Evolution of the U.S. Spot Market for Natural Gas*, 37 JOURNAL OF LAW AND ECONOMICS 477–517.

in Order No. 636 for completing its restructuring of interstate pipeline services.[9] Exercising its authority under Section 5 of the *Natural Gas Act*, the Commission found the pre-Order No. 636 regulatory structure, which included the terms of existing pipeline transportation service, unduly discriminatory and anticompetitive.[10] Although unbundling of sales and transportation services had largely taken place, the Commission was of the opinion that consumers did not have adequate access to the competitive wellhead market, alleging that pipelines refused to provide open-access transportation services that were "comparable" to transportation services embedded in their own merchant services. The Commission concluded that its unbundling of pipeline transportation services would "have a significant beneficial impact on the natural gas industry by furthering the creation of an efficient national wellhead market. . . ."[11] To achieve this goal, Order No. 636 mandated that pipelines unbundle their sales and transportation service, and provide open-access transportation services equal in quality for all gas supplies, whether purchased from the pipeline or elsewhere.

Transition Cost Recovery

The Commission recognized that divestiture would impose certain "transition costs" on the pipelines, and that these costs would generate significant implementation delays unless dealt with at an early stage. In particular, the Commission recognized unbundling would create four types of costs: (1) unrecovered gas purchase costs resulting from the adoption of market-based gas pricing in lieu of a purchased gas adjustment mechanism; (2) gas supply realignment ("GSR") costs resulting from the need to revise or terminate existing contracts with gas suppliers; (3) costs incurred in connection with providing bundled sales service that could not be directly assigned to customers of bundled service (which the FERC explicitly labeled "stranded costs"); and (4) costs of new facilities required to implement the Order.

The Commission's position was that pipelines would be allowed to collect all prudently incurred costs, but the question was: who would bear the costs in each specific category? In the end, the burden was spread. Pipelines recouped unrecovered gas purchase costs from their former bundled, firm sales customers through a direct billing mechanism; the majority of GSR costs were recovered through negotiated exit fees or reservation fee surcharges in firm transportation contracts (ten percent of GSR costs were recovered in rates for interruptible service); and stranded costs, consisting mainly of the costs of gas in storage and capacity on upstream pipelines that could not be assigned to customers of unbundled services, as well as the costs of new facilities, were recovered in general rate cases.

The Commission's recognition of transition costs, and its approach for dealing with them, differed from its position five years earlier when, in Order

---

[9] Order No. 636, Final Rule (April 8, 1992) and Subsequent Order Nos. 636–A (August 3, 1992) and 636–B (November 27, 1992).
[10] Order No. 636 at 39–40.
[11] Order No. 636–A at 40–41.

No. 436, it declined to take direct action to alleviate the burden uneconomic take-or-pay contracts placed on pipelines. That burden increased significantly in the early 1980s when the Commission eliminated the variable cost component of the minimum-bill obligations for pipeline customers in Order No. 380. By removing costs associated with maintaining supplies of gas available for purchase from pipelines minimum commodity bills, the Commission effectively eliminated the requirement that pipelines customers purchase any minimum quantity of gas. Pipelines holding reciprocal long-term gas purchase agreements with take-or-pay provisions were left holding an empty bag. By the end of 1986, ten billion dollars worth of contracts were involved in lengthy take-or-pay disputes.[12]

In *American Gas Distributors*, the U.S. Court of Appeals for the District Court of Columbia faulted the Commission for failing to address the effect of regulatory change on pipelines take-or-pay obligations.[13] The Court noted pipelines were "caught in an unusual transition" as a result of regulatory changes beyond their control.[14]

With respect to its current effort to restructure the electric industry, the Commission notes:

> The Courts reasoning in [American Gas Distributors] concerning the restructuring of the gas industry is also applicable to the current move to competitive bulk power markets in the electric industry. Once again, a regulated industry is faced with an "unusual transition" to a more competitive market. Once again, one result of the transition is the possibility that utilities will be left with large unrecoverable costs.[15]

The Coming Problem of Stranded Costs in the Electric Industry

In contrast to the natural gas industry, electric power has long been supplied by large, vertically integrated utilities. These utilities own and operate generation, transmission, and distribution facilities and sell, as a bundled service, delivered power to wholesale and retail customers.[16] There are over 3,500 separate electric systems in the U.S., of which the largest 200 provide approximately ninety percent of the industrys generating capacity and serve nearly eighty percent of final customers. In contrast, the remaining 3,300 systems own little or no generation or transmission facilities; instead, they function as distributors of electric energy purchased at wholesale.

Federal regulation governs the licensing and operation of non-federal hydroelectric projects on federal waterways and the interstate transmission and sale of power at wholesale. The Commission's jurisdiction over wholesale electric rates amounts to approximately 28 percent of the industrys total domestic sales. Remaining sales involve retail electric power subject to the jurisdiction of state public utilities commissions.

---

[12] *See* Wald, M. (November 7, 1988), *Gas Producers See an End to Disputes with Pipelines*, NEW YORK TIMES.

[13] *American Gas Distributors v. FERC*, 824 F.2d 981, 998 (D.C.Cir 1987).

[14] *Id.* at 1021.

[15] Notice at 157.

[16] *See* Federal Energy Regulatory Commission, (1981), POWER POOLING IN THE UNITED STATES, Washington D.C.: Government Printing Office, p. 5.

The Structure of the Industry in the 1960s

In the post-war era, the electrification of America was a national priority. From 1950 to 1959, electricity sales grew at an average annual rate of 22 percent.[17] In the early 1960s, the expectation was that demand would continue to grow, but at rates less than previously observed. Inflation rates, interest rates, and fuel pries were low and stable. These conditions, combined with substantial technological advances, made electric generation a declining-cost industry. In the expanding economy, assisted by a regulatory system that stayed out of the way, utility stocks provided low risk and steady returns to capital market investors.

The perception that utilities were stable investments was reinforced by an implicit arrangement known as *the regulatory compact*. Under that compact, an investor-owned utility ("IOU") was granted an exclusive franchise to serve a specific geographic area and an opportunity to earn a "fair" return on prudently incurred expenses. In return, the utility had to offer rates deemed "just and reasonable" by regulation and accept a "duty" or "obligation" to serve.[18] Under rate-of-return regulation, the compact can be expressed as the requirement that the present value of the stream of quasirents (i.e., revenues minus operating costs) allowed by regulation exactly equal initial investment costs.[19]

By the late 1960s, conditions affecting the industry began to change. Inflation emerged as a major problem facing the U.S. economy and nominal interest rates increased. During this period, construction of nuclear and other capital-intensive baseload facilities made on the expectation that demand would continue to grow contributed to rising power costs. From 1960 to 1969, the average retail price of power increased by thirty percent (in real terms).[20]

The Troubled 1970s

In the early 1970s, increased U.S. and domestic demand for oil outpaced the country's ability to "back up" imported oil in case of supply disruptions. Public and governmental concern led many utilities to consider options for reducing their dependence on crude oil, such as coal (an old option) and nuclear (a new option). Rapidly escalating crude oil prices resulting from the OPEC oil embargo in 1973, which led the American Petroleum Institute in 1974 to forecast that crude oil prices would reach forty dollars a barrel by 1980,[21] accelerated the actions of utilities in reducing their dependence on foreign oil. In many parts of the country, coal-fired generation was restricted, as air emissions standards became more stringent under the recently enacted *Clean Air Act*.

---

[17] *See* Energy Information Administration, (1992), ANNUAL REVIEW OF ENERGY, p. 223.
[18] *See Hope Natural Gas Co. v. Federal Power Commission*, U.S. 591 (1944).
[19] Under rate-of-return regulation, the revenue earned by a utility in each period equals the sum of its operating cost, depreciation, and a market (fair) rate of return applied to the value of the rate base at the beginning of the period.
[20] *See supra* note 17, at 233.
[21] *See* American Petroleum Institute, (1974), PETROLEUM DATA BOOK, Table 8.

In November 1973, with long lines at gasoline stations and growing public frustration over the rising price of energy, President Nixon announced "Project Independence," an ambitious plan to achieve an independent U.S. energy system by the end of the decade. That plan anticipated nuclear power would be relied upon for thirty to forty percent of U.S. electricity requirements. In 1975, President Ford presented his own version of Project Independence, calling for 200 nuclear power plants in the U.S.

Attempts to diversify away from expensive fossil fuels, however, did not produce the intended results. Delays in nuclear power construction and escalating construction costs exerted pressure on utility earnings. In 1980, capital spending, largely for the construction of new generation facilities, exceeded $28 billion, seven times the level of expenditures in 1965.[22] With interest rates on newly issued bonds rising from 4.6 percent in 1965 to 13.5 percent in 1980, Moody's average stock price for electric utilities declined by over fifty percent, from $117 per share in 1965 to just under $55 per share in 1980.[23] Market-to-book ratios declined steadily to a low of 0.66 in 1980.[24]

The Moral Equivalent of War

In response to increased pressure from environmentalists and a desire to diversify away from fossil fuel plants, the *Public Utility Regulatory Policies Act of 1978* ("PURPA") was passed as part of President Carter's "Energy Plan."[25] PURPA was enacted to stimulate the use of alternative and renewable energy sources in the generation of electric power.[26] The Act required FERC to establish regulations for utility purchases of power from Qualifying Facilities ("QFs") which were defined as nonutility power producers meeting certain operating, efficiency, and fuel-use standards.[27] QFs included producers who used renewable energy and alternative energy sources such as hydro, wind, solar, and geothermal energy, and cogenerators who generated electricity using thermal energy created during manufacturing processes. PURPA required a utility to interconnect with, and buy power from, QFs at an estimate of the utilitys avoided costs (defined as what it would cost the utility to generate the same power, including the cost of new capacity required to meet load growth). Many state commissions established "standard offer" contracts that allowed QFs to sell long-term power (up to ten years) to the utilities based on forecasts of avoided costs that assumed oil prices would be three times their current level.[28]

[22] Hyman, L. (1992), AMERICA'S ELECTRIC UTILITIES: PAST, PRESENT, AND FUTURE, Arlington, VA: Public Utilities Reports, Table 14–5.
[23] *Id* at 31, Table 14–7.
[24] *Id* at 31, Table 14–7.
[25] 16 U.S.C. § 2601–2645, 2701–2708 (1988).
[26] PURPA also encouraged utilities to consider rate designs and load management programs to conserve energy.
[27] Under PURPA, QFs are defined as power producers with capacities less than eighty megawatts or cogenerators for which at least five percent of their total energy output is in the form of useful thermal energy.
[28] In the state of New York, the "Six Cent Law" required utilities to pay a minimum of $0.06 per kWh for projects less than 80 megawatts, although the utilities long-run marginal costs were less than half that value. Although ultimately repealed for future contracts, many existing contracts were "grandfathered" under this requirement.

PURPA also outlined procedures and requirements for ratemaking and the promotion of energy conservation. The legislation mandated the offering of load management options to all users, thus ushering in the age of "demand-side management" ("DSM") and the "negawatt." Justified on the basis that consumers would not make cost-effective investments in energy conservation on their own, state public utility commissions ordered utilities to develop programs to encourage consumers to purchase energy-efficient technologies and adopt energy conscious behavioral practices. When zero-cost financing and appliance rebates failed, utilities were asked to give away weatherization and other demand-reducing devices. In 1991, one analyst expected that utility DSM expenditures would exceed $165 billion over the next ten to fifteen years.[29]

The Development of Nonutility Power

During the 1980s the ownership profile of electric generation capacity began to change. Power purchased from QFs grew as state commissions promoted their development through inefficient avoided-cost pricing rules. At the same time, technological advances allowed economies of scale to be achieved at smaller levels of output, challenging the embedded price of large-scale plants brought on line in the 1970s. Smaller and more efficient gas-fired, combined-cycle generation facilities, for example, were brought on line at costs significantly less than operating coal or nuclear plants.[30]

Advances in transmission technology were also realized, making it feasible to transport power over longer distances at higher voltage levels. Producers with low-cost power could now, in principle, reach previously isolated systems where customers had been captive to higher-cost generation.

Impediments to the development of nonutility generation remained, however. In particular, ownership restrictions in the *Public Utility Holding Company Act* ("PUHCA") limited entry into generation and failed to implement the open-access transmission policies required for nonutility generators to compete.[31] Lacking the authority to remove PUHCA restrictions, the Commission encouraged the development of independent power producers ("IPPs") by authorizing market-based rates for their power sales on a case-by-case basis. As was the case with PURPA, inefficient entry was again encouraged: nonutility generators selling power at market-based rates could undercut the prices of existing utilities burdened with cost-of-service tariffs and procedural delays in achieving approvals for selective discounting. Eventually, the Commission implemented market-based rates for IOUs as well as IPPs and marketers, in return for IOUs opening their transmission systems to competitors.

---

[29] *See* Hirst, E. (1991), *Fulfilling the Demand-side Promise*, 128 PUBLIC UTILITIES FORTNIGHTLY 31.

[30] *See* Energy Information Administration, (1993) ELECTRIC POWER PLANT COST AND POWER PRODUCTION EXPENSES 1991; and Bayless, C. (December 1, 1994), *Less is More: Why Gas Turbines Will Transform Electric Utilities*, 132 PUBLIC UTILITIES FORTNIGHTLY.

[31] 15 U.S.C. § 79–79z–6.

To further enhance the development of nonutility generation, Congress passed the *Energy Policy Act of 1992* amending the *Public Utility Holding Company Act*.[32] The *Energy Policy Act* relaxed ownership restrictions of PUHCA that inhibited companies from entering the generation business. To do this it created "exempt wholesale generators" ("EWGs") and allowed both utilities and nonutilities to form EWGs without triggering holding company provisions. The Act also allowed the Commission to order (upon application), wholesale, but not retail, transmission access on a case-by-case basis and transmission service by utilities, subject to certain provisions.

The growth of nonutility electric power generation grew at a rapid pace. By 1992 the number of QFs increased to 1,179 nationwide, with an installed capacity of 43,760 megawatts.[33] The number of facilities brought on line by IPPs increased to 629 by 1992, with an installed capacity of 13,054 megawatts.[34] Thus, by 1992 the total capacity of nonutility generators represented approximately ten percent of the generating capacity of U.S. electric utilities. Since 1992, generating capacity added by IPPs has exceeded capacity additions of electric utilities.[35]

By 1993, the electric utilities ship had struck ground far from shore. Weighted down by the high embedded cost of previous investments, and rate structures containing cross subsidies, the utilities faced competition from nonutility generators free from the encumbrances of rate regulation and obligations to serve. With the advent of open access and the wholesale "wheeling" of power, even prudent costs may become stranded. With retail wheeling, their situation is "very dismal indeed."

The Magnitude of The Stranded Cost Problem in the Electric Industry and the FERC's Response

> "I believe that the reader of this will not think strange if I confess that these anxieties, these constant dangers I lived in, and the concern that was upon me now, put an end to all invention and to all the contrivances that I had laid for my future accommodations and conveniences."
> Robinson Crusoe

In its March 1995 Notice, the FERC defined stranded costs caused by wholesale wheeling in the electric industry as:

> any legitimate, prudent and verifiable cost incurred by a public utility or a transmitting utility to provide service to: (i) a wholesale requirements customer that subsequently becomes, in whole or in part, an unbundled wholesale transmission services customer of such public utility or transmitting utility or (ii) a retail customer, or newly created wholesale power sales customer, that subsequently becomes, in whole or in part, an unbundled wholesale transmission services customer of such public utility or transmitting utility.[36]

---

[32] Pub. L. No. 102–486, 106 State. 2776 (1992).
[33] Energy Information Administration, (1994), ELECTRIC POWER ANNUAL 1992, p. 125
[34] *Id.* at 125.
[35] *Id.* at 23.
[36] Notice at 198.

The FERC's definition is in essential agreement with that offered by Professors Baumol, Joskow, and Kahn, who defined stranded costs as:

> past investments, contractual commitments, and deferred recoveries of expenses, previously reviewed and approved (and, in some cases, mandated) by regulators, that have not yet been fully recovered by the utility companies, and that could not be recovered in a fully competitive market because competitors would bear no such burdens.[37]

There is near unanimity that stranded costs in the electric industry loom large. According to one analyst, stranded costs "are as high as $200 – $300 billion, versus total shareholder equity of $175 billion." Another analyst estimates stranded costs will run "$30 to $40 billion per year for the next several years assuming 100 percent retail access." Thus, not only are stranded costs larger than the Gross Domestic Product of Mexico, they surpass total shareholder equity in every investor-owned utility in the U.S.

Who Should Pay?

In its Notice, the FERC concluded that stranded costs should not be borne by utilities shareholders because that "could threaten the stability of the industry and the service it provides. . . ."[40] The Commission concluded that stranded costs should be prevented by a "direct assignment of stranded costs to the departing wholesale customer. . . . We believe it only appropriate that the departing customer, and not the remaining customers (or shareholders), bear its fair share of the legitimate and prudent obligations that the utility undertook on that customers behalf."[41]

In its determination that stranded costs should be paid for by departing customers, the FERC chose a different and more restricted set of customers than was chosen in its restructuring of the natural gas industry. In the implementation of Order No. 636, the FERC chose to recover stranded costs from all customers in general transportation rate cases for interstate pipelines. The difference in the two sets of customers, departing customers in the electric industry versus all customers in the natural gas industry, follows from the fact that unbundling in the gas industry was essentially complete by 1992 when Order No. 636 took effect. Recall that by 1991, bundled sales accounted for

---

[37] Baumol, W., Joskow, P., and Kahn, A. (December 1994), *The Challenge for Federal and State Regulators: Transition from Regulation to Efficient Competition in Electric Power*, Appendix A of the Comments of the Edison Electric Institute in Response to FERC, Notice of Proposed Rulemaking on Recovery of Stranded Costs by Public Utilities and Transmitting Utilities, Docket No. RM94–7–000 (June 1994). *See also* Baumol, W., and Sidak, J. G., Stranded Costs, 18 HARVARD JOURNAL OF LAW AND PUBLIC POLICY 1–15.

[38] Flaim, T. (March 1994), *Stranded Investment – $300 Billion Anchor or "Tonya Harding" Issue?*, 6 ELECTRICITY JOURNAL 17.

[39] Kahal, M. (November 1994), *An Economic Perspective on Competition and the Electric Utility Industry*, prepared for the Electric Consumers' Alliance's Comments in Response to FERC, Notice of Proposed Rulemaking on Recovery of Stranded Costs by Public Utilities and Transmitting Utilities, Docket No. RM94–7–000 (June 1994).

[40] Notice at 169.

[41] Notice at 175–176.

only 16 percent of throughput on interstate pipelines.[42] Since 84 percent of pipeline throughput was for customers who had stopped receiving bundled sales prior to 1992, the FERC could not reasonably ask only the remaining 16 percent of customers to pay for stranded costs caused by Order No. 636 since its own open-access policies, starting with Order No. 436 in 1985, had encouraged customers to purchase unbundled transportation services. As the Commission noted in its March 1995 Notice, "the direct assignment approach for addressing stranded costs for the electric industry differs from the approach eventually taken for the natural gas industry. . . . by the time the Commission issued Order No. 636, changes in the natural gas industry had progressed to such a point that it was not possible for the Commission to use a strict cost causation approach. Many natural gas customers had already left their historical pipeline suppliers' systems."[43]

The Commission's determination that stranded costs should be paid for by departing customers stands in stark contrast to that of other commentators. For example, Michaels (1994) asserted that shareholders should pay all stranded costs.[44] He argued that any assets held by utilities whose market value falls below book value (net of depreciation) are casualties of competition for which ratepayers owe nothing. Michaels advocated treating utilities' assets in the same way that the competitive process treats the assets of firms competing in unregulated markets. The market value of the assets of any firm equals its present discounted net cash flows. If market conditions change so that the present discounted value of an assets net cash flows equals zero, the asset is worthless but not "stranded" in the sense that the firm has no claim on any market participant to reimburse it for the assets lost value. In Michaels' colorful language: "No other industry can tap widows and orphans to undo $300 billion of retrospective mistakes."[45]

Identifying and Quantifying Stranded Costs

In its March 1995 Notice, the FERC determined that whether or not a particular electric utility industry cost was stranded should be determined on the basis of a "reasonable expectation standard." This standard states that a utility claiming that an exiting wholesale customer should be assigned stranded costs must show that "it incurred the costs based on a reasonable expectation when the costs were incurred that the applicable [wholesale power] contract would be extended."[46] Assuming that a utility can make a showing that it meets the "reasonable expectation standard," the FERC addressed the issue of how precisely to quantify the dollar value of the stranded costs.

The Notice suggested that stranded costs should be quantified by estimating the revenues lost by a utility as a result of wholesale customer bypass. That is, stranded costs should be calculated by "subtracting [1] the competitive market

---

[42] See Doane and Spulber, note 8.
[43] Notice at 176–177.
[44] Michaels, R. (October 1994), *Unused and Useless: The Strange Economics of Stranded Investment*, 7 ELECTRICITY JOURNAL 12–22.
[45] *Id.* at 20.
[46] Notice at 201.

value of the power the customer would have purchased from the utility (and the basic revenues from the transmission service) had the customer continued to take service under its contract from [2] the revenues that the customer would have paid the utility."[47] The Commission noted that calculating the monetary values of these two items could be problematic. For example, in calculating the revenues a customer would have paid the utility had the customer continued to take service from the utility, should the existing rate and service levels be used, or should adjustments be allowed based on forecasts of future rates and demands? The Commission also pointed out that defining the period in which the two revenue streams should be calculated could be difficult. Should the period be the life of the remaining contract; or the length of one additional contract extension; or the utilitys planning horizon?

Does the FERC's "Revenue Lost" Mechanism Meet Established Economic Criteria?

"When I waked it was broad day, the weather clear, and the storm abated, so that the sea did not rage and swell as before."
Robinson Crusoe

If investors are to be compensated for stranded costs, what economic criteria should guide the design of mechanisms for the recovery of stranded costs? The first economic criterion of relevance is that of productive or technical efficiency, which states that the costs of producing any given output should be as low as possible. Thus, for example, the costs of producing a given quantity of electric power should be minimized. The second economic criterion is that of efficiency in exchange or Pareto optimality, which states that an allocation of products is efficient if no individual can be made better off without necessarily making another individual worse off.[48] The final economic criterion is that prices should equal marginal costs so as to maximize economic welfare.[49]

Whether or not the FERC's "revenue loss" mechanism meets these economic criteria turns out to depend on whether the incumbent utilitys marginal costs are more or less than the competitive price in the bulk power market. This is an empirical question for which some evidence can be provided. There are two cases to be considered, the first in which the nonutility generator has not sunk the capital costs of constructing generation facilities, and the second in which it has sunk these costs.

In the first case, the average incremental costs in dollars per kilowatt hour (kWh) of nonutility generators for different technologies have been estimated as those shown in Figure One. For low-capacity generation plants, e.g., less than 20 megawatts, diesel engine generation facilities are the most efficient, for example the average incremental cost (including capital costs) for a 10 megawatt plant equals $0.085 per kWh. This cost approximately equals the

---

[47]   Notice at 216.

[48]   *See, e.g.,* Nicholson, W. (1985), MICROECONOMIC THEORY: BASIC PRINCIPLES AND EXTENSIONS, Chicago: Dryden Press, at 610.

[49]   Of course, if a firm operates with declining average costs, its price must exceed marginal cost. In this case, nonlinear prices must be charged to maximize the sum of consumers and producers surplus. *See* Wilson, R. (1994), NONLINEAR PRICES, New York: Oxford University Press.

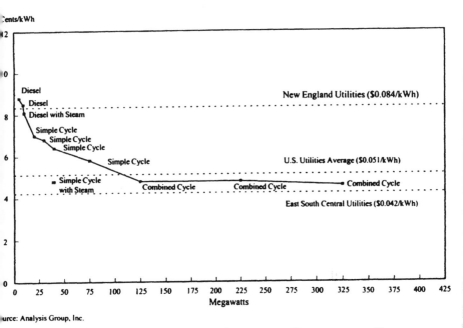

Source: Analysis Group, Inc.

FIGURE 1   COST OF NON-UTILITY ELECTRIC GENERATION IN COMPARISON WITH UTILITIES
AVERAGE INDUSTRIAL RATES

average industrial rate charged by electric utilities in New England during the
period July 1993 to June 1994, which was $0.084 per kWh. For larger capacity
generation plants, e.g., up to 75 megawatts, simple-cycle combustion turbine
generation plants are most efficient, with average incremental costs ranging
from approximately $0.070 per kWh to $0.058 per kWh, although the addition
of a heat recovery steam generator reduces costs to less than $0.050 per kWh.
This compares with the average industrial rate charged by U.S. electric utilities
during this period of $0.051 per kWh. Finally, for generation plants with larger
capacities, e.g., up to 350 megawatts, combined-cycle combustion turbine
plants are most efficient, with average incremental costs as low as $0.046 kWh.
This compares with the lowest-cost region in the U.S. (the East South Central,
consisting of Kentucky, Alabama, and Mississippi) which had an average
industrial rate of $0.042 per kWh during this period.[50]

If attention is restricted to smaller generation plants used by cogenerators
and industrial end-users, the average incremental costs (including capital
costs) are those shown in Figure Two. As indicated in the figure, the addition
of a heat recovery steam generator lowers average costs by approximately
$0.02 per kWh, so that a simple-cycle generation plant with a steam energy
source can achieve an average incremental cost of approximately $0.047 per
kWh even with a plant capacity of only 40 megawatts.

In the second case in which the nonutility generator has already sunk its

---

[50]   The lowest cost state in the 1993 to 1994 period was Idaho ($0.028 per kWh), while the highest
cost state was New Hampshire ($0.094 per kWh). See Edison Electric Institute (1994), TYPICAL
RESIDENTIAL COMMERCIAL, AND INDUSTRIAL BILLS.

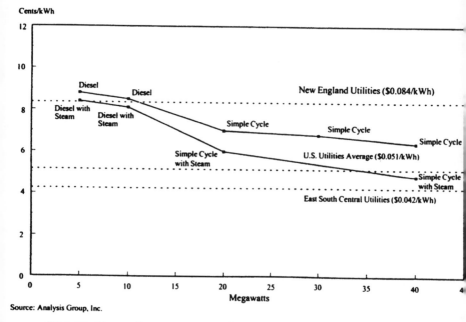

Cents/kWh

Source: Analysis Group, Inc.

FIGURE 2 COST OF COGENERATION AND SELF-GENERATION IN COMPARISON WITH UTILITIES
AVERAGE INDUSTRIAL RATES

capital costs, the above cost estimates would be reduced. For example, for a
20 megawatt simple-cycle combustion turbine generation plant, capital costs
amount to approximately 20 percent of total plant costs. Therefore, if a
nonutility generator has sunk the capital costs of a 20 megawatt simply-cycle
plant, its average variable cost would be approximately 20 percent less than
the average incremental cost shown in Figure Two, which was based on the
assumption that capital costs had not yet been sunk. Thus, a 20 megawatt
simple-cycle plant with a heat recovery steam generator would have average
variable costs of approximately $0.048 per kWh rather than average incremen-
tal costs (including capital costs) of $0.060 per kWh. The other generation
facilities shown in Figures One and Two also would have commensurately
lower average variable costs if plant capital costs were sunk.

This discussion of electric generating costs shows that the marginal costs of
nonutility generators can be less than the industrial rates charged by U.S.
utilities. However, this does not mean that nonutility generators are more
efficient. Utilities industrial rates are based on embedded costs (historical
value of the rate base net of depreciation) and so can exceed their marginal
costs. Non-utility generators are more efficient than utilities only if their
marginal costs are less than utilities marginal costs. This is ultimately an
empirical question to be answered on a case-by-case basis. In sum, Figures
One and Two illustrate that nonutility generators can have marginal costs
lower than utilities industrial rates (which causes the bypass incentive in the
first instance), but not necessarily lower than utilities marginal costs.

TABLE 2   ALTERNATIVE BYPASS SCENARIOS (DOLLARS PER kWh)

Utility's Wholesale Price	$0.07
Competitive Price in Bulk Power Market	$0.05
Case One:	
Utility's Marginal Cost of Serving Wholesale Customer	$0.06
Case Two:	
Utility's Marginal Cost of Serving Wholesale Customer	$0.04

Returning to the central question of whether or not the FERC's "revenue loss" mechanism meets the economic criteria of productive efficiency, Pareto optimality, and setting prices equal to marginal costs, consider the example shown in Table Two. In Case One, the utility's marginal cost of serving the wholesale customer is more than the competitive price in the bulk power market, while in Case Two the utility's marginal cost is less than the competitive price.

The "competitive price" in the bulk power market would be set by the marginal cost of the least efficient supplier in that market. The marginal cost of this supplier would include capital costs if the plant were not yet constructed. But if the plant already existed, the suppliers marginal cost would equal its average variable cost, which excludes sunk capital costs required to build the plant.

According to the FERC's "revenue lost" mechanism for calculating stranded costs, a wholesale customer leaving the utility in this example must make a direct payment equal to $0.02 per kWh (i.e., $0.07 per kWh minus $0.05 per kWh), which makes the customer indifferent if the transition cost were assumed to continue indefinitely. The FERC, however, takes the position that the customer benefits in the long-run as competition in the bulk power market is enhanced.[51]

Productive Efficiency

Does the Commission's stranded cost recovery mechanism promote the first criterion of productive efficiency? The answer is, in general, no. Consider Case One in which the utilitys marginal cost exceeds the competitive price in the bulk power market. According to the Commission's "revenue lost" method, stranded costs equal $0.02 per kWh (i.e., $0.07 per kWh minus $0.05 per kWh), but the customers contribution to margin equals only $0.01 per kWh (i.e., $0.07 per kWh minus $0.06 per kWh). In this instance, the customer exits the system, which achieves productive efficiency since the marginal cost in the bulk power market is less than the utility's marginal cost, i.e., bypass is economic.

[51]   Under the Commission's "reasonable expectation standard," if the transition cost were assumed to exist for a finite period, the customer would benefit by exiting the system since the present value of payments would be lower. That is, if the customer remained with the utility, she would pay the present value of $0.07 in perpetuity, but if she exits, her costs equal the present value of $0.05 in perpetuity plus the present value of $0.02 for a finite period.

Now consider Case Two, in which the utility's marginal cost of supplying wholesale power to the customer is less than the competitive price in the bulk power market. In this case, bypass is uneconomic in that the competitive, wholesale power market produces power at a higher marginal cost than the utility. Under the Commission's "revenue lost" method, stranded costs equal $0.02 per kWh (i.e., $0.07 per kWh minus $0.05 per kWh), but the customers contribution to margin equals $0.03 kWh (i.e., $0.07 per kWh minus $0.04 per kWh). In this case, the Commission's "revenue lost" method does not achieve the goal of productive efficiency since it fails to prevent uneconomic bypass.[52]

Notice that the problem would be solved if stranded costs were calculated as the difference between the utilitys price and its marginal cost, i.e., the contribution to margin. In this case, the stranded cost payment would equal $0.03 per kWh (i.e., $0.07 per kWh minus $0.04 per kWh), so the customer would not exit since the utilitys price of $0.07 per kWh is less than the sum of the stranded cost payment ($0.03 per kWh) and the competitive price in the bulk power market ($0.05 per kWh).

Pareto Optimality

Does the Commission's stranded cost recovery mechanism achieve Pareto optimality? Again, the answer is, in general, no. In Case One, in which the utility's marginal cost of serving the wholesale customer exceeds the competitive price in the bulk power market, stranded costs again equal $0.02 per kWh (i.e., $0.07 per kWh minus $0.05 per kWh). The customer's contribution to margin, however, equals only $0.01 per kWh (i.e., $0.07 per kWh minus $0.06 per kWh), so the remaining customers are over-compensated by the exit, meaning that the utility will have no difficulty in maintaining the *status quo* prices. Therefore the wholesale customer's exit will not reduce the welfare of remaining customers or shareholders, so the Pareto optimality condition is met.

Now consider Case Two in which the utility's marginal cost of supplying power to the wholesale customer is less than the competitive price in the bulk power market. Stranded costs remain at $0.02 per kWh, but the customer's contribution to margin equals $0.03 kWh (i.e., $0.07 per kWh minus $0.04 per kWh), so the remaining customers are under-compensated by the exit, forcing the utility to increase rates to some remaining customers or recover lost revenues from shareholders. In either case, Pareto optimality is not maintained as either remaining ratepayers or shareholders are made worse off by the lost contribution to margin. As before, the problem would be solved if stranded costs were calculated as the difference between the utility's price and its marginal cost because uneconomic bypass would be prevented in the first instance.

---

[52] This result occurs when the incumbent is prevented from reducing its rate to deter entry. If the incumbent is allowed to reduce its rate to prevent uneconomic entry, Pareto optimality is violated because remaining customers must bear a rate increase if the firm is to achieve its break-even condition.

Allocative Efficiency

Finally, does the Commission's stranded cost recovery mechanism meet the goal of allocative efficiency, i.e., equating prices with marginal costs? We know from above that in Case One, in which bypass is efficient, the Commission's "revenue lost" calculation of stranded costs results in remaining customers being over-compensated for the wholesale customer's exit. In this case, the exit places no competitive pressure on the incumbent utility to rebalance rates to remove existing cross subsidies. So the Commission's stranded cost recovery method fails to force prices in the direction of marginal costs. In this instance, calculating stranded costs as the difference between a utility's prices and marginal costs offers no assistance to the effort to push prices in the direction of marginal costs, since the stranded cost payment exactly equals the wholesale customer's contribution to margin.

The fact that neither the Commission's stranded cost recovery mechanism nor the alternative mechanism equate prices with marginal costs should not be taken as a criticism. Given the massive cross subsidies in existing utility rate structures, and the fact that both mechanisms effectively indemnify remaining customers to preserve Pareto optimality, the inability of these two mechanisms to force prices to marginal costs should not be surprising. The stranded cost forum does not offer FERC a policy tool with which to eliminate cross subsidies. As noted by one observer: "If uneconomic bypass threatens a utility whose rates are based on average rather than marginal cost, the indicated remedy is not to impose [stranded cost recovery] but to redesign rates."[53]

However, even though the payment of stranded costs protects remaining rate payers from rate increases likely to be in the direction of marginal costs, the Commission's efforts to introduce competition into bulk power markets through wholesale wheeling will no doubt increase pressure on public utilities commissions to eliminate cross subsidies. As one commentator has noted: "Competition will eliminate cross subsidies from large customers to small customers (or vice versa); it will not lead to cross subsidies going in a different direction."[54]

Finally, in Case Two, in which the utility's marginal cost is less than the competitive wholesale market, we know from above that when bypass is inefficient, remaining customers are under-compensated. That is, some of the contribution to margin made by the departing wholesale customer must be borne by either remaining customers or shareholders. In this case, there would be competitive pressure on the utility to move its rates toward marginal costs, unless shareholders picked up the tab.

These results are summarized in Tables Three and Four, which illustrate the advantages of the alternative method of calculating stranded costs, i.e., the utility's

[53] *Supra note* 44 at 16.
[54] Black, B. (October 1994), *A Proposal for Implementing Retail Competition in the Electric Utility Industry*, 7 ELECTRICITY JOURNAL 67.

TABLE 3 FERC's STRANDED COST RECOVERY MECHANISM AND
ECONOMIC CRITERIA

	Utility's Marginal Cost Greater Than Competitive Price in Bulk Power Market	Utility's Marginal Cost Less Than Competitive Price in Bulk Power Market
Does FERC's Stranded Cost Recovery Mechanism Meet the Criterion of Productive Efficiency?	Yes	No
Does FERC's Stranded Cost Recovery Mechanism Meet the Criterion of Pareto Optimality?	Yes	No
Does FERC's Stranded Cost Recovery Mechanism Meet the Criterion of Equating Prices and Marginal Costs?	No	Partially

price minus its marginal cost.[55] As noted, neither method meets the criterion of equating prices with marginal costs. This should not be regarded as a problem with the two methods, but rather an indication that eliminating welfare losses caused by cross subsidies cannot be accomplished with any method designed to solve the stranded cost problem[56]. The most that can be achieved in the current forum is to increase the extent of competition in markets for electric power, which will in the long run place competitive pressure on public utilities commissions to move prices in the direction of marginal costs.

Conclusions

"It now occurred to me that the time of our deliverance was come. . . ."
Robinson Crusoe

By all measurements, the stranded cost problem facing the electric utility industry exceeds all such previous transitional costs caused by the introduction

[55] The alternative proposal put forth here is equivalent to the "efficient component pricing rule" put forward by William Baumol and Gregory Sidak in the context of establishing prices to be paid by non-regulated firms when they use a regulated firm's facilities. *See* Baumol, W. and Sidak, J. Gregory (forthcoming 1995), *Pricing of Services Provided to Competitors by the Regulated Firm*, HUME PAPERS ON PUBLIC POLICY. In addition, the alternative proposal for recovering stranded costs in the electric utility industry discussed here parallels a method proposed by Paul MacAvoy to allow local gas distribution companies to recover stranded costs resulting from bypass. *See* MacAvoy, P. (1994), *Supplemental Report of Dr. Paul W. MacAvoy on Stranded Cost Issues*, Before the Federal Energy Regulatory Commission, Docket No. CP93-258-000. MacAvoy's efficiency argument for stranded cost recovery dates to testimony provided before the FERC in 1985. *See* Docket No. CP85-437, Exhibit SG-3.

[56] *See, however*, Economides, N. and White, L. (1995), *Access and Interconnection Pricing: How Efficient is the "Efficient Component Pricing Rule"?*, Working Paper, New York University. They argue that the failure of the efficient pricing rule to force prices in the direction of marginal costs may be socially harmful.

TABLE 4   ALTERNATIVE STRANDED COST RECOVERY MECHANISM (UTILITY'S PRICE
MINUS ITS MARGINAL COST) AND ECONOMIC CRITERIA

	Utility's Marginal Cost Greater Than Competitive Price in Bulk Power Market	Utility's Marginal Cost Less Than Competitive Price in Bulk Power Market
Does the Alternative Stranded Cost Recovery Mechanism Meet the Criterion of Productive Efficiency?	Yes	Yes
Does the Alternative Stranded Cost Recovery Mechanism Meet the Criterion of Pareto Optimality?	Yes	Yes
Does the Alternative Stranded Cost Recovery Mechanism Meet the Criterion of Equating Prices and Marginal Costs?	No	Partially

of competition into U.S. regulated markets. The FERC's recent restructuring of the natural gas industry offers valuable lessons in minimizing stranded costs and in designing efficient cost recovery mechanisms. However, the FERCs "revenue lost" recovery mechanism fails to meet established economic efficiency criteria. We offer an alternative cost recovery mechanism that better achieves these efficiency goals, and in particular, meets the criteria of productive efficiency and Pareto optimality in circumstances when the Commissions "revenue lost" mechanism fails to meet these goals. The hope expressed here is that market participants, consisting of utilities, nonutility generators, ratepayers, and capital market investors, will not be stranded like Robinson Crusoe, wasting away for years on their own version of Mas-a-tierra Island, waiting for their ship to come in.

Bibliography

15 U.S.C. § 79–79z-6.
15 U.S.C. § 717–717w (1988).
15 U.S.C. § 3301–3432 (1988).
16 U.S.C. § 2601–2645, § 2701–2708 (1988).
American Gas Distributors v. FERC, 824 F.2d 981, 998 (D.C.Cir 1987).
American Petroleum Institute, (1974), PETROLEUM DATA BOOK, Table 8.
Baumol, W., Joskow, P., and Kahn, A. (December 1994), *The Challenge for Federal and State Regulators: Transition from Regulation to Efficient Competition in Electric Power,* Appendix A of the Comments of the Edison Electric Institute in Response to FERC, Notice of Proposed Rulemaking on Recovery of Stranded Costs by Public Utilities and Transmitting Utilities, Docket No. RM94-7-000 (June 1994).
Baumol, W., and Sidak, J. G., *Stranded Costs*, 18 HARVARD JOURNAL OF LAW AND PUBLIC POLICY 1–15.

Baumol, W. and Sidak, J. Gregory (forthcoming 1995), *Pricing of Services Provided to Competitors by the Regulated Firm*, HUME PAPERS ON PUBLIC POLICY.

Bayless, C. (December 1, 1994), *Less is More: Why Gas Turbines Will Transform Electric Utilities*, 132 PUBLIC UTILITIES FORTNIGHTLY.

Black, B. (October 1994), *A Proposal for Implementing Retail Competition in the Electric Utility Industry*, 7 ELECTRICITY JOURNAL 67.

Blanchard, O., Froot, K., and Sachs, J. (eds.) (1994), THE TRANSITION IN EASTERN EUROPE: VOLUME 1, COUNTRY STUDIES; VOLUME 2, RESTRUCTURING, Chicago and London: University of Chicago Press.

Breyer, S. and MacAvoy, P. (1974), ENERGY REGULATION BY THE FEDERAL POWER COMMISSION, Washington, D.C.: The Brookings Institution.

Doane, M. and Spulber, D. (1994), *Open Access and The Evolution of the U.S. Spot Market for Natural Gas*, 37 JOURNAL OF LAW AND ECONOMICS 477–517.

Economides, N. and White, L. (1995), *Access and Interconnection Pricing: How Efficient is the "Efficient Component Pricing Rule?"*, Working Paper, New York University.

Edison Electric Institute (1994), TYPICAL RESIDENTIAL, COMMERCIAL, AND INDUSTRIAL BILLS.

Energy Information Administration, (1992), ANNUAL REVIEW OF ENERGY, p. 223.

Energy Information Administration, (1993) ELECTRIC POWER PLANT COST AND POWER PRODUCTION EXPENSES 1991.

Energy Information Administration, (1994), ELECTRIC POWER ANNUAL 1992, p. 125.

FERC (March 29, 1995), NOTICE OF PROPOSED RULEMAKING AND SUPPLEMENTAL NOTICE OF PROPOSED RULEMAKING, RECOVERY OF STRANDED COSTS BY PUBLIC UTILITIES AND TRANSMITTING UTILITIES, DOCKET NO. RM94-7-001, 70 FERC ¶ 61,357

Federal Energy Regulatory Commission, (1981), POWER POOLING IN THE UNITED STATES, Washington D.C.: Government Printing Office, p. 5.

Flaim, T. (March 1994), *Stranded Investment – $300 Billion Anchor or "Tonya Harding" Issue?*, 6 ELECTRICITY JOURNAL 17.

Hirst, E. (1991), *Fulfilling the Demand-side Promise*, 128 PUBLIC UTILITIES FORTNIGHTLY 31.

Hope Natural Gas Co. v. Federal Power Commission, U.S. 591 (1944).

Hyman, L. (1992), AMERICAS ELECTRIC UTILITIES: PAST, PRESENT, AND FUTURE, Arlington, VA: Public Utilities Reports, Table 14–5.

Kahal, M. (November 1994), *An Economic Perspective on Competition and the Electric Utility Industry*, prepared for the Electric Consumers Alliances Comments in Response to FERC, Notice of Proposed Rulemaking on Recovery of Stranded Costs by Public Utilities and Transmitting Utilities, Docket No. RM94-7-000 (June 1994).

MacAvoy, P. and Pindyck, R. (1975), THE ECONOMICS OF THE NATURAL GAS SHORTAGE (1960–1980), New York, NY: North Holland Publishing Company.

MacAvoy, P. (1985), *The Effects of Bypass of the Gas Distribution Pipelines in the California Natural Gas Market*, Before the Federal Energy Regulatory Commission, Docket No. CP85-437, Exhibit SG-3.

MacAvoy, P. (1994), *Supplemental Report of Dr. Paul W. MacAvoy on Stranded Cost Issues*, Before the Federal Energy Regulatory Commission, Docket No. CP93-258-000.

Michaels, R. (October 1994), *Unused and Useless: The Strange Economics of Stranded Investment*, 7 ELECTRICITY JOURNAL 12–22.

Nicholson, W. (1985), MICROECONOMIC THEORY: BASIC PRINCIPLES AND EXTENSIONS, Chicago: Dryden Press, at 610.

Order No. 636, Final Rule (April 8, 1992) and Subsequent Order Nos. 636-A (August 3, 1992) and 636-B (November 27, 1992).

Philips Petroleum Co. v. Wisconsin, 347 U.S. 672 (1954).

Pub. L. No. 102–486, 106 State. 2776 (1992).

Wald, M. (November 7, 1988), *Gas Producers See an End to Disputes with Pipelines*, NEW YORK TIMES.

Wilson, R. (1994), NONLINEAR PRICES, New *York: Oxford University Press.*

The Emerging Coexistence of Competition and Regulation in Natural Gas Transportation

Adam B. Jaffe and Stephen D. Makowka

Synopsis

In the past twenty years, major aspects of the U.S natural gas industry have been deregulated and exposed to the discipline of competitive market forces. Authors Jaffe and Makowka describe the natural gas industry in the U.S. and summarize the positive impacts that unbundling and deregulation of gas services have had on the efficiency and reliability of gas markets. However, some aspects of the natural gas industry, such as transportation, that are perceived to have significant natural monopoly characteristics, continue to face traditional regulatory control. Although deregulation of competitive functions is a necessary condition for efficiency in this industry, it is not sufficient given the negative impacts of traditional regulation on these remaining "monopoly" functions. The authors suggest that deregulation of prices in the "secondary" market for pipeline capacity, combined with implementation of more flexible regulation of pipeline transportation, are the necessary next steps in the effort to transform the natural gas industry to one based on market forces and efficiency.

* * * *

Introduction

Twenty years ago the natural gas industry in the U.S. was almost completely controlled by government regulation. Today, major aspects of this system have been removed from the regulatory arena and are instead governed by competitive market forces. As a direct result, the efficiency and reliability of gas markets have improved significantly. Natural gas is an often-cited deregulation success story.[1] Regulation of the natural gas industry, however,

---

[1] See e.g. Clifford Winston, "Economic Deregulation: Days of Reckoning for Microeconomists," J. of Economic Literature, Vol. XXXI, September, 1993, at 1263; and Jerry Ellig and Joseph Kalt, eds., New Horizons in Natural Gas Deregulation (Westport, Connecticut: Greenwood Publishing Group, 1995)[forthcoming] .

remains pervasive. Depending on the class of customer – industrial, commercial or residential – approximately 40% to 70% of the "burner tip" cost of gas to consumers is determined by regulation rather than by market forces. To some extent, this is because not all potentially competitive functions in the supply chain from the wellhead to the burner tip have been deregulated. More fundamentally, important aspects of this supply chain have significant natural monopoly characteristics, and hence may not be suitable for deregulation. Hence the challenge for policy makers is now shifting from effectuating deregulation to reforming the regulation that remains in order to make it as efficient and compatible with competition as possible.

In this paper, we first give a brief overview of the economics of the natural gas industry and summarize the process by which market forces have replaced regulation in crucial aspects of the industry over the last two decades. Second, we describe important ways in which regulation continues to hamper the extent to which competitive forces could foster efficient allocation of natural gas transportation capacity. Finally, we describe modifications to the form of continued monopoly regulation that would further increase the efficiency of the natural gas system.

Economics and Historical Background

Economics of Natural Gas

Natural gas is produced from wells by literally thousands of competitive producers. The only economical transport mechanism for gas over land is via pipelines. Wells are connected to pipelines by gathering systems. Pipelines carry the gas from the producing areas to consuming areas, where it is delivered either to local distribution companies (LDCs) or to large retail customers who may be connected directly to the pipeline. LDCs distribute the gas to final customers. Connected to this system are a number of ancillary services: the gas coming from the ground is processed before injection into the main pipeline system, to remove impurities and higher molecular weight hydrocarbons, and many pipelines and LDCs operate gas storage facilities (often depleted wells), into which gas is injected during periods of low demand and released during periods of peak demand.

Over the long term, wellhead prices for gas are determined by a combination of the Hotelling resource-exhaustion process, technological change and the prices of other fuels. In the short run, however, gas prices are highly sensitive to the short-run demand/supply balance, because wells have very low operating costs once sunk and the high cost of transporting gas over water eliminates arbitrage with markets outside of North America. As discussed further below, this has led in recent years to large unpredicted swings in gas prices. The demand for gas is also highly seasonal, leading to a more predictable seasonal spot-price variation. Given the volatility of gas prices and the high fixed and sunk costs of gas-producing, transporting and consuming equipment, one would expect that markets would evolve for long-term gas sales, as well as for options, futures and other hedging instruments. Up until 1978, such markets were rendered irrelevant by regulation, but the process of deregulation has unleashed an explosion in the variety of both physical and financial instruments for the management of gas price risk.[2]

Pipeline technology exhibits significant economies of scale in both the short and long run. In the short run, the marginal cost of moving gas in quantities up to the capacity of an existing pipeline is close to zero. In the long run, the unit cost of capacity declines with increasing capacity over much of the relevant capacity range. As a result, most consuming areas are served by only one or a small number of pipelines, and some producing areas have only one or a few pipelines into which gas can be delivered. Because of the seasonal nature of demand, most pipelines are capacity-constrained during some part of the year. As discussed further below, pipeline transportation has historically been regulated on an average-cost-of-service basis, with capacity purchased on an annual basis. This means that the price of pipeline transportation on peak days is far below the opportunity cost or market-clearing price. Conversely, regulated prices during off-peak periods are typically well above marginal cost.[3] Thus better allocation of scarce capacity on peak days, and the creation of incentives to shift demand from peak to off-peak or otherwise take advantage of the low marginal cost of off-peak transportation are necessary to maximize the efficiency of the system.

Synopsis of Gas Industry Regulation and Deregulation

Until 1978, the natural gas industry in the United States was highly regulated. The Federal Power Commission (FPC), later replaced by the Federal Energy Regulatory Commission (FERC), regulated the price paid by interstate pipelines to purchase gas from gas producers (the "well-head price").[4] The interstate pipelines then resold this gas, again at federally-regulated prices, to local distribution companies ("LDCs"). LDCs then resold this gas to residential, commercial and industrial customers "behind the city gate."[5] These retail prices were (and still are) regulated by state public utility commissions.

Under federal oversight, interstate gas pipelines developed as merchants, selling bundled gas services to their customers. Pipelines traditionally purchased gas at regulated prices at the wellhead, gathered the gas into their

---

[2] See Adam B. Jaffe and Joseph P. Kalt, "*Oversight of Regulated Utilities' Fuel Supply Contracts: Achieving Maximum Benefit From Competitive Natural Gas and Emission Allowance Markets*," The Economics Resource Group, April, 1993.

[3] For many pipelines, the prices based on average historical cost are also well below the replacement cost of the pipeline and/or the incremental cost of capacity expansion. Thus, for many pipelines, if they simply charged market-clearing prices for their capacity at all times throughout the year, they would recover revenues that exceeded historical costs, but capacity expansion might still not be economical. A crucial issue in the debates over pipeline regulatory policy, though one that is usually implicit rather than explicit, is who should get the rents associated with existing capacity (see section III).

[4] Gas that did not enter interstate commerce was not subject to federal jurisdiction and was generally unregulated.

[5] The transfer of gas from interstate pipelines to LDCs is said to occur at the "city gate," regardless of whether it happens to be a city border.

systems, transported it from producing areas to the "city-gate," and sold it there to local distribution companies (LDCs). The sales price that a pipeline could charge for its deliveries of gas was regulated on a cost-of-service basis, with revenues limited to recovery of the components of cost, including the transporting pipeline's capital investments, operating expenses and gas acquisition costs.

In order to finance the construction of pipeline systems and fulfill service obligations to customers, pipelines typically entered into long-term supply contracts with their customers and long-term purchase contracts with their suppliers. The supply contracts typically obligated the pipelines to take minimum quantities of gas or else pay substantial penalties. The pipelines balanced these "take or pay" obligations with LDC sales contracts that obligated the LDCs to purchase minimum quantities at cost-based prices ("minimum bills").

When world energy prices began to rise in the early 1970s, regulated gas well-head prices diverged increasingly from market-clearing levels. With pipeline gas merchants restricted to the passing through of regulated wellhead prices, the pipeline sales market was inherently characterized by excess demand. The primary LDC customers were themselves limited, by state level cost-of-service regulation, to the passthrough of their gas acquisition prices – at below market-clearing levels. With prices of gas below market-clearing levels, there was always an implicit (when rationing by priority was effective) or explicit (in the case of the memorable periods of shortage) queue of unsatisfied demand for gas. In this environment, pipelines and LDCs – each worried about their ability to satisfy their service obligations – signed extremely long contracts for guaranteed supplies of gas, with little foreseen risk that these costs would not be recovered from customers. In short, perpetually short supplies of gas relative to demand and the business of regulatorily supported cost "passthrough" meant that the transportation and sale of gas were conducted largely outside the discipline of market forces.

After implementation of the Natural Gas Policy Act of 1978 (NGPA), which was passed in response to dramatic shortages of natural gas in the interstate market in the 1970s, the traditional natural gas system began to unravel. By phasing in the deregulation of wellhead prices of natural gas, the NGPA introduced the forces of competition into the wellhead gas market.[6] After decades of being held below market-clearing levels, wellhead gas prices in freshly struck contracts rose sharply in the late 1970s and early 1980s. Pipelines, seeing rising prices, cognizant of their contractual obligations to deliver sufficient gas to their LDC customers, and confident of their ability to recover their costs in their sales prices, entered into large numbers of contracts to supply gas at prices that were several times the historical norm. These high prices spurred increased interest in developing new gas resources.

As new gas supplies where brought to market and oil prices receded from

[6] The phased deregulation was complicated, with different prices permitted depending on when wells were constructed and the type of well. By the late 1980s, most of the remaining ceilings had become non-binding as market prices fell. The last regulatory restrictions on well-head prices ended on January 1, 1993.

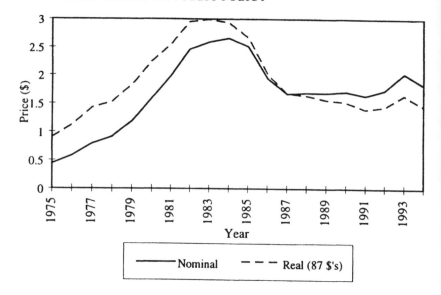

FIGURE 1 AVERAGE WELLHEAD PRICES OF MARKETED PRODUCTION

their early 1980s peak, however, natural gas prices began to soften. This cycle of rising and then falling natural gas prices, coupled with the traditional industry practice of signing long-term supply contracts at fixed prices, created a severe economic dilemma for gas pipelines. The 1980 situation of current spot prices far above the average of prices in existing long-term contracts dramatically reversed itself by the mid-1980s. Faced with spot prices at the wellhead well *below* their average acquisition cost under long-term contracts, pipelines struggled to find markets for their high priced gas.

By the mid-1980s, the FERC correctly perceived that the existing system of pipeline regulation was inhibiting the flow of benefits from well-head deregulation and competition through to gas customers. As the sole providers of bundled transportation and gas sourcing services under the traditional regulatory scheme, pipelines often represented the only purchasers at the wellhead and the only sellers at the city-gate. This severely limited the ability of customers to go shopping for gas and created pressure on the regulators to open up the wellhead markets to additional buyers.

In order to allow the benefits of deregulation to flow through to the customer, the FERC began a regulatory transformation that removed many of the regulatory obstacles to a more competitive market. Most importantly, the FERC abrogated the contractual "minimum bills" under which LDCs committed to pay for minimum levels of gas available from interstate pipelines. This expanded the ability of the customers to seek supplies directly from producers, or through brokers or resellers rather than pipelines if they so chose.

Ending the requirement that LDCs contract for minimum amounts from pipelines was insufficient, however, to give these customers effective access to the wellhead market, due to the fact that pipelines continued to control the transportation of natural gas supplies. In order to facilitate the development of a market for gas sources from non-pipeline alternatives, the FERC correctly reasoned that potential customers and suppliers would require effective access to the transportation network at prices and conditions that would allow them to compete with the pipelines' own bundled sales. In other words, by unbundling a transportation-only option, the FERC made it possible for LDCs to access competitive supplies and then move those supplies, at regulated rates, to the city gate.

This unbundling process proceeded in steps and was largely completed by FERC Order No. 636, issued in 1992. Under Order No. 636, all pipeline customers have the option of purchasing gas themselves at the wellhead, or purchasing gas from marketing intermediaries and then transporting that gas to their city-gate under an unbundled transportation-only tariff. Pipeline companies are permitted to engage in the unregulated gas marketing business, but they must do so through affiliates that are functionally separated from the transportation business, and transportation services must be structured in such a way as to offer comparable service to all shippers. In addition, Order No. 636 permits transportation customers to acquire the right to use pipeline capacity at regulated prices to resell that capacity to another party in a "secondary market." The Commission also acted to propagate the forces of competition by requiring that pipelines unbundle other potentially competitive activities such as storage from the regulated transportation function. Finally, Order No. 636 changed the rate structure for pipeline transportation, establishing a simple two-part tariff for "firm" pipeline transportation service, under which customers pay a demand charge based on their maximum capacity allocation and a commodity charge for each unit of gas shipped.[7] The demand charge is calculated so that the aggregate capacity reservations recover all of the pipeline's fixed costs (operation and maintenance, depreciation, amortization and return on capital), with only the variable operating costs recovered in the commodity charge.

By ordering the unbundling transmission-related services, Order No. 636 created the possibility of direct competition from non-pipeline entities into the markets for many of the services previously available only on a bundled basis. Although somewhat constrained by legislative requirements that they provide for "just and reasonable" rates, federal regulators, supported by the courts, have reasoned that in instances where there is no evidence of market power, market-based rates are a viable alternative to traditional cost-of-service determinations. The success of unbundling under Order No. 636 can be seen in the demand for new services such as capacity aggregation, balancing, and management for peaking and no-notice services, which are supplied by a new group of players including brokers, marketers and pipelines. Figure 2 demonstrates that Order No. 636 has largely completed the transformation of the pipeline industry from a bundled to an unbundled one. The competition that this has

---

[7] "Firm" service means that the customer has the right to transport an amount of gas up to the maximum daily quantity except under extreme circumstances. Pipelines also offer "interruptible" service, under which shippers can move gas on a capacity-available basis.

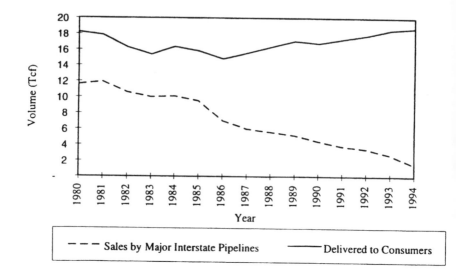

FIGURE 2   SALES OF NATURAL GAS BY MAJOR INTERSTATE PIPELINES VS.
DELIVERIES TO CONSUMERS

facilitated has brought significant improvement to the performance of the gas
industry; even under severe conditions such as pipeline accidents and extreme
weather, we have not witnessed the "shortages" and rationing of natural gas
that occurred repeatedly in the 1970s. Customers who have access to unbundled gas now have a powerful array of contractual and financial options
available for managing their gas costs. Gas futures and options are traded on
the New York Mercantile Exchange, and more complex and long-term hedges
and swaps are available in a growing over-the-counter market.

A final strand of the regulation and deregulation story relates to the
regulation of pipeline construction and expansion. Under the Natural Gas
Act, the federal regulators must find that additions of pipeline capacity serve
the "public convenience and necessity." Historically, this meant that a pipeline
had to prove that adequate demand existed to make the capacity economical.
Other pipelines and other parties could intervene to argue against capacity
expansion. In return, pipelines were entitled to rates that recovered their costs,
regardless (in principle) of whether the pipeline was fully utilized. Declines in
demand were (at least eventually) offset by rate increases. In parallel with
well-head deregulation and unbundling of pipeline transportation and merchant functions, the FERC beginning in 1986 created a new mechanism for
approving pipeline construction. If pipelines are willing to bear the financial
risk of under-utilization, they do not need to prove that they are needed for
the public convenience and necessity.[8] Indeed, the FERC approved the

---

[8]   Accepting the risk of under-utilization means agreeing to a regulatory framework in which
rates are determined on the basis of a fixed usage rate (originally 95%, now 100%) regardless
of actual usage.

construction of three competing pipeline proposals to bring additional pipe-line capacity into California, explicitly deciding that it would let the market determine which, if any, of the pipelines would actually be built.[9]

Remaining Restrictions on Efficient Competition

This historical overview illustrates the significance of restructuring in the natural gas industry and how these changes have led to the development of a more efficient market for many gas services. For much of the industry, however, regulatory oversight and traditional ratemaking remain a persistent fact of life. We now turn to an examination of these remaining regulated pieces of the gas marketplace and explore the current policy problems facing regulators. First, however, it is worth summarizing the broad policy criteria by which natural gas regulation is measured in the United States. With the wellhead markets essentially deregulated, remaining regulatory attention concentrates on the transportation and distribution of natural gas, as well as on ancillary services, such as storage, brokering and balancing.[10] For these services, the regulators first, and most fundamentally, wish to prevent the inefficient ex-ploitation of monopoly power over consumers who have access to a limited number of competitive alternatives. In addition, though this is not often explicitly stated, it is clear that regulators also seek to prevent regulated entities from extracting any other rents from their assets, including short-run scarcity rents or quasi-rents associated with the fact that replacement cost of capacity is above original construction cost. Attempting to mitigate monopoly behav-ior and avoid rent extraction sharply curtails the regulator's ability to rely on the action of unregulated market forces to determine prices.

A number of additional policy problems associated with gas regulation arise from the desire to recreate certain desirable features of competition, while controlling the ability of service providers to extract rents. For example, it is important that the residual regulatory framework does not distort the func-tioning of markets for well-head gas, gas brokering services, gas storage and other activities that have been found to be competitive. Also, it is important that existing scarce pipeline capacity is allocated efficiently, that services are produced efficiently, and that an efficient array of service options are available to consumers. Finally, it is essential to create appropriate incentives for investment in new pipeline capacity.

---

[9]   The issue is more complicated with respect to existing pipelines, because in addition to deciding if the expansion should take place, the FERC must determine whether the new capacity should be sold to new customers on an incremental cost basis, or whether the costs of the expansion should be "rolled in" to the costs of the existing system and overall average rates used. The FERC has a rulemaking pending that examines this generic issue.

[10] Although there has been significant deregulation of some of these ancillary services, pipeline companies themselves continue to be the largest providers of many of these services, at regulated rates, across broad geographic markets within the United States.

Pipeline Transportation

With respect to the interstate pipeline transportation system, the current system of regulation does a pretty good job of solving problems of monopoly power, rent extraction and, through incremental pricing, investment in new capacity. However, the problems associated with allocative, productive, and varietal efficiency remain to be adequately addressed. In part the tardiness of the regulator in these areas stems from the uncertainty about the most appropriate means to reconcile the sometimes conflicting policy goals outlined above. For example, though market-based pricing has been widely adopted for many segments of the industry, it is not clear that these lessons are directly transferable to transportation because of the "sunkenness" of the assets involved. At the very least, these concerns, correctly, cause regulators to examine the issues of market power for transportation services with a much keener eye. While is seems plausible that portions of the transportation industry will be found to be competitive, such as those found on the U.S. Gulf Coast where the large number of interconnected pipelines offer numerous alternatives to shippers, it is clear that straight market-based pricing for most of the interstate transportation system would result in a large rent transfer from pipeline customers to pipeline owners. It seems unlikely that the political/regulatory process will permit this.

The federal regulators are aware that traditional forms of regulation are not effective at dealing with the remaining efficiency goals of policy. In 1992, the FERC issued an incentive policy statement encouraging gas services providers to propose alternatives to traditional cost-of-service ratemaking.[11] This invitation for proposals adopted two basic principles that any proposal would have to meet: it must encourage efficiency and it must allow for initial rates that conform to traditional cost-of-service standards. To date, however, no pipeline has successfully implemented any alternative rate design under this policy statement, in part due to the heavy industry preoccupation with the restructuring taking place pursuant to Order No. 636.

More recently, the FERC has refocussed on the issues of alternatives to traditional ratemaking by initiating a proceeding to determine the appropriate, generic criteria required to evaluate requests for market-based rates, as well as by reopening the discussion of other, non-market-based, alternatives to traditional cost-of-service approaches.[12] Faced with a variety of potential

[11] *Policy Statement on Incentive Regulation*, PL92-1-000, 61 F.E.R.C. P61,168, October 30, 1992.
[12] See Alternatives to Traditional Cost-Of-Service Ratemaking for Natural Gas Pipelines, RM95-6-000, 70 F.E.R.C. P61,139, February 8, 1995. The methodology, proposed by the FERC here as a basis for comments, relies heavily on the market power analysis established by the Department of Justice and the Federal Trade Commission in the *Horizontal Merger Guidelines*. In general, this is the methodology used by the FERC staff and commissioners to approve market-based rates for oil pipelines and storage services. However, uncertainty remains over how to most appropriately apply these broad guidelines, if at all, to the natural gas transportation function. Among the questions raised by the FERC are: 1) Is the use of the Horizontal Merger Guidelines appropriate; 2) Are the guideline criteria too strict; 3) Should there be different standards for different services; 4) Does the existence of large buyers offset the problems associated with large sellers; 5) Is capacity release a good substitute for firm transportation; and 6) Are there other methods that would better serve goals of flexible, efficient transmission pricing?

methodologies to replace traditional rate making. the FERC is attempting to develop a framework within which to evaluate the appropriateness of these alternatives. We propose that the question of how to induce more efficient pipeline behavior in transportation can be satisfactorily answered via the types of regulatory reforms outlined in the next section. First, however, we turn to a brief discussion of other segments of the natural gas industry that currently face regulatory restrictions that inhibit efficient resource allocation.

Capacity Release

Order No. 636 provided for a host of changes that individually and in combination provide significant opportunities for more efficient pipeline use. One of the cornerstones of Order No. 636 is the requirement that individual pipeline companies permit shippers to "release" (resell or sublet) their firm capacity. Deal information, bid prices, and capacity availability are made publicly available though electronic bulletin boards (EBBs) maintained by each pipeline. The creation of this secondary market is intended to increase efficiency in gas transportation by creating an incentive for firm shippers to re-allocate capacity to those users who place the highest value on such capacity. In essence, the availability of capacity release creates competition among numerous providers of transportation capacity where, prior to Order 636, the pipeline itself was the only provider. In this way, a competitive secondary market could achieve the objective of efficient allocation of scarce pipeline capacity, while ensuring that scarcity rents accrue to customers rather than to the pipeline.

The primary effect of the capacity release program is to create incentives for firm transportation customers who do not need their full capacity allocation during off-peak periods to resell that capacity to others. Though the capacity-release program is relatively new, this is already occurring. According to a recent study by the Interstate Natural Gas Association of America (INGAA), during the first nine months of 1994, capacity release exhibited rapid growth and wide participation on most interstate natural gas pipelines. During this period, there were over 36,000 individual transactions resulting in over 13,500 awards averaging 79.3 Bcf/day of released capacity.[13]

There is ample evidence that industry participants are utilizing capacity release to redistribute rights to capacity more efficiently. In addition, the existence of the secondary market for firm capacity provides direct competition for interruptible and short-term firm capacity sales by pipelines. An important feature of capacity release that increases its viability as an alternative to pipeline-provided service is the ability of acquiring shippers to designate alternative receipt and delivery points for that capacity. Thus, the value of released capacity is enhanced because new shippers are not restricted to receiving and taking gas at the same points as original shippers.

Regulators continue to fine-tune this program based on the growing

---

[13] "Capacity Release Activity in the First Three Quarters of 1994," INGAA, Rate and Policy Department, Report No. 95-1, February 1995, at 5–7.

experience of the industry with this new market. For example, the capacity release guidelines originally required that transactions of 30 days or more be posted for bidding, causing parties interested in prearranged deals to engage in unnecessarily complex paired transactions of 29 days and 1 day each. This restriction has subsequently been determined to be unnecessary and has been removed. Industry opinion, however, remains divided over how effectively capacity release competes against the primary market for long-term firm capacity transactions. Although release can be permanent, most transactions are for a defined period of time and are subject to various recall provisions.

The secondary market as currently administered cannot, however, achieve efficient allocation of capacity during peak periods because the FERC has chosen to retain a price ceiling in the secondary market equal to the "as-billed" or regulated capacity cost. Since the opportunity cost of capacity is far above these prices during peak periods, there is little or no incentive for capacity to move to its highest value use. Since the secondary market on most or all pipelines is highly competitive, the retention of a price ceiling in this market cannot be justified on grounds of preventing exercise of market power. Indeed, imposing a price ceiling on a party that cannot be compelled to sell at that price achieves *no* apparent policy objective: rather than forcing the seller to lower the price, the ceiling merely prevents the transaction from taking place. Removing the ceiling would not lead to monopoly prices (because of competition in the secondary market); it would merely permit pipeline customers to capture the full value of the rents associated with any difference between the primary regulated price and the secondary market price. Although it is always risky to claim that any policy change is a true Pareto improvement, it is difficult to see how any pipeline customer could be made worse off by the removal of the secondary market ceilings.[14]

Local Distribution

The competitive benefits associated with the deregulation and unbundling of services at the federal level for customers of interstate pipeline services are also limited because state regulators have not extended 636-like unbundling to the retail level. Because LDCs responsible for distribution behind the city-gate remain unbundled monopolies under traditional cost-of-service ratemaking, we are still stuck on the policy goal of not letting the regulatory framework interfere with the workings of existing competitive markets. The unbundling process largely completed for interstate pipelines with Order No. 636 has barely begun at the state level and, as a result, the vast majority of retail customers have no option but to purchase a bundled gas-sales/gas-distribution service from their local gas company.

[14] While speculation in political economy is always dangerous, the motivation for retaining this ceiling appears to be a jurisdictional one, namely, that state regulators would then get involved in telling LDCs under their jurisdiction when and how to resell capacity and what to do with the profits. While inappropriate behavior by state regulators could clearly limit the benefits of secondary market competition, it is difficult to see how nonprofit-maximizing behavior by primary capacity holders could reduce efficiency relative to what obtains with ceilings in place.

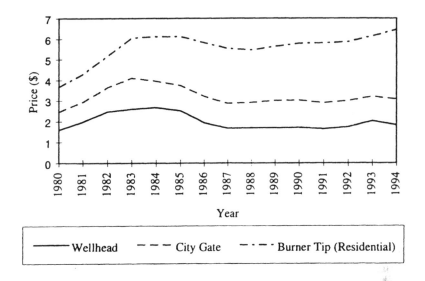

FIGURE 3   NATURAL GAS PRICES FROM THE WELLHEAD TO THE BURNERTIP:
US NATIONAL DATA

This fact is important because the distribution function itself represents a significant portion of the overall delivered cost of gas to the burner tip. As Figure 3 illustrates, as wellhead and interstate transportation prices have fallen, the distribution portion of delivered cost is becoming a larger piece of the cost structure. In fact, for the residential customer, these costs have been increasing in nominal terms. While there may be doubt as to whether the benefits of unbundling would exceed the transactions costs for small customers, it is clear that implementation of 636-like unbundling for large customers could have significant benefits. Even the transactions costs associated with smaller customers could be addressed through the activities of load aggregators who could offer even small customers viable alternatives to LDC procurement services if they had access to the distribution pipe on a non-discriminatory basis. At the very least, unbundling of the LDC's physical delivery from the acquisition of gas offers substantial potential benefits.

Some state regulators are moving to address these issues through a variety of different mechanisms.[15] In California, for example, Pacific Gas and Electric (PG&E), an LDC serving northern California, has requested approval of its Core Procurement Incentive Mechanism (CPIM).[16] Under the CPIM proposal,

[15]   The following summary of state activity is not meant to be exhaustive. Rather, it is intended to be representative of the type of thinking currently taking place at the state level. These discussions are by no means universal, however. Regulators in some states have moved much less towards a review of these issues than their counterparts elsewhere.

[16]   Pacific Gas and Electric, Core Procurement Incentive Mechanism, Prepared Testimony dated December 29, 1994.

PG&E would continue to purchase natural gas for its customers, but instead of a traditional reasonableness review of its gas costs, PG&E would be rewarded or punished based on its actual cost compared to a market-based benchmark. In New York, recent PSC polices are intended to direct local distribution companies in their adjustment to the more competitive environment.[17] Specifically the PSC has allowed LDCs to price services to non-core customers at comparable levels to alternative energy sources subject to some maximum limits. This pricing flexibility is coupled to a band around allowed rates of return beyond which savings would be shared with core customers and shortfalls would be eliminated. In Wisconsin, the staff of the PSC's Natural Gas Division has prepared a report that recommends that the PSC should examine the scope of the utility franchise in the context of emerging competition over traditional monopoly services and whether utility services that are not monopoly services should be offered as either utility or non-utility services in the context of emerging competition.[18]

The Next Step for Pipeline Regulation

As the previous section has shown, there are important respects in which unbundling and deregulation have not yet been carried to their logical conclusions. Completion of the job of fostering competition where possible – by deregulating the secondary capacity market and carrying unbundling through to the burner tip – will yield significant additional efficiency benefits. The final step in the regulatory reform process will then be to move to "incentive regulation" of the primary pipeline capacity markets to create good efficiency incentives.[19]

There is by now a burgeoning literature on incentive-regulation mechanisms, as well as increasing practical experience with such mechanisms in various industries and jurisdictions.[20] Such mechanisms seek to achieve three objectives: (1) reduction of the administrative cost and burden of the regulatory process; (2) improvement of the incentives for cost-minimization relative to those created by regulatory lag under cost-of-service regulation; and (3) creation of incentives for innovation, involving both new technologies and new forms and structures for service offerings.

The particular technological and institutional structure of the pipeline industry helps a lot in choosing among different incentive regulation models. In particular, the traditional firm transportation tariff, combined with the competitive secondary capacity market provides a base for a more flexible

17   Re Restructuring of the Emerging Competitive Natural Gas Market, Case 93-g-0932, Opinion No. 94–26, December 20, 1994.
18   "Approaches to Natural Gas Regulation in Wisconsin, " Public Utilities Commission of the State of Wisconsin, Report 05-SG-100, April 25, 1994.
19   The issues of pipeline regulation will be discussed in this section in the context of interstate pipelines. All of the concepts discussed would also apply to LDC transportation. Indeed, even states that do not implement LDC unbundling could improve LDC efficiency by applying incentive-based regulation to the bundled LDC sales function.
20   See, e.g. Michael Crew, ed., Incentive Regulation for Public Utilities, 1994.

regulatory structure. The two components of the regulatory model that we propose are (1) replacement of the existing cost-of-service-based firm transportation tariff with an inflation-indexed price cap; and (2) creation of regulatory flexibility that would permit pipelines to offer any other transportation service that they desire, with terms and conditions to be freely negotiated between the pipeline and the customer.

The price cap or "RPI – X" mechanism is now well-established. The main issues that must be resolved in any particular application are what inflation index to use, and how to determine the productivity factor "X." One of the current authors has explored these issues in some detail with different co-authors in a related paper.[21] In that paper, he proposes developing a pipeline-specific producer-price index using subcomponents of the published PPI with weights determined from pipeline operating data collected by the FERC. We estimate that the productivity factor, based on pipeline operations in the recent past ought to be approximately .6% per year.

An additional issue that must be addressed is the period of time over which the index mechanism is left in place. This issue is complicated in the pipeline context by the legal framework of pipeline regulations. Under Section 5 of the Natural Gas Act, any customer has the right to initiate a pipeline rate case, in which the customer can try to prove that the pipeline's rates are not just and reasonable under the Act. Therefore, even if a pipeline and the Commission agreed that rates would not be subject to review for some fixed period of time, it is not clear how customers could be prevented from "undoing" the incentive mechanism by invoking their Section 5 rights.

To implement the price-cap mechanism, a pipeline would go through a "last" rate case to determine the cost-of-service rates that are to be the base for the inflation-indexed rate. The key part of this tariff would be the determination of the demand charge or first part of the two-part tariff for firm service, which is essentially the sum of the pipeline's fixed costs divided by its (reserved) capacity. We propose that, at this time, pipelines also be given blanket authority to offer any other transportation services, provided that the regulated firm transportation tariff remains available to all customers that have the contractual right to service under that tariff. This model for more flexible regulation has been dubbed "recourse rate" regulation, because privately negotiated terms and conditions for service are deemed to be just and reasonable and otherwise lawful by virtue of the fact that the customer always has "recourse" to a regulated service. Any customer that chooses to substitute a different set of terms and conditions will do so only if it is thereby better off.[22]

The purpose of the recourse-rate proposal is to address the fact that the traditional pipeline regulation framework has admitted an incredibly limited variety of transportation service offerings. Essentially, pipelines offer two

[21]   Amy B. Candell, et. al., "*Indexing Natural Gas Pipeline Rates*," The Economics Resource Group, Inc., 1995.
[22]   "Incentive Regulation For Natural Gas Pipelines: A Specific Proposal With Options," Technical Report 89–1, Office of Economic Policy, Federal Energy Regulatory Commission, September 1989.

flavors of service: firm and interruptible.[23] Whatever conditions are associated with these services, such as limitations on hourly and daily variations in receipts and deliveries, balancing penalties, etc., must be accepted as given. The reality, of course, is that different customers have different needs, and hence different degrees of willingness to pay for flexibility in service terms. The recourse-rate regime creates a framework in which customers can tailor their pipeline transportation service to meet their needs.

This approach is particularly attractive because, at least to some extent, the pipeline will be offering new forms of service in competition with its own customers, who will be entering the market as resellers of primary pipeline capacity, as well as brokers and other third parties who can take capacity from primary customers and repackage it for sale in other forms. Thus the combination of a deregulated secondary capacity market with a pipeline given the flexibility to negotiate contract terms with customers who have the backstop of the regulated recourse rate creates the maximum opportunity for efficient operation and allocation of pipeline capacity while ensuring that all rents embedded in the existing pipeline go to customers by virtue of the regulated recourse rates.

We believe that there are only two additional regulatory safeguards necessary to ensure that the recourse-rate-based negotiating flexibility operates efficiently and to the benefit of customers. First, since pipeline companies are permitted to operate gas marketing affiliates under the Order No. 636-unbundling regime, so long as they do not give their affiliates better transportation service than they give to other shippers, it is appropriate that protections be put in place to prevent negotiating flexibility from being used to create affiliate preferences. Such protection could take the form, for example, of a requirement that affiliate deals be made public and offered to all similarly situated shippers.[24]

Finally, to the extent that the pipeline controls the decision to add additional capacity, it could use this power to extract additional rents in return for capacity-using service enhancements under the recourse-rate proposal. Therefore, it would be appropriate to impose on pipelines that are given negotiating flexibility an obligation to expand capacity if there is sufficient demand to make expansion economical. Essentially, given the obligation to sell its existing capacity at a regulated rate in the primary capacity market, the only opportunity for the pipeline to engage in monopolistic witholding of supply is with respect to new capacity. This can be prevented by an obligation to expand capacity whenever there are customers who stand ready to pay the incremental cost of such capacity.

---

[23] Some pipelines do have multiple classes of interruptible service, with differing priorities. Pipelines are also required under Order 636 to offer a "no-notice" transportation service, which is designed to ensure that customers have effective access to competitive gas markets.

[24] Service terms that are not with affiliates should not be public, and pipelines should not be required to offer the same terms to all shippers. The system should reward the pipeline if it can figure out ways to squeeze additional value out of its assets by, for example, negotiating a discount with one or more shippers in return for their agreeing to additional restrictions on their service, which restrictions give the pipeline the operational flexibility necessary to offer value-enhancing modifications to other shippers. To create good incentives, the pipeline has to be free to negotiate the best deals it can with each customer.

The past 15 years of natural gas regulation at the federal level has witnessed many accomplishments. Consumers have benefited from wellhead gas prices that have remained far below the peak levels reached in the late 1970s and early 1980s. The ability of the system to allocate pipeline capacity has also been improved by the creation of the capacity release program. There remain, however, significant constraints on the system's efficiency, and the removal of these constraints is the natural next step for gas policy. Specifically, many potentially competitive markets such as those for gas storage remain largely regulated, price ceilings on released capacity limit the allocative efficiency of the system, and traditional cost of service regulation for transportation services limit the incentive of pipelines to innovate and reduce costs thereby raising the cost of transportation above competitive levels.

The process of regulatory reform in the gas sector has been like peeling an onion. In successive stages, we have peeled away layers of regulation, replacing them with market forces as the mechanism for "regulating" prices, and thereby increasing the economic efficiency of the sector. After peeling off the layers that can be subject to competition, we are left with the unbundled pipeline transportation function where the tailoring of products to the needs of market participants is only in its nascent stages. For some parts of the pipeline system, even that core function may be subject to sufficient competition that market forces can be relied upon to ensure that rates and terms of service are just and reasonable. But for much of the pipeline system, competition alone may not be adequate to ensure just and reasonable rates for the primary transportation capacity, making market-based rates inappropriate. The problem becomes, therefore, how to design a regulatory system that comes as close as possible to duplicating the outcome of a competitive market, and which maximizes the ability of the residual regulated part of the system to work efficiently with the competitive parts of the system.

This question is an important one because the residual regulated transmission function is still a significant fraction of the city-gate or burner-tip cost of gas. As competition has driven the evolution of gas markets, pipeline service offerings, constrained by traditional regulation, have not been able to keep pace and meet the demands of the marketplace. As a direct result of regulatory inflexibility, limitation in the types of pipeline transportation services now constitute the key constraint on the overall efficiency of the pipeline system. That is, pipeline transportation is now the "weak link" in terms of flexibility and efficiency in the chain from the wellhead to the city-gate or burner tip. Although discounting of interruptible service is permitted and is common, and under special conditions firm service may be allowed to be supplied at rates other than full cost of service levels,[25] in general, the transportation products offered by pipelines come in "one size fits all." This lack of product variety is inconsistent with the development of an efficient natural gas industry on both

---

[25] In many cases, faced with the possibility of uneconomic bypass, pipelines have sought and received approval for offering discounted firm tariffs to certain customers under the assumption that, as long as the discounted rates are above marginal cost, these customers will make some contribution to the fixed cost of the pipeline, thus reducing cost recovery from remaining customers.

the supplier and the user sides of the transportation system. In fact, because transportation constitutes an indispensable link in the chain of services that bring natural gas from wellhead to end-use market, it is not plausible that the efficient set of transportation service offerings consists solely of "plain vanilla" firm and interruptible options. Thus the logical next step in the evolution of gas policy is to strengthen this weak link, by giving the pipeline transportation function the flexibility and incentives to evolve efficiently in conjunction with the competitive industry segments.

Conclusion

The natural gas industry has been transformed from one that was almost completely regulated from gas wells to gas burners into one in which many of the structurally competitive functions have been unbundled from natural monopoly functions and deregulated. A number of lessons emerge from this experience. First, unbundling works. It is possible to devise rules for access to a monopoly facility that foster competition. A second and related point is that vertical de-integration is not a necessary condition for effective competition. Most gas pipelines retain gas marketing affiliates, and many own significant gas producing operations. The "open access" and affiliate-dealing rules under Order 636 have created an environment in which all kinds of entities seem to thrive. While no such rules are perfect, there seems to be a general sense that pipeline transportation approximates the long-sought mythical "level playing field."

A third lesson is that regulators have a hard time letting go. The notion that the price of pipeline capacity on a cold winter day might go to 10 or even 100 times its allocated historical cost seems to create cold feet, even if that price is a secondary market one that will be received by a customer (in competition with dozens of other capacity holders) rather than a monopolist. But a fourth lesson is that this reluctance must confront the fact that competition tends to propagate itself through the system. Deconcontrol of well-head prices created the overwhelming pressure that forced interstate unbundling, and the unbundled competitive markets are now beating on the LDC city gates, demanding retail unbundling.

The final lesson and our overall theme is that deregulation of competitive functions is a necessary but not sufficient condition for efficiency. Reform of residual regulatory mechanisms is also extremely important. The natural gas industry is, in our view, close to the end of its long process of regulatory transformation. We hope that the understanding of the need to create a policy framework that is conducive to efficiency will not run out before these final steps are taken.

Bibliography

Alternatives to Traditional Cost-Of-Service Ratemaking for Natural Gas Pipelines, RM95-6-000, 70 F.E.R.C. P61,139, February 8, 1995.

"Approaches to Natural Gas Regulation in Wisconsin." Public Utilities Commission of the State of Wisconsin, Report 05-SG-100, April 25, 1994.

Candell, Amy B. et. al. "Indexing Natural Gas Pipeline Rates." The Economics Resource Group, Inc., working paper, 1995.

"Capacity Release Activity in the First Three Quarters of 1994." Interstate Natural Gas Association of America, Rate and Policy Department, Report No. 95–1, February 1995: 5–7.

Crew, Michael A, ed. *Incentive Regulation for Public Utilities* (Boston: Kluwer Academic Publishers, 1994).

Ellig, Jerry and Joseph Kalt, eds. *New Horizons in Natural Gas Deregulation* (Westport, CT: Greenwood Publishing Group, forthcoming).

"Incentive Regulation For Natural Gas Pipelines: A Specific Proposal With Options." Federal Energy Regulatory Commission, Office of Economic Policy, Technical Report 89–1, September 1989.

Jaffe, Adam B. and Joseph P. Kalt. "Oversight of Regulated Utilities' Fuel Supply Contracts: Achieving Maximum Benefit From Competitive Natural Gas and Emission Allowance Markets." The Economics Resource Group, Inc., working paper, April 1993.

Pacific Gas and Electric, Core Procurement Incentive Mechanism. Testimony filed before the California Public Utilities Commission, December 29, 1994.

Policy Statement on Incentive Regulation, PL 92-1-000, 61 F.E.R.C. P61,168, October 30, 1992.

Re Restructuring of the Emerging Competitive Natural Gas Market, Case 93-G-0932, NYPSC, Opinion No. 94-26, December 20, 1994.

U.S. Department of Justice and the Federal Trade Commission. *Horizontal Merger Guidelines* (Washington, DC: U.S. Government Printing Office, April 2, 1992).

Winston, Clifford. "Economic Deregulation: Days of Reckoning for Microeconomists." *Journal of Economic Literature* 31 (September 1993): 1263.

Cheaper SO$_X$, Same Old NO$_X$:
A Look at Implementation of Title IV
of the Clean Air Act Amendments of 1990

Todd Strauss

Synopsis

Title IV of the Clean Air Act Amendments of 1990 pertains to acid rain. Targeted almost exclusively at electric power plants burning fossil fuel, Title IV includes both the heralded market mechanism for sulfur dioxide (SO$_2$), and traditional-style command-and-control regulation of nitrogen oxides (NO$_x$). Implementation (to date) of the provisions of Title IV is briefly described here. The SO$_2$ program has begun and appears headed for success; the NO$_x$ program has been delayed and its success is in doubt.

*   *   *   *

Introduction

The U.S. environmental regulatory system has long been criticized, by economists and others, for reliance on technological standards and other "command-and-control" regulation rather than market-oriented mechanisms such as taxes or tradeable pollution permits. The call was finally heeded in Title IV of the Clean Air Act Amendments of 1990 (CAAA). Title IV, the acid rain provision, includes the first environmental program in the U.S. *designed* as a market system (rather than merely tacked on afterwards). Title IV created tradeable emissions allowances for SO$_2$. Beginning in 1995, the allowances constrain national SO$_2$ emissions.

The CAAA also contain much command-and-control style regulation. Title IV, which applies almost exclusively to electric power plants burning fossil fuel, calls for command-and-control regulation of NO$_x$ emissions from coal-burning electric power plants.

Title IV thus provides an important opportunity to compare the two regulatory regimes directly yet empirically. While it is much too early to assess impact of the U.S. national acid rain program, we can look at implementation to date. Current contrasts between Title IV's SO$_2$ and NO$_x$ programs are vivid enough to make some inference about the empirical merits of the two regulatory programs.

In this paper, experience with the market mechanism for SO$_2$ emissions is compared to the experience with command-and-control NO$_x$ regulation under Title IV of the CAAA. For each pollutant, technical aspects of emissions and abatement, statutory and regulatory provisions of Title IV, and implementation to date are described. These experiences are then compared.

SO$_2$

First, some facts about SO$_2$ emissions and electricity production. SO$_2$ is the primary precursor of acid rain. Chemical reactions in the atmosphere transform SO$_2$ into sulfate and other sulfur oxides (SO$_x$), and sulfuric acid. "Acid rain" is technically acid deposition, may be wet or dry, and includes sulfur- and nitrogen-containing chemical species. The harmful effects of acid rain in the U.S. are felt primarily in the northeastern U.S. and in Canada, and are largely produced by SO$_2$ emissions from coal-burning electric power plants in the Midwest.

The effects of acid rain have been studied by the federal National Acid Precipitation Assessment Program (NAPAP).[1] Lakes and streams are harmed, particularly in the Adirondack Mountains of upstate New York. Building materials are corroded. Haze occurs in some rural areas. SO$_2$ emissions can also have severe impacts on public health, but these appear to have been mitigated in the U.S. (partly because of other provisions of the Clean Air Act); acidic aerosols may have some public health effects. Valuing the damages of all these effects is difficult and fraught with uncertainty. By 1990, damage valuation had been done for limited categories, such as recreational trout fishermen in the Adirondacks. At any rate, the legislators and regulators crafting the acid rain provisions of the CAAA largely ignored the NAPAP study.[2]

SO$_2$ in the U.S. is largely emitted by electric power plants that burn coal. Coal plants spew forth about two-thirds of total annual U.S. SO$_2$ emissions.[3] Coal plants also generate more than half of the electricity in the U.S.[4]

The sulfur content of coal varies by geological deposit. In the U.S., Midwestern coal has high sulfur content (greater than 1.5 lbs. per million Btu (MMBtu)), while western coal and some Central Appalachian coal are very low in sulfur (less than 0.85 lbs. per MMBtu).[5]

[1] National Acid Precipitation Assessment Program, *1990 Integrated Assessment Report* (Washington, D.C.: NAPAP Office of the Director, 1991).
[2] Marshall Yates, "Congress Approves Historic Clean Air Legislation," *Public Utilities Fortnightly*, 6 December 1990, p. 53; Michael Weisskopf, "With Pen, Bush to Seal Administration Split on Clean Air Act," *The Washington Post*, 15 November 1990, p. A23.
[3] NAPAP, p. 179; U.S. Energy Information Administration, *Electric Power Annual 1993* (Washington, D.C.: U.S. Government Printing Office, Report No. DOE/EIA-0348(93), 1994), pp. 126, 130.
[4] U.S. Energy Information Administration, *Electric Power Annual 1993*, pp. 17–18, 76.
[5] U.S. Energy Information Administration, *Coal Industry Annual 1993* (Washington, D.C.: U.S. Government Printing Office, Report No. DOE/EIA-0584(93), 1994), pp. 178–179.

The standard technology to reduce SO_2 emissions from coal-burning power plants is commonly known as a "scrubber," in which postcombustion gases are passed through tanks containing wet limestone or other sorbent that retains SO_2. Scrubbing is expensive. Capital costs of scrubbing are estimated to be between $175 and $275 per kW. Operating and maintenance expenses are about $9 per kW per year, and 0.2 cents per kWh. For a retrofit on a power plant with 15 years remaining service, the costs amount to more than $500 per ton SO_2 abated.[6]

CAAA Details

Title IV of the CAAA applies to "affected sources," almost exclusively electric generating units burning fossil fuel. An electric power producer must possess an allowance for each ton of SO_2 it emits from an affected source (or pay a penalty of $2000 per ton, a fine much higher than both typical emissions abatement costs and the projected and realized prices of allowances). Each allowance entitles its possessor to emit one ton of SO_2 during or after the year in which the allowance is issued. Allowances may be bought, sold, and traded.

Approximately nine million allowances will be issued annually, beginning in the year 2000, when the SO_2 emissions allowance program will begin to apply to almost all electric power plants burning fossil fuel.[7] In comparison, U.S. electric power plants emitted approximately 16 million tons of SO_2 annually during the mid-1980s.[8] Thus, total annual U.S. emissions of SO_2 from electric power plants are scheduled to be cut by almost half from mid-1980s levels. The explicit goal in the CAAA is a total annual reduction of 10 million tons from 1980 U.S. SO_2 emission levels.[9]

In Title IV, a general formula is employed to specify the number of allowances to be allocated to individual electric generating units. The formula has the following structure: a performance standard multiplied by a "baseline" divided by a conversion factor. The performance standard is expressed as the sulfur content of fuel (lbs. SO_2 per MMBtu). The baseline specified is typically the average annual quantity of fuel consumed during the mid-1980s, with some

---

[6] U.S. Energy Information Administration, *Electric Utility Phase I Acid Rain Compliance Strategies for the Clean Air Act Amendments of 1990* (Washington, D.C.: U.S. Government Printing Office, Report No. DOE/EIA-0582, 1994) [hereinafter cited as *Compliance Strategies*], pp. 29–33, 83–93; Andrew J. Van Horn, *et al.*, *Integrated Analysis of Fuel, Technology, and Emission Allowance Markets: Electric Utility Responses to the Clean Air Act Amendments of 1990* (Palo Alto, California: Electric Power Research Institute, Report No. TR-102510, 1993) [hereinafter cited as *Utility Responses*], pp. A-19 to A-21. Detailed assumptions associated with these estimates are included in the two reports.

[7] Some electric generating units are exempt from Title IV regulation. For example, certain independent power producers, such as qualifying facilities under the Public Utility Regulatory Policies Act (PURPA), are exempt. Also, generating units with capacities of less than 25 MW are exempt. A provision of Title IV provides for exempt sources, and sources other than electric generating units, to join the SO_2 emissions allowance program voluntarily.

[8] NAPAP, p. 179.

[9] The CAAA cap annual SO_2 emissions at 5.6 million tons from sources other than electric utilities. Non-utility sources may choose either to implement specified command-and-control measures, or participate in the allowance program.

provisions for generating units that operated at atypically low levels during this time. The conversion factor is 2000, to convert lbs. into (short) tons.

Between the years 1995 and 1999, the SO$_2$ emissions allowance program applies to only 261 electric generating units (110 power plants).[10] This is known as Phase I. These 261 generating units are explicitly listed in Title IV. Located in 21 states in the eastern U.S., each of these generating units has a generating capacity of at least 100 megawatts (MW). The aggregate capacity of the Phase I units is 89 gigawatts (GW). These units constitute about 27% of current U.S. coal-burning electric capacity, 11% of total U.S. electric capacity, and 22% of total electric capacity in the three NERC regions where most of these plants are located.[11]

Title IV explicitly lists the number of allowances each of these 261 generating units is to be issued annually during Phase I. The historical SO$_2$ emissions of Phase I generating units were particularly high; these large generating units typically burned coal with a high sulfur content and did not utilize scrubbers. In 1985 these 261 units emitted 9.3 million tons of SO$_2$, about 58% of total U.S. SO$_2$ emissions from electric power plants in 1985.[12] In Phase I, 5.5 million allowances will be issued annually, based on a performance standard of 2.5 lbs. SO$_2$ per MMBtu.[13]

Beginning in the year 2000, this performance standard tightens to 1.2 lbs. SO$_2$ per MMBtu and applies to almost all electric generating units burning fossil fuel. This is known as Phase II. Again, the performance standard simply specifies the number of annual allowances endowed to existing generating units; an individual generating unit may emit more SO$_2$ if it possesses the necessary number of additional allowances. In any case, the number of allowances issued annually is capped at 8.95 million.[14] Thus, the level of average annual national SO$_2$ emissions is capped. If necessary, the performance standard will be adjusted downward so the cap is not exceeded. Therefore, the "performance standard" is not technology-based, but merely a mechanism to describe the allocation of allowances; the true constraint is the number of allowances issued annually.

To better understand implementation of Title IV, a few more details are

[10] Title IV specifies 261 generating units, e.g., units 1–4 of Tennessee Valley Authority's Gallatin plant, and unit 3 of TVA's Paradise plant.

[11] Industry statistics are frequently reported by NERC (North American Electric Reliability Council) region. The 48 states of the contiguous U.S. (excluding Alaska and Hawaii) are divided into nine NERC regions. The three NERC regions referred to in the text are MAIN, ECAR, and SERC. These comprise part or whole of 18 states in the Midwest and South. Sources: U.S. Energy Information Administration, *Inventory of Power Plants in the United States 1993* (Washington, D.C.: U.S. Government Printing Office, Report No. DOE/EIA0095(93), 1994), pp. 24, 30–31, and Table 20; U.S. Energy Information Administration, *Electric Power Annual* 1993, p.121.

[12] U.S. Energy Information Administration, *Compliance Strategies*, pp. 53–58; NAPAP, p. 179.

[13] In addition to the 5.5 million annual allowances specifically issued during Phase I to individual units, "extension" allowances are issued to Phase I units installing scrubbers. There are several other provisions for additional allowances. In sum, the average annual allocation of allowances during Phase I is approximately 6.3 million allowances.

[14] There are also provisions for some additional allowances to be issued between the years 2000 and 2009.

needed. New electric generating units – whether owned and operated by a regulated electric utility or an independent power producer – have no endowed allowances, and must acquire sufficient allowances to match their SO_2 emissions output. On the other hand, owners of retired generating units retain their allowances in perpetuity. To promote development of a market and guarantee new power plants some source of allowances, approximately 2.8% of allowances are withheld from the allocation to existing power plants and sold at an annual auction conducted by the Chicago Board of Trade and sponsored by the EPA. In addition, some allowances are withheld from electric utilities and may be purchased from the EPA at a fixed price of $1500 per allowance.

Monitoring compliance – matching a source's SO_2 emissions with the allowances it possesses – requires more precise data on source emissions than previously gathered. Continuous emissions monitoring is required on generating units subject to the SO_2 emissions allowance program. The capital cost associated with a monitoring system is estimated at $850,000, and annual operating costs are about $425,000.[15]

Importantly, the SO_2 emissions allowance program is layered on top of already existing environmental and price regulation. First, Title IV does not supersede National Ambient Air Quality Standards (Title I) for SO_2, which aim, for public health reasons, to limit local, temporal concentrations in the air. State environmental regulations remain in effect. For example, Wisconsin mandated that, by 1993, each electric utility in the state must average no more than 1.2 lbs. SO_2 per MMBtu. Second, Title IV repeals the SO_2 percent reduction requirement of the revised New Source Performance Standards (NSPS) mandated in the Clean Air Act Amendments of 1977, but maintains the original NSPS of 1.2 lbs. SO_2 per MMBtu. The NSPS are true technology-forcing performance standards. Third, Title IV does not override traditional state regulation of investor-owned electric utilities. There is also no guarantee that Congress or the EPA will not change the rules midstream, since SO_2 emissions allowances are explicitly not property rights.

More details about the SO_2 emissions allowance program may be found in the original legislation and among the many works of exegesis and commentary.[16] Since the program's goal is to reduce national SO_2 emissions, there has been some concern about the program's impact on acid rain and its effects in

---

15 U.S. Energy Information Administration, *Compliance Strategies*, p. 108.
16 The Clean Air Act Amendments of 1990 are Public Law 101-549. The acid rain program is codified at 42 U.S.C.7651. Works of explanation and commentary include: Reinier Lock and Dennis P. Harkawik, eds., *The New Clean Air Act: Compliance and Opportunity* (Arlington, Virginia: Public Utilities Reports, 1991); J.C. Molburg, J.A. Fox, G. Pandola, and C.M. Cilek, *Analysis of the Clean Air Act Amendments of 1990: A Forecast of the Electric Utility Industry Response to Title IV, Acid Deposition Control*, (Argonne, Illinois: Argonne National Laboratory, Report No. ANL/EAIS/TM-81, 1991); Ian M. Torrens, J. Edward Cichanowicz, and Jeremy B. Platt, "The 1990 Clean Air Act Amendments: Overview, Utility Industry Responses, and Strategic Implications," *Annual Review of Energy and the Environment* (1992) 17: 211-233; K.A. Bailey, T.J. Elliott, L.J. Carlson, and D.W. South, *Examination of Utility Phase I Compliance Choices and State Reactions to Title IV of the Clean Air Act Amendments of 1990* (Argonne, Illinois: Argonne National Laboratory, Report No. ANL/DIS/TM-2, 1993); and U.S. Energy Information Administration, *Compliance Strategies*.

local areas such as the Adirondacks.[17] While this is a crucial point, it is an issue of program objective and design. Policy analysis had indicated that allowance trading would not attenuate the Adirondack cleanup effected by the CAAA cap on total national SO$_2$ emissions.[18] Here we focus on Title IV as it has been implemented by the EPA and interpreted by the judiciary, given the law as written by Congress.

Market Activity

The market for SO$_2$ emissions allowances was slow in developing. With the beginning of Phase I in 1995, the allowance market has developed more rapidly. Allowances are now traded in standardized forums, price information is more readily available, and prices are much lower than initially anticipated. However, the volume of interutility allowance transactions remains disappointing to most observers.

The market was nearly nonexistent at first. Until the EPA-sponsored auction of allowances conducted by the Chicago Board of Trade on 29 March 1993, there were only between five and 10 publicly announced sales, one proposed option transaction, and one charitable donation.[19] In the remainder of 1993 there were 10 more transactions.[20] Even when transactions were publicly announced, transaction details such as price were often not disclosed. (This has been the source of some tension, for operations in the electric utility industry are typically under scrutiny by regulators and interveners in regulatory hearings.)

High negotiation costs were associated with these early, customized transactions.[21] Unfavorable publicity and state political maneuvers also hindered allowance transactions. Allowances were often described in the popular or mass media as "permits to pollute," and the market for allowances was described as a "stink market."[22] When a transaction appeared to send allowances from a coastal New York utility (LILCO) to a supplier of high-sulfur

17   George Lobsenz, "New York Officials Ask Court To Review EPA SO$_2$ Rules," *The Energy Daily*, 16 March 1993; U.S. Environmental Protection Agency, *Acid Deposition Standard Feasibility Study* (Draft Report No. 430-R-95-001, February 1995).

18   Renee Rico, "The U.S. Allowance Trading System for Sulfur Dioxide: An Update on Market Experience," *Environmental and Resource Economics* (1995) 5: 118; NAPAP, p. 447.

19   U.S. General Accounting Office, *Allowance Trading Offers an Opportunity to Reduce Emissions at Less Cost* (Washington, D.C.: U.S. General Accounting Office, Report No. GAO/RCED-95-30, 1994) [hereinafter cited as *Allowance Trading*], p. 33. Also, as reported in various issues of *Electric Utility Week*.

20   U.S. General Accounting Office, *Allowance Trading*, p. 33.

21   Susan Beck, "Negotiating the First Pollution-Credits Deal," *The American Lawyer*, July/ August 1992, p. 110; Matthew L. Wald, "He Doesn't Call Them Dirty Deals," *New York Times*, 13 May 1992, p. D4; "Trading Firms Turn Up Heat in Vying for Central Role in Allowance Market," *Electric Utility Week*, 21 September 1992, p. 7.

22   Typical of the popular press is the report in *The New York Times* of the March 1993 EPA auction (Barnaby J. Feder, "Sold: The Rights to Air Pollution," *The New York Times*, 30 March 1993, p. D1). Fear of bad publicity from allowance transactions was reported in the trade press ("Allowance Market at Risk from Poor Public Relations, Proponents Fear," *Utility Environment Report*, 29 May 1992, p. 1).

Midwestern coal (AMAX), the State of New York sued the EPA.[23] Illinois, to preserve its high-sulfur coal mining industry, passed a law requiring Illinois utilities to consume in-state coal.[24]

In accord with the provisions of the CAAA, the EPA worked to promote the formation of a liquid market for allowances. The Chicago Board of Trade was chosen to conduct annual EPA-sponsored auctions of allowances. Three auctions have been held. Privately-sponsored auctions by the Chicago Board of Trade and others had been delayed because the EPA had not developed the necessary software to record transactions. The EPA's allowance tracking system finally became operational in March 1994.[25]

Several organizations have now established themselves as allowance brokers or clearinghouses. There were at least one dozen allowance transactions during 1994.[26] Activity increased as Phase I began. One firm claimed to have brokered 11 transactions in January 1995. It is estimated that, since 1991, interutility transactions for more than two million allowances have occurred. Innovative deals have been negotiated, including allowance options, bundling allowances with coal, and a swap of SO_2 emissions allowances for carbon dioxide emissions credits.[27]

Price information is more readily available, particularly on electronic bulletin boards and trading systems. Price indices are published regularly in the trade press.[28] Prices for allowances have declined over the past three years, while EPA auction prices and private transaction prices have converged. As of May 1995, the price of a 1995 allowance was approximately $135, far below 1991 estimates and below the estimated discounted value of a 1995 allowance saved ("banked") for Phase II.[29] The spread between offers to buy and offers to sell allowances is perhaps $5, or less than 4% of the price of an allowance.

The volume of interutility allowance transactions has disappointed most

---

[23] The LILCO-AMAX transaction and response by State of New York are described in Lobsenz, *supra* note 17.

[24] Federal courts later declared the Illinois Coal Act in violation of the Constitution's Commerce Clause. The case is described in "Court Affirms Unconstitutionality of Ill. Law Favoring In-State Coal," *Electric Utility Week*, 23 January 1995, p. 10. Indiana took similar steps to protect its high-sulfur coal mining industry, and was similarly rebuffed.

[25] Jeffrey Taylor, "CBOT Plan for Pollution-Rights Market Is Encountering Plenty of Competition," *Wall Street Journal*, 24 August 1993, p. c1; "EPA Issues Final NO_x Rules, Puts Allowance Tracking System On Line," *Electric Utility Week*, 7 March 1994, p. 9.

[26] U.S. General Accounting Office, *Allowance Trading*, p. 33.

[27] George Lobsenz, "Allowance Trading Takes Off," *The Energy Daily*, 27 January 1995; "Three SO_2 Brokers Agree: Price Index Key in Rate Treatment of Allowances," *Utility Environment Report*, 9 December 1994, p. 5; "Utilities Encouraging Coal Suppliers to Bundle SO_2 Allowances With Bids," *Electric Utility Week*, 3 April 1995, p. 18.

[28] "Cantor Fitzgerald EBS Devises New Monthly SO_2 Allowance Price Index," *Utility Environment Report*, 3 February 1995, p. 8.

[29] The 1995 auction results are described in Denise Warkentin, "Duke Power Buys 53% of Allowances Sold at Auction," *Electric Light & Power*, May 1995, p. 3. April 1995 brokerage allowance prices and bid-ask spreads are reported in "Cantor Fitzgerald EBS SO_2 Allowance Prices," *Utility Environment Report*, 12 May 1995, p. 3. Current prices are contrasted with earlier forecasts and expectations in Matthew L. Wald, "Acid-Rain Pollution Credits Are Not Enticing Utilities," *New York Times*, 5 June 1995, p. A11. Also see U.S. General Accounting Office, *Allowance Trading*, p. 36.

observers, however. Dampening the allowance market are Internal Revenue Service rules for the tax treatment of allowances. Also a factor has been uncertainty in ratemaking treatment of allowances by state and federal regulatory agencies.[30] Resistance by the stodgy electric utility industry to innovative ideas has also been blamed.

Nonetheless, a prime virtue of the SO$_2$ emissions allowance program is the flexibility afforded to electric utilities in abating SO$_2$ emissions. To determine whether the allowance program has reduced the cost of SO$_2$ emissions abatement, an examination of utility compliance plans is necessary.

Compliance Plans

The discussion here is focused on Phase I, because electric utilities have already been compelled to take action to comply with Phase I. Title IV of the CAAA sets a performance standard of 2.5 lbs. SO$_2$ per MMBtu for Phase I generating units. To comply, an electric utility has four choices for a coal-burning generating unit without a scrubber: i) the scrubbing option: retrofit scrubbers and continue to burn high-sulfur coal; ii) the allowance option: acquire additional allowances and continue to burn high-sulfur coal; iii) the coal-switching option: reduce consumption of high-sulfur coal by switching to lower sulfur coal; and iv) reduce utilization of the generating unit by switching to another fuel source such as natural gas, implementing demand-side solutions, or purchasing power from other electricity producers.

Utilities were required to file Phase I compliance plans with the EPA in 1993. Table 1 summarizes the compliance strategies chosen. Switching to lower-sulfur coal is the favored strategy, declared by roughly 60% of affected Phase I units. Acquiring allowances will be employed by roughly 15% of affected Phase I units. Scrubbing, the technological option typically mandated under

TABLE 1   PHASE I COMPLIANCE PLANS[31]

Compliance Option	Number of Generators	Capacity (GW)
i) scrubbing	27	14
ii) acquiring additional allowances	39	14
iii) coal-switching	162	53
iv) retiring, switching to gas, etc.	8	2
previously implemented controls	25	6
Total	261	89

[30] These issues are examined in Bailey *et al.*, *supra* note 16, and in U.S. General Accounting Office, *Allowance Trading*, pp. 43–60.

[31] Based on Table 3 in U.S. Energy Information Administration, *Compliance Strategies* and Table B-1 in Van Horn, *Utility Responses*. Actual fulfillment of these plans cannot be verified until allowance transactions are reported in the EPA Allowance Tracking System database, and scrubber deployment and annual fuel consumption are reported by the Energy Information Administration. While partial verification can be done at the end of 1995, complete verification of Phase I compliance plans cannot be concluded until Phase I ends in 1999.

a command-and-control regulatory regime, will be employed by less than 16% of affected Phase I capacity.

The most striking figures in Table 1 are for the levels of coal-switching. These levels are much greater than generally anticipated in 1990 and 1991. Moreover, apparently 35% or more of the additional demand for lower-sulfur coal will come from the Central Appalachian region in the east, rather than the Powder River Basin in the west.[32] Flexibility created by Title IV has revealed a previously underutilized and undervalued resource for reducing SO_2 emissions: Central Appalachian coal with low to moderate sulfur content (less than 1.6 lbs. SO_2 per MMBtu). Converting a power plant from consuming Midwestern coal to Central Appalachian coal is easier technically and much less expensive than converting to Powder River Basin coal. Coal prices have already begun to reflect a slight premium for Central Appalachian low-sulfur coal over Power River Basin coal.[33]

The level of retrofit scrubbing is much less than anticipated initially. Producers of scrubbing equipment have faced reduced demand, and have been spurred to make their technology more cost-competitive.[34]

The compliance plans offer additional evidence for the success of the market mechanism for SO_2 emissions abatement. As indicated above, allowance prices are much lower than expected. One reason for low allowance prices could be that utilities have relied heavily on scrubbers as a compliance strategy, thus obviating the need for allowances and creating excess allowances. However, the low level of scrubbing for Phase I compliance suggests this is not true. Lower-than-anticipated prices for allowances have apparently increased the demand for allowances by Phase II power plants, and decreased their demand for scrubbers.[35]

However, the compliance plans also indicate flaws in the market. In a perfectly efficient market with full information, the marginal cost of SO_2 emissions reduction would be equal for all affected sources, and the price of an allowance would equal that marginal cost. Clearly, the price of an allowance is much less than the cost of scrubbing, yet scrubbers will be installed at some generating units. This suggests some problem with the market. It is unclear whether the problem is caused by the discrete and irreversible nature of investment in scrubbing, by uncertainty or incomplete information, or by inadequate management of information (and inadequate tools for managing information).

Phase I is a transition stage. Generating units that will comply by switching

[32] U.S. Energy Information Administration, *Compliance Strategies*, pp. 22–23; Van Horn, *Utility Responses*, pp. 1–6 to 1–13.

[33] Jerry Vaninetti and Todd Myers, "Calculating What the Market Will Bear During Phase I," *Coal*, February 1995, p. 25.

[34] U.S. General Accounting Office, *Allowance Trading*, p. 29; Samuel Goldreich, "Industry Banking on the Clean Air Act," *Baltimore Business Journal*, 2 December 1994, p.13; "ABB: Advances Make 'Stealth' Scrubber More Competitive with Fuel Switching," *Utility Environment Report*, 20 January 1995, p. 14.

[35] "Competitive Pressures Discouraging Utilities From Installing Scrubbers," *Utility Environment Report*, 12 May 1995, p. 4; "Utilities Delay Deciding on Scrubbers, But Wildcards May Force Their Hands," *Energy Report*, 1 May 1995.

TABLE 2 PROJECTED ANNUAL COMPLIANCE COSTS[36]
(BILLIONS OF 1992 DOLLARS)

Flexibility	Phase I	Phase II
Unit	1.3	4.9
Intrafirm	1.1	3.1
Interfirm	–	2.0

coal sources in Phase I may still install scrubbers in Phase II, or even reduce output. Nonetheless, the available evidence shows that innovative attempts to comply have been and will be made, and that retrofitting scrubbers – the typical command-and-control option[37] – will be utilized less. Recent moves to restructure the U.S. electric industry and promote competition may further discourage investment in scrubbers; such capital expenditures may be "stranded" by restructuring. Whatever the development of the allowance market, electric utilities can pursue options such as fuel-switching and intrafirm allowance trades. The cost-effectiveness of these strategies is suggested by Table 2.

Table 2 presents cost estimates for three scenarios: unit flexibility, intrafirm flexibility, and interfirm flexibility. Unit flexibility means that each affected generating unit must comply with the appropriate performance standard.[38] Scrubbing and fuel-switching are compliance options included in this scenario. Intrafirm flexibility means that compliance is measured at the firm level, such that the average of a firm's emissions meet its performance standard (the average and performance standard are Btu-weighted). In other words, it represents a scenario that supposes no interutility trading occurs under the current allowance program. Interfirm flexibility represents the current allowance program supposing a fully efficient allowance market develops.

Table 2 suggests that the Title IV SO$_2$ emissions allowance program will be cost-effective even if an efficient allowance market does not develop.[39] Intrafirm flexibility is projected to result in Phase I compliance cost savings of approximately 15%, or $0.2 billion annually. Phase II compliance cost savings are estimated to be about 37%, or $1.2 billion annually. Development of an efficient allowance market may yield additional savings of $1.0 billion annually.

[36] Based on Table I.1, U.S. General Accounting Office, *Allowance Trading*, p. 74. Cost for Phase I intrafirm trading scenario is based on Phase I utility compliance plans. Intrafirm scenario includes interfirm trades that had been announced by September 1994.

[37] Installing scrubbers, closing the unit, and obtaining a compliance waiver might be the typical options available under command-and-control regulation. Whether switching coal sources would be feasible is questionable; for a description of the politics involved in setting the percentage reduction requirement (revised NSPS) of the Clean Air Act Amendments of 1977, see Bruce A. Ackerman and William T. Hassler, *Clean Coal/Dirty Air* (New Haven: Yale University Press, 1981).

[38] A reminder: the performance standard for Phase I is 2.5 lbs. SO$_2$ per MMBtu; for Phase II, 1.2 lbs. SO$_2$ per MMBtu. Again, these are multiplied by baseline (mid-1980s) energy inputs.

[39] Costs associated with monitoring and enforcement are not included. Such costs must be incurred under both command-and-control and market mechanism regimes. For SO$_2$ emissions, such costs seem similar under both regimes, when compared to the size of compliance cost savings.

In other words, more than half the benefit of the allowance program does not depend on an efficient allowance market, but simply intrafirm flexibility in compliance. Clearly, the SO_2 emissions allowance program is considerably more cost-effective than a command-and-control program would have been.

NO_x

NO_x, like SO_2, is a precursor of acid rain. However, compared with SO_2, NO_x is a minor contributor to acid rain.[40] The primary environmental problem associated with NO_x is urban smog and ozone formation. Hence, while attention here is focused on the NO_x control provisions of Title IV (Acid Rain), most CAAA discussion of NO_x is in Title I (Ambient Air Quality).

Atmospheric chemistry associated with NO_x is more complicated than that associated with SO_2.[41] Nonetheless, the acid rain effects of NO_x emissions are less dispersed and closer to the emissions source than for SO_2. More important for emissions abatement, the sources of NO_x are more varied than the sources of SO_2. Natural causes such as lightning and soils are responsible for perhaps 10% of total U.S. NO_x emissions. Yet like SO_2, NO_x emissions are primarily associated with burning fossil fuels. In the U.S., electric power plants emit about 32% of total U.S. anthropogenic NO_x emissions. Cars and trucks are the largest source of NO_x emissions, accounting for 43% of total U.S. anthropogenic NO_x emissions. Total U.S. anthropogenic NO_x emissions were 20 million tons in 1985.[42]

U.S. coals have more homogeneous nitrogen content than sulfur content. However, NO_x emissions depend mostly on the combustion process, unlike SO_2 emissions, which are mostly related to the sulfur content of the coal. Thus, available NO_x control technologies may involve combustion process modification ("low NO_x burners" or "overfire air") or postcombustion processing of flue gases (e.g., selective catalytic reduction). The Department of Energy's Clean Coal Technology program includes projects using more advanced techniques such as fluidized bed combustion and coal gasification. For Title IV regulation, the applicable technology is currently low NO_x burners. Title I regulation (Ambient Air Quality) may include more expensive controls, such as overfire air or selective catalytic reduction, in certain nonattainment areas.

Low NO_x burner control technology for electric power plants is less expensive than SO_2 scrubbers. The capital cost of retrofitting low NO_x burner technology is $10 to $25 per kW, compared with $175 to $275 per kW for SO_2 scrubbers.[43] The incremental operating cost of low NO_x burner technology is negligible. With low NO_x burner technology, the cost of abatement is generally less than $500 per ton NO_x for existing utility boilers.[44]

[40] NAPAP, p. 177.
[41] For a detailed discussion, see NAPAP, pp. 175–208.
[42] NAPAP, p. 189.
[43] Energy Information Administration, *Compliance Strategies*, pp. 81–100.
[44] Frank T. Princiotta, "Technological Options for Acid Rain Control," *The New Clean Air Act: Compliance and Opportunity*, pp. 123, 127.

CAAA Details

Title IV provisions regarding NO$_x$ emissions are straightforward compared with the provisions for SO$_2$ emissions.[45] The provisions apply only to coal-burning electric generating units to which the SO$_2$ emissions provisions also apply. The annual average emissions rate (in lbs. NO$_x$ per MMBtu) of each generating unit is capped, according to the type of boiler technology employed. Actual emissions rate limits are set by the EPA, subject to guidelines set forth in the CAAA.[46] Deadlines for the promulgation of these limits are stated. Electric utilities may petition the EPA for easement of the emissions rate limit if the limit cannot be met using the technology on which the limit was based. Such easement is called an "alternative emission limitation" (AEL). A petition for an AEL must include operating and monitoring data for 15 months, during which the "appropriate control equipment" was "properly installed" and "properly operated."

Some flexibility is allowed. Rather than complying with the limit on each individual generating unit, an electric utility may average emissions across units (within the firm) to meet an aggregate, Btu-weighted limit. Moreover, no particular control technology is prescribed. To meet the limit, improvements in NO$_x$ control technology may be employed. Both averaging and substituting different control technologies are subject to the typical permitting and licensing procedures.

Nonetheless, the hallmark of command-and-control style regulation is evident. Technology-based performance standards are set. A generating unit may be in compliance (by employing the required technology) yet still not attain the performance standard. Even if the performance standard is met, the environmental goal explicitly stated in the CAAA – to reduce U.S. annual NO$_x$ emissions by two million tons, from 1980 levels – may not be achieved. Unlike the SO$_2$ program, there is no actual cap on total NO$_x$ emitted by the affected sources. Nor is there a system of tradeable allowances.[47]

[45] Quoted phrases are taken from section 407 of the CAAA (codified at 42 U.S.C. 7651f), which details the NO$_x$ emissions reduction program of Title IV.

[46] The NO$_x$ emissions rate for tangentially fired boilers must be no greater than 0.45 lbs. per MMBtu. The NO$_x$ emissions rate for dry-bottom, wall-fired boilers, excluding cell burners, must be no greater than 0.50 lbs. per MMBtu. (These two types of boilers are called Group I by the EPA.) The emissions rate limits for Group I boilers may be set higher if the EPA finds that the specified numerical limits cannot be attained with low NO$_x$ burner technology. Limits for other types of boilers are to be set based on retrofitting with "the best system of continuous emission reduction, taking into account available technology, costs and energy and environmental impacts; and which is comparable to the costs of NO$_x$ controls" for tangentially fired and dry-bottom, wall-fired boilers (excluding cell burners).

[47] Interpollutant allowance trading of NO$_x$ and SO$_2$ was permitted in early versions of both the bill submitted by the Bush Administration and the bill submitted by Senate Democrats. During negotiations, however, NO$_x$ emissions were eliminated from the allowance trading program (Marshall Yates, "Clean Air Compromise Achieved Between Senate and the Administration," *Public Utilities Fortnightly*, 29 March 1990, p. 30). Section 403(c) of the CAAA (42 U.S.C. 7651b) specifies that, by 1 January 1994, the EPA "shall furnish to the Congress a study evaluating the environmental and economic consequences of amending [Title IV] to permit trading SO$_2$ allowances for NO$_x$ allowances." The EPA has not done so. Currently there is little political impetus for such a report, and the EPA is continuing to work on the study.

Implementation

The deadline for establishing regulations on Group I boilers was not met. According to the CAAA, emissions rate limits for Group I boilers were to have been set by the EPA within 18 months of passage of the CAAA. Final rules were not issued until March 1994. This delay of almost two years, while greater than the delays associated with other EPA rulemaking on Title IV, is consistent with usual EPA practice; on average, EPA rulemaking takes more than three years.[48]

These rules were promptly challenged by electric utilities and the coal industry. They charged that the EPA had overstepped its authority in setting emissions rate limits based on overfire air NO_x controls rather than simply low NO_x burners. An appellate court agreed. The EPA scrapped its Title IV NO_x regulations and delayed implementation of the program. Revised rules were issued on 13 April 1995. Title IV NO_x provisions are currently scheduled to take effect on 1 January 1996.[49] Because of the delay, as of May 1995 electric utilities were still implementing compliance plans, and no petitions for AELs had been filed yet.

Inferences

It is premature to judge how well Title IV has reduced acid rain. It is even premature to assess how well Title IV has been implemented. After all, 1995 is the first year a national SO_2 emissions cap is in effect (and it is in effect on just the Phase I electric generating units). The market for SO_2 emissions allowances is still developing. Rules for the NO_x reduction program have just been established, and electric utilities must begin complying next year.

Nonetheless, in contrast with some previous clean air regulation, it does appear that compliance with the SO_2 emissions allowance program will occur. Program compliance ensures that annual U.S. SO_2 emissions are capped. Therefore, it appears that the environmental goal of reducing annual U.S. SO_2 emissions by 10 million tons from 1980 levels will be met. Cost-effectiveness of the program—how much it costs to attain the environmental goal of reducing annual U.S. SO_2 emissions by ten million tons from 1980 levels—appears good, especially when compared with cost estimates for a more traditional program requiring mandatory installation of scrubbers.

In contrast, the NO_x control program appears similar to previous environmental regulation of coal-burning electric power plants. The cost-effectiveness of the program is likely to be dismal. Even program enforcement and compliance may result in failure to attain the environmental goal. In short, the SO_2

---

[48]   U.S. General Accounting Office, *Clean Air Rulemaking: Tracking System Would Help Measure Progress of Streamlining Initiatives* (Washington, D.C.: U.S. General Accounting Office, Report No. GAO/RCED-95-70, 1995), p. 3.

[49]   The contest is described in George Lobsenz, "EPA's New NO_x Rules Abide by Court Ruling," *The Energy Daily*, 19 April 1995. The EPA's revised rules may be found in 60 Federal Register 18751.

reduction program appears on course toward success; for the NO$_x$ reduction program, success is doubtful.

What can we learn from the experiences described above? The SO$_2$ reduction program works because flexibility is afforded to electric utilities trying to comply with the emissions cap. The utility compliance plans for Phase I illustrate this well. A second reason has been the effect of competition on substitutes. Suppliers of scrubbers, brokers of allowances, and purveyors of low-sulfur coal have been competing for business in previously unimagined ways, to the general benefit of electric utilities (the consumers). While electric utilities have lower compliance costs, the targeted environmental goal, once established, is unlikely to be compromised by industry lobbying or litigation.

In contrast stands the NO$_x$ reduction program. The technological standards have become firmly entrenched after the legal battle. It is now perhaps more prayer than policy that compliance, when it begins, will result in the targeted reductions in NO$_x$ emissions.

Those interested in how markets form and how markets can be made to work better have already begun to analyze the SO$_2$ emissions allowance market and its apparent inefficiency. Some have pointed to the annual allowance auction and suggested tweaking the rules for setting market-clearing prices.[50] Some have focused on the effects of state utility regulation on the allowance program.[51] Some have focused on the two-phase design of the program, suggesting that the market began slowly because Phase I did not include all participants, but only units likely to be sellers of allowances.[52]

Whether the actual cap on SO$_2$ emissions in Phase II is anything near the optimal level remains mostly speculation. As it is, the EPA may ratchet down the Phase II emissions cap in future years. One hopes that compliance experiences (and social preferences) inform that decision.

While these insights have merit, this forum on the U.S. regulatory system calls for a broader perspective. The market has been tried, and it works better than command-and-control. The theoretical insight of economists and policy analysts will pass its first major field trial. A second lesson from these experiences, clear but often overlooked in these times of ideological dismantling of the regulatory state, is that markets are created; they do not simply happen. Information is crucial. Without the aggressive efforts of the allowance brokers,

[50] U.S. General Accounting Office, *Allowance Trading*, pp. 53–55; Timothy N. Cason, "Seller Incentive Properties of EPA's Emission Trading Auction," *Journal of Environmental Economics and Management* (1993) 25: 177–195.

[51] Douglas R. Bohi and Dallas Burtraw, "Avoiding Regulatory Gridlock in the Acid Rain Program," *Journal of Policy Analysis and Management* (1991) 10: 676-684; Douglas R. Bohi and Dallas Burtraw, "Utility Investment Behavior and the Emission Trading Market," *Resources and Energy* (1992) 14:129–153; Barry D. Solomon and Kenneth Rose, "Making a Market for SO$_2$ Emissions Trading," *The Electricity Journal*, July 1992, pp. 58–66; Daniel J. Dudek and Joseph Goffman, "Can Preapproval Jump-Start the Allowance Market?" *The Electricity Journal*, June 1992, pp. 12–17; Jay S. Coggins and Vincent H. Smith, "Some Welfare Effects of Emission Allowance Trading in a Twice-Regulated Industry," *Journal of Environmental Economics and Management* (1993) 25: 275–297.

[52] Joseph Goffman, Testimony on *Implementation of Acid Rain Provisions of the Clean Air Act*, Senate Committee on Environment and Public Works, Subcommittee on Clean Air and Nuclear Regulation, 21 October 1993.

the data logged in the EPA allowance tracking system, and the widespread discussion of compliance strategies in the trade press and conferences, there would be no market at all. For their efforts, we salute them.

Bibliography

Ackerman, Bruce A., and William T. Hassler (1981). *Clean Coal/Dirty Air.* New Haven: Yale University Press.

Bailey, K.A., T.J. Elliott, L.J. Carlson, and D.W. South (1993). *Examination of Utility Phase I Compliance Choices and State Reactions to Title IV of the Clean Air Act Amendments of 1990.* Report No. ANL/DIS/TM-2. Argonne, Illinois: Argonne National Laboratory.

Bohi, Douglas R., and Dallas Burtraw (1991). "Avoiding Regulatory Gridlock in the Acid Rain Program." *Journal of Policy Analysis and Management* 10: 676–684.

Bohi, Douglas R., and Dallas Burtraw (1992). "Utility Investment Behavior and the Emission Trading Market." *Resources and Energy* 14:129–153.

Cason, Timothy N. (1993). "Seller Incentive Properties of EPA's Emission Trading Auction." *Journal of Environmental Economics and Management* 25:177–195.

Coggins, Jay S., and Vincent H. Smith (1993). "Some Welfare Effects of Emission Allowance Trading in a Twice-Regulated Industry." *Journal of Environmental Economics and Management* 25: 275–297.

Dudek, Daniel J., and Joseph Goffman (1992). "Can Preapproval Jump-Start the Allowance Market?" *The Electricity Journal,* June, pp. 12–17.

Goffman, Joseph (1993). Testimony on Implementation of Acid Rain Provisions of the Clean Air Act. Before Senate Committee on Environment and Public Works, Subcommittee on Clean Air and Nuclear Regulation, 21 October.

Lock, Reinier, and Dennis P. Harkawik, eds. (1991). *The New Clean Air Act: Compliance and Opportunity.* Arlington, Virginia: Public Utilities Reports.

Molburg, J.C., J.A. Fox, G. Pandola, and C.M. Cilek (1991). *Analysis of the Clean Air Act Amendments of 1990: A Forecast of the Electric Utility Industry Response to Title IV, Acid Deposition Control.* Report No. ANL/EAIS/TM-81. Argonne, Illinois: Argonne National Laboratory.

National Acid Precipitation Assessment Program (1991). *1990 Integrated Assessment Report.* Washington, D.C.: NAPAP Office of the Director.

Princiotta, Frank T. (1991). "Technological Options for Acid Rain Control." In *The New Clean Air Act: Compliance and Opportunity,* edited by Reinier Lock and Dennis P. Harkawik. Virginia: Public Utilities Reports, pp. 112–130.

Solomon, Barry D., and Kenneth Rose (1992). "Making a Market for SO_2 Emissions Trading." *The Electricity Journal,* July, pp. 58–66.

Torrens, Ian M., J. Edward Cichanowicz, and Jeremy B. Platt (1992). "The 1990 Clean Air Act Amendments: Overview, Utility Industry Responses, and Strategic Implications." *Annual Review of Energy and the Environment* 17: 211–233.

U.S. Energy Information Administration (1994). *Coal Industry Annual 1993.* Report No. DOE/EIA-0584(93). Washington, D.C.: U.S. Government Printing Office.

U.S. Energy Information Administration (1994). *Electric Power Annual 1993.* Report No. DOE/EIA-0348(93). Washington, D.C.: U.S. Government Printing Office.

U.S. Energy Information Administration (1994). *Electric Utility Phase I Acid Rain Compliance Strategies for the Clean Air Act Amendments of 1990.* Report No. DOE/EIA-0582. Washington, D.C.: U.S. Government Printing Office.

U.S. Energy Information Administration (1994). *Inventory of Power Plants in the*

United States 1993. Report No. DOE/EIA-0095(93). Washington, D.C.: U.S. Government Printing Office.

U.S. Environmental Protection Agency (1995). *Acid Deposition Feasibility Study.* Draft Report No. 430-R-95-001, February.

U.S. General Accounting Office (1994). *Allowance Trading Offers an Opportunity to Reduce Emissions at Less Cost.* Report No. GAO/RCED-95-30. Washington, D.C.: U.S. General Accounting Office.

U.S. General Accounting Office (1995). *Clean Air Rulemaking: Tracking System Would Help Measure Progress of Streamlining Initiatives.* Report No. GAO/RCED-95-70. Washington, D.C.: U.S. General Accounting Office.

Van Horn, Andrew J., *et al.* (1993). *Integrated Analysis of Fuel, Technology, and Emission Allowance Markets: Electric Utility Responses to the Clean Air Act Amendments of 1990.* Report No. TR-102510. Palo Alto, California: Electric Power Research Institute.

The Strategy for Privatization in the United States

Dennis E. Logue

Synopsis

Since the late 1970s, all levels of governments in the United States have privatized, deregulated, and contracted out to the private sector a wide variety of activities which had previously been subject to highly politicized decision making. For a wide range of activities, decision rights have been shifted from the public to the private sector. While state and local governments have continued moving in this direction, the Federal government effort to depoliticize seems to have stalled. The reason for this is not obvious. A large body of empirical work shows that prior efforts have been successful in enhancing economic efficiency, and much analysis supports the view that there are still many areas that are ripe for privatization and deregulation. The most plausible reason for the slowdown is politics. Without state owned enterprises and heavily regulated activity, the importance of political office is diminished. The value of access to elected officials is reduced. This reasoning suggests that a viable long run strategy of privatization requires that electoral reforms must first be enacted before much further depoliticization of economic decision-making can be expected.

*   *   *   *

Introduction

Twenty years ago, "privatization" was not even officially recognized as a word. Now the term is commonly applied in the financial, economic, and political press. It describes activity taking place in virtually every country around the world. It pertains to a process of moving economic activity under the control of government to the private sector. It means the depoliticization of economic decisions. Privatization means that the array of choices open to businesses and individuals is enhanced, and it also means that government officials are given greater freedom in choosing the ways in which to implement policy.

Privatization occurs with any one of several of these motivations:[1] (1)

---

[1] Adopted from Hanke (1987), p. 2.

depoliticization of economic decision making or at least raising the costs of political intervention in enterprise behavior or other economic activities; (2) cost reduction and improved economic performance of an activity; (3) raising revenues through asset sales; (4) reducing public outlays to sustain un-economic public enterprises; (5) reducing the power of public sector unions and other government employees; (6) promoting popular capitalism through widespread ownership of shares, and (7) reducing, generally, the size and scope of government.

The process of privatization in the U.S. began in the late 1970s as a number of large, heavily regulated industries began to be deregulated. Europe, led by Prime Minister Thatcher's Britain, began to withdraw government from industrial activity via the sales of state owned enterprises to the public. Finally, as the realization that Marxist-Leninist thinking eventually leads to economic hardship became overwhelming, this decadent philosophy was replaced by a more capitalist, freedom-oriented ideology. Accordingly, the former Communist countries began the process of transferring very large fractions of their state owned enterprises to private ownership. Indeed, as of this essays writing the pace of privatization world-wide is accelerating as Latin America and Asia increasingly turn to markets to replace government control over their economies.

Despite what seems to be a world-wide trend, the U.S., once a leader, now seems to be slowing its pace of privatization. Several key industries have been largely deregulated, but others have not. Moreover, market-based solutions to regulations cutting across industry bounds are not being implemented as rapidly as they might. Indeed, Paul MacAvoy's (1995) essay shows that privatization activities, though visible and heralded, have barely kept pace with regulatory and other interventional policies; he notes that in 1970 the regulated sectors of the economy represented 15.8% of GDP, in 1980 27% of GDP, and in 1992 21.3% of GDP. To be sure, state and local governments remain active in many areas of privatization, but curiously passive in others. They are rapidly turning to private contractors to provide services on a competitive bid basis, but continue to maintain stringent, sometimes unusual licensing procedures, and a few even continue to run state liquor monopolies. The Federal government, however, has slowed markedly in substituting private for political decision making and in a few areas has even fallen back, by renewing regulation in old areas, as with an enhanced and binding Community Reinvestment Act, or entering new areas such as student loans.

This essay will provide an overview of privatization activity and strategy in the U.S. It begins by suggesting reasons why so much economic activity got to be controlled by all levels of government in the first place. The various modes of privatization activity are then considered, followed by a review of the evidence supporting the view that privatization has brought economic benefit to the nation. Following that, I offer some hypotheses regarding why the privatization process has slowed, especially at the Federal level, despite the new seemingly economically liberal regime in Washington. The paper concludes (perhaps recklessly) by offering some predictions for the future.

Government and the Market

During the Progressive Era – the latter nineteenth and early twentieth centuries – the Federal, state and local governments began their serious expansion into the previously private arena of economic decision making. Woodrow Wilson, for example, asserted in 1887 that "the American founders' arguments for limited government were based on 'paper pictures and 'literary themes." He proposed a greatly expanded role for government – "guided by technically expert civil servants prepared by schooling and drilled, after appointment, into a perfected organization, with an appropriate hierarchy and characteristic discipline."[2]

This expansionary view of government gained impetus in the Great Depression as growth of government, already something that could be popular with bureaucrats and professional politicians, gained intellectual support from the Keynesian vision of activist government in the face of economic fluctuations and broad public support as a consequence of the insufferability of Depression era economic life. It continued through the early 1970s which witnessed the passage of much onerous regulation, including wage and price controls and the nationalization of the nation's passenger railroads.

Over that period, politicians searched for reasons to intervene in economic activity. Believing that America's problems could be solved by more good people in government, power-seeking bureaucrats and citizens whose actions were genuinely motivated by compassion in the face of various crises, e.g. the environment, automobile safety, drug safety, etc., searched for reasons for intervention in economic activity. Like their forebears, these politicians found many markets that were not working as the textbook version of perfect competition suggests, and hence sought government intervention to improve economic (as well as social) performance.

The *Economic Report of the President* (1982) documents the growth in regulatory activity. It shows that in 1900 there were fewer than ten Federal regulatory agencies. By 1980, there were more than fifty. (p. 135)

Efficiency Motives for Intervention

There are valid reasons for proposing intervention in economic decision-making. One of the most commonly cited reasons for proposing regulation or some other sort of government intervention is "Natural Monopoly." This situation occurs when there are such economies of scale that the existence of competing firms would keep each from operating as efficiently as they might. In the extreme case, destructive competition results. Since several firms may have marginal costs below average costs, marginal cost pricing will force some firms out of business and even financially hamper the survivors. Consumers, of course, will pay more than they must to cover costs of services either with competition or if the natural monopolist were left unregulated. Hence,

---

[2] Reported in Mitchell and Simmons (1994), p. 210.

natural monopoly is controlled by restrictions on entry and rate of return regulation.

Fear of natural monopoly motivated the regulation of electric utilities as well as telephone service. Surprisingly, it was also one of the reasons offered by the New York Stock Exchange to support its position that it should be allowed to set fixed, minimum commissions on trades executed by the Exchange's member firms; without minimum commissions trades would take place in different settings, despite the Exchange's natural monopoly position. Overall costs would rise as a consequence of fragmented order flow. Natural monopoly type arguments also supported price fixing of passenger air transportation services by the Civil Aeronautics Board (CAB).

Technology has seemingly put to rest the idea that long distance telecommunications services constitutes a natural monopoly. Experience has shown that the natural monopoly argument advanced by the New York Stock Exchange was inaccurate in that the abandonment of fixed minimum commissions in 1975 brought no ill consequences for the Exchange itself or the member firm community as a whole. Security trading is still heavily concentrated on the New York Stock Exchange. Nor have consumers suffered at all; indeed, they have been big winners.[3] Moreover, state regulatory bodies have discovered that some integrated services such as electricity supply can be unbundled into natural monopoly components, say distribution systems, and competitive components say electricity generation. Indeed, many states are moving rapidly toward competitive structures for parts of previously regulated entities. Sometimes the natural monopoly argument seems to have been extended to considerations of "excessive" competition, rather than "destructive" competition – this was, for instance, the case for heavily regulating interstate trucking. Back in the period of great regulatory growth, government, as a policy matter, motivated perhaps by strong union support, decided more trucks were better than fewer, and higher transport prices better than lower.

A second general reason for government intervention has to do with two types of market failures. One type of market failure occurs when there are externalities. Externalities or spillover effects can sometimes cause an entity to produce too much of some (collectively) undesirable products such as pollution or too little of some other products such as Research and Development where much of the gains to society cannot be captured by the risk-taking innovator. Sometimes the positive spillover is termed the free-rider problem; public goods, such as defense, would not be produced in adequate quantity, without government intervention to control free-rider issues.

A second type of market failure has to do with the cost of producing and disseminating information. Once information is produced, the cost of dissemination is trivial and hard to protect. Thus, too little information may be produced. The social gain to producing information, as with automobile safety standards, or obviating the private need for producing information, as with providing small savers with bank deposit insurance or preventing unsafe drugs

---

[3] See MacAvoy (1993).

from going to market, often outweighs the total cost of doing so in many instances.

Indeed, one could even push this impacted information argument to the point where, say, a mandatory Social Security System is justified because ordinary consumers do not know enough about their futures, their life expectancies, and their late life earning prospects to do sufficient private saving. Failure to do so creates an externality that demands address by a humane society, one which is unwilling to let old people starve. Accordingly, some sort of system may be preferable to none.

Sometimes the impacted information type of market failure may lead to a paternalistic response. This is not an intended economic motive for government intervention, but many sorts of interventions based on impacted information arguments are subconsciously (and sometimes consciously) really motivated by paternalism or, more formally, interdependent utility functions. This motive may also contain additional economic reasons, as in the case of Social Security.

Political Motives for Intervention

The third broad motive for government intervention in the economy is a public finance motive. There may be legitimate public interests served in some instances while others may represent self-interested rent-seeking to a very refined degree. One type of public finance motivation is what has been termed "rent control."[4] Sometimes events create sudden economic rents, as they did in the case of the oil crisis in the 1970s. Because of the perceived "unfairness" associated with such sudden, fortuitous events, politicians and public interest advocates pleaded for government intervention intended to remedy the hardships suffered by those on the other side of the rent creating action. To the extent such redistribution creates a safer and more congenial environment for all, there may be an efficiency justification for it.

Richard Posner (1971) reveals that a common consequence of public finance motivated regulation and intervention is cross-subsidization. Sometimes government intervention is used to correct an apparent monopoly problem or market failure problem, but really just leads to a transfer from one group to another. That is, some groups are pressed to pay more so others can pay less. Indeed, for many years long distance telephone rates were maintained at higher levels than economically necessary in order to generate excess funds to subsidize local telephone service. Similarly, the cost of service concept does not play a role in keeping first-class postal rates the same for all letters no matter how far any one letter is sent.

Posner (1971) writes:

> "The internal subsidy ... is an aspect of public finance in what is at once a more exact and a more natural sense. Taxation in common parlance refers to the powers of the state to extract money from its citizens in order (1) to defray the cost of services that the politically dominant elements in the state wish to provide and that

[4] See Breyer (1982), p. 21

the market would not produce in the desired quantity and at the desired price, (2) to transfer money from one group to another, or (3) often, to do both. By this test, regulation is part of a system of taxation or public finance. The basic mechanism is the internal subsidy." (p. 28–9)

One rough example of a regulated activity which might be characterized this way is the corporate pension plan. The Employee Retirement Income Security Act (ERISA) of 1974 was enacted in order to protect employees from employers who might renege on pension promises. There were certainly elements of market failure problems, namely spillover effects – if promised pensions are not paid, an added strain would be put on public welfare services, and the Social Security System – and impacted information – related to how employees could ever understand enough about the value of an employer commitment to pay a pension, including the solvency of the pension plan, to insist upon a high enough current salary to compensate for the risk of pension insolvency. But real as these things seemed, there had been comparatively few instances of corporations firing employees just before retirement to save on pension expense or defaulting pension plans. Moreover, most analysts believed unionized employees were compensated through wages for any default risk in their pension plans.[5] (The case of Studebaker in the early 1960s is always recalled; here thousands of workers were left pensionless because of an unfunded pension plan. The reason why this example is always cited is because there are no comparably large or harmful alternative examples.) ERISA made pensions safer, but for these employees, mostly union members whose wages already reflected risky pension plans, ERISA resulted in a gratuitous transfer from employers to employees.[6] Employees were being compensated for risks they did not bear. This is one illustration of a situation in which market failure considerations were publicly presented but where transfer considerations privately dominated the enactment of the legislation.

Indeed, reading commentary in the popular press, one can easily get the impression that the transfer aspect of regulation is one of its most important contributions. As a strident opponent of privatization, Sclar (1994) writes about the transfer question:

"... [support for] privatization ... is rooted in its ideological desire to shrink government ... particularly programs like education, transportation, medical care, and housing, which foster a redistribution of goods and services to those at the bottom of the social order ... it pursues its ideological goal under the banner of a pragmatic concern for government efficiency." (p. 300).

One problem with government intervention is it is generally difficult to determine whether the costs associated with the cure for market failure, most broadly construed, exceed the benefits. Rather than being rooted in a desire to shrink government, one inference from the privatization movement is intervention has gone too far. Indeed, the net benefits of government involve-

---

[5] The case of Studebaker which occured in the early 1960s was always cited as an example of a company with an underfunded pension plan which defaulted on its pension obligations. The fact that it is the only large company example ever cited suggests the rarity of the event.

[6] See Ippolito (1986, 1988) and Logue (1979b, 1991).

ment are now in many instances negative. There are occasions where imperfect markets work better than after they are subjected to the best of government intervention designed and implemented by bureaucrats with limited knowledge and imperfect measuring sticks. There are many opportunities, then, for improving the efficiency or cost effectiveness of any given type of intervention.

The Push for Privatization

Despite the growth of the U.S. government during the early and mid-twentieth century, there were always a few voices which argued against it. However, because the arguments were couched in relatively abstract ideological and philosophical terms the wisdom of a Hayek or a Rand, for example, never really had a powerful direct influence on the vast majority of policy-makers. People like Hayek and Rand viewed freedom as a zero sum game. The bigger the government, the less free the individual. The argument is abstract and thus can easily be misconstrued as promoting a concern for self and a lack of concern for other human beings.[7]

Respectability of the Idea of Privatization

In the early 1960s, the idea of privatization, if not limited government generally, gained much more intellectual respectability largely because it was demonstrated that a humane society and limited government could coexist. Milton Friedman (1962) is credited by some with this intellectual breakthrough because he showed that gains could come from limited government without sacrificing concern for others.[8] He made at least three significant points.

First, he emphatically underscored the fact that government is a monopoly. In the U.S., we have had a long-standing, almost visceral distaste for monopolies. Even if one enjoyed all the consequences of government action, one could still find unpleasant the prospect of dealing with a monopoly service provider. In some sense, Friedman provided a motivation for government contracting out; by suggesting that contracting with private providers to do things that government at some level or another had provided was an alternative way of delivering services.

Second, Friedman argued that government was anti-consumer at a time when Americas interest in consumerism began to gain popularity. Government robbed individuals of choices in some cases and it caused higher prices in others. For example, trade barriers were easily shown to be harmful to consumers either by raising prices or cutting off the importation of some goods. He further argued that an anti-consumer government was preventing consumer choice regarding services such as mail delivery.

Finally, Friedman demonstrated that government could fulfill its obligations

---

[7] For instance, one of Ayn Rand's books was *The Virtue of Selfishness*. The title alone invites criticism on humanitarian grounds.

[8] See Henig (1989–90).

to citizens without actually providing the services. Government could fulfill its responsibility to educate, for instance, without actually running the schools. Instead it could offer education vouchers to parents who could use them at any school they pleased.

Friedman's contribution showed how a conversation about privatization could take place without the support of an abstract "natural law" discussion about the relative responsibilities of government and individuals. As a result, he fostered much experimentation at state and local levels with certain kinds of privatization and certainly stimulated debate within the Federal government about the actual size, if not the scope, of its responsibilities. The concept of privatization gained respectability.

Modes of Privatization

There are various types of privatization activities, activities which devolve decision rights from the public to the private sector. For our purposes, separating these into five categories is sufficient:

1. *Deregulation or Regulatory Reform.* This is the privatization activity that the U.S. government has pursued. Beginning in the late 1970s, airlines, trucking, financial services, and telecommunications all experienced reduced regulatory interference. The government has tried to test the quality of markets. Seemingly, government has experimented in those instances where the cost of regulation seemed to have risen above its benefit. Deregulation is akin to privatization in the sense that market forces rather than bureaucrats or commissioners will govern the behavior of enterprises. For example, under the broad rubric of deregulation, private entry into fields such as next day mail delivery has been allowed.

2. *Contracting Out.* This has been tried extensively by state, local, and the Federal government. Here a governmental unit chooses a private contractor to perform a service for which it is responsible. Garbage collecting and school busing were among the first things contracted out to private suppliers largely because performance for such activities is easily monitored. In recent years, activities where monitoring is technically difficult and costly, and contracts are complex are being contracted out. These include prison management and even the management of public school systems.

3. *Vouchers/Grants.* These are transfers to individuals or groups which allow them to acquire government provided goods or services from suppliers of their choice. Subsidized Medicare and Medicaid are examples. Recipients can visit a variety of health providers, they are not restricted to government clinics.

4. *Asset Sales.* State owned enterprises such as Conrail are being sold, but at an excruciatingly slow pace in the U.S. Foreign governments have pursued this course of action far more enthusiastically than the U.S.

government has. But this comparison may be deceiving. Many foreign government asset sales are of the type of companies that in the U.S. were regulated, but not state owned, telephone companies for example. Further, foreign governments were more willing to subsidize failing industrial firms, such as the Jaguar motor car company, and therefore increased the incidence of their ownership of industrial firms. The U.S. government generally only guarantees loans, as in Chrysler Corporations case. Foreign governments have more to sell than the U.S. government, and the U.S. government has more to deregulate.

The U.S. has plenty to sell nonetheless. The only significant asset sales by the U.S. government have been Conrail in 1987, some loans, and some radio frequencies. The U.S. government aborted plans to sell public lands in the early 1980s and seems to have little enthusiasm for selling any of the 50 or so public enterprises, such as the Postal Service or the Tennessee Valley Authority, that the U.S. government still owns and operates. (See MacAvoy and McIsaac (1995)).

5. *Cessation of Public Programs and Disengagement of Government.* These are the most important manifestations of privatization. There are two aspects to the downsizing of government. At one level one can envision a high level of government ceding to a lower level of government responsibility for an activity. This moves decision-making closer to the electorate. An example of this would be pushing environmental regulation to the state level so that local economic conditions can be taken into consideration when rules are made. At a second level, this sort of privatization means government passes on its perceived responsibility to private markets and to individual conscience. An example might be the Federal governments end to regulation of the banking system.

Progress

In 1986, President Reagan established a working group to investigate privatization opportunities. The objective was not necessarily to eliminate government provided services, but to (1) make private alternatives available, (2) ensure the production of services demanded by consumers, not government bureaucrats, (3) lead to more efficient, lower cost production of these services, and (4) remove government imposed constraints on competition.[9]

Table 1 is a 1989 compilation of the significant privatization initiatives of the Federal government. It heralded the great success of the Reagan administration in getting government "off the backs of the people." Unfortunately, there is very little need to update the list, except if we were to note areas of backsliding or added government action, as with the Clean Air Act of 1990.

---

[9] Based upon *Economic Report of the President* (1986), p. 9.

TABLE 1   PRIVATIZATION ACTIVITIES

Year	Initiative	Effect
1971	Specialized common carrier decisions (FCC)	Allowed entry by tele-communications carriers into interstate markets
1972	Domestic satellite open skies policy (FCC)	Allowed competition among communications satellites
1975	Abolition of fixed brokerage fees (SEC)	Eliminated fixed minimum commission charges by NYSE/ASE firms
1976	Railroad Revitalization and Reform Act	Limited ICC jurisdiction over maximum freight rates to non-competitive markets
1977	Air Cargo Deregulation Act	Allowed fee splitting amongst shippers
1978	Airline Deregulation Act	Abolished CAB rate setting by December 1984
	Natural Gas Policy Act	Partial decontrol of natural gas prices
	Standards revocation (OSHA)	Reduced some requirements
	Emissions trading policy (EPA) different sorts of emissions	Allows firm to trade off of
1979	Deregulation of satellite earth stations (FCC)	Eliminate price regulation and entry structures on satellite earth Stations
	Urgent-mail exemption (Postal Service)	Allowed electronic mail
1980	Motor Carrier Reform Act	Federal controls on discretionary power of state rate making bureaus
	Household Goods Transportation Act	Allowed movers to set rates
	Staggers Rail Act	Eliminated ICC certification requirements regarding market entry and exit for rail carriers
	Depository Institutions Deregulation and Monetary Control Act	Phase out of interest rate controls, broadened lending and investing power of thrift institutions
	International Air Transportation	Eliminated international price fixing of air fares for

	Competition Act	U.S. carriers
	Deregulation of cable television (FCC)	Allowed cable operators to carry additional signals
	Deregulation of customer premises equipment and enhanced services (FCC)	Allowed private attachments to to phones
1981	Decontrol of crude oil and refined petroleum products (Executive Order)	End of price controls on oil and natural gas
	Truth-in-lending simplification (FRB)	Simplified disclosure requirements
	Automobile industry regulation relief package (NHTSA)	Softened regulations regarding the introduction of auto safety requirements
	Deregulation of radio (FCC)	Eliminated controls on amount of commercial messages
1982	Bus Regulatory Reform Act	Deregulated intercity bus traffic
	Garn-St. Germain Depository Institutions Act	Raised FDIC insurance limits, expanded lending powers of thrift institutions
	AT&T settlement	Split up AT&T; enhanced completion amongst long distance telecommunications providers
	Antitrust merger guidelines	Reduced restrictions on business combinations
1984	Space commercialization	Simplified procedures for companies wishing to launch space vehicles
	Cable Television Deregulation Act	Ended price regulation of cable TV services
	Shipping Act	Shippers allowed to set their own point-to-point charges
1986	Trading of airport landing rights	Airlines allowed to buy or sell landing right allotments
1987	Sale of Conrail	Sale of government owned railroad to the public
	Elimination of fairness doctrine (FCC)	Eliminated rule requiring coverage of all sides of controversial issues
1988	Proposed rules on natural gas and electricity FERC)	Allowed open access to pipelines and possible deregulation of energy production

Source: *Economic Report of the President*, 1989, p. 196.

The President's Report on Privatization (1988) identified many areas that were targets of privatization: Low Income Housing, Housing Finance, Federal Loan Programs, Air Traffic Control, Educational Choice, the Postal Service. It also identified prospective asset sales: Amtrak, the Petroleum Reserves, Public Lands, and Power Production and Marketing. Nevertheless, virtually none of the recommendations have been followed.

As the table makes clear, most of the privatization, or essentially regulatory reform, has occurred in the regulated industries. Very little, however, has been done to make regulated activities, environmental rules as opposed to rules on industry behavior, more market oriented. Most of the progress in allowing for market solutions has been confined to changes in regulatory behavior. There is little progress to report regarding the use of market forces to regulate activities as opposed to industries. There appears to be only one significant instance where market forces have been allowed to work, and this is the auctioning of air pollution rights. Apart from this, little has been done to allow markets to allocate regulatory burdens efficiently.

Privatization Strategy

It would be helpful to our ability to forecast the future of privatization if there appeared to be a theme to Federal governments efforts to this point. But there is no discernible theme, no discernible strategy. Why would Conrail be sold, but the Tennessee Valley Authority retained? Why is the airline industry deregulated, while huge maritime subsidies are continued?

From the viewpoint of economic efficiency, uncolored by public choice considerations, there seems to be little rhyme nor reason to the way government has gone about privatizing. It has not chosen to privatize based on any criteria of prioritization such as privatizing areas with the greatest deadweight costs or areas where technology and knowledge have clearly eliminated the conditions which prompted government intervention in the first place. Rather, it appears a privatization strategy of a sort has emerged from the complex and curious interplay of economic and political forces.[10]

Benefits of Privatization

Regarding the effect of deregulation, there is little doubt government withdrawal has been beneficial. Where market failures exist, there seems to be a broad consensus that, when possible, outsourcing has been very effective. The data reviewed in the next section support these views. Where government intervention principally involves large transfers from politically powerful groups, privatization has been difficult because maintaining the status quo is too attractive to those groups and legislators who are close to those groups alike.

---

[10] In a very interesting article. Winston and Crandall (1994) relate presidential voting patterns to the type of regulation the incumbent party sponsored during its presidential administration.

Deregulation

The most extensive work on the benefits of privatization has focused on deregulation. Two survey papers summarize the results of many studies. Paul MacAvoy (1993) reports on the price reductions of industries that were being regulated to control prices. For example, his digest of many studies reveals that: (1) commission rates in the brokerage industry dropped by 16% after fixed commissions were eliminated, (2) prices fell by 14.3% in the rail freight business, by 7.2% in the trucking industry, and by 7.0% in the passenger airline industry, after deregulation, and (3) prices fell by 6.7% for petroleum products following the removal of well-head price controls. Another extensive survey by Clifford Winston (1993) critically evaluates and agrees with studies that show significant consumer gains from deregulation, substantially lower producer losses, and total net benefits in the vicinity of $36–$46 billion (1990 dollars) per year in just a few industries. This amounts to significant gain to the economy.

Despite the resounding success of deregulation, the pace of deregulation has slowed considerably. For example, one area that has been a candidate for serious regulatory reform for decades and was singled out for special attention in Vice President Quayle's Council on Competitiveness Report (1992) is the banking system. Despite a long history of getting the regulation wrong,[11] rather than giving over the industry entirely to market forces, the deregulatory efforts seem to be leaning toward a piecemeal relaxation of rules. Indeed, of the three pieces of legislation under consideration at this date only the bill introduced by Senator DAmato represents a true freeing of the banking system from bureaucratic control.[12] But even as legislators are considering some measures that may ease banks' regulatory constraints, the Federal Reserve Board is tightening the regulatory noose by more stringently interpreting laws such as the Community Reinvestment Act.[13]

Along these same lines, Richardson and Ziebart (1995) point out that the number of Federal regulations in 1985 dropped from the number in 1980; the number fell from 121,670 to 101,963. However, by 1993 the number had risen to 128,615. (p. 4). There are other instances of foot dragging as well. This is indeed surprising in light of the resounding success of deregulation so far. We will soon see why.

Contracting Out

State and local governments have taken the lead in contracting out. They are enthusiastically contracting out a wide variety of activities which they feel

[11] Even the government admits regulation contributed to the Savings and Loan debacle of the late 1980s and early 1990s. See *The Economic Report of the President* (1993), p. 193–196.

[12] See Wallison (1995).

[13] A recent newspaper report reveals that banks will have heightened Community Reinvestment Act responsibilities, requiring them, among other things, to report small business loans by regions so that regulators may determine whether enough loans are being made in economically depressed areas. See Taylor and Gaylord, "New Banking Rules to Allow Scrutiny of Regional Loans," *Wall Street Journal*, April 19, 1995, p. C13.

politically responsible to provide and where clear performance guidelines can be developed, performance can be monitored, and contracts can be easily enforced. These include general administrative services such as parking ticket collection. They are even contracting out activities that are more difficult to handle on an agency basis; these include corrections (prisons), education, health, mental health/retardation, social services, and transportation.[14] The reported savings are significant, though they vary widely across areas and states.

The Federal government is a large user of contract services at considerable cost savings. In 1986, when enthusiasm for privatization was running high, the General Accounting Office identified other opportunities for contracting out that could result in moving 95,000 to 500,000 government positions to the private sector at savings ranging from $.9 billion to $4.6 billion.[15] No subsequent published report, however, clearly revealed how much of this plan was actually implemented.

Asset Sales

The U.S. government has been quite slow in the area of asset sales. Conrail, some Federal loans, and radio frequencies have been sold, but very little else. The U.S. government runs at least fifty major enterprises, employing more than 800,000 people, generating annual revenues of more than $50 billion. MacAvoy and McIsaac (1995) studied several of the largest of these and compared their performance to private sector counterparts. In no dimension of economic performance did the federally owned enterprises perform better than their private counterparts. Indeed, they conclude:

> "These were the results because management has had greater discretion to serve particular influence groups rather than the more broadly conceived market for final goods and services ... with fault on the public corporate structure so fundamental, then divestiture of the enterprises from government ownership appears to be the only possible means for correction in the long run." (p. 34)

We can look abroad and confirm MacAvoy and McIsaacs predictions. In other countries, the economic performance of those state owned enterprises that have been sold has been excellent.

A recently published study by Meggenson *et al.* (1994) compared the pre and post privatization financial and operating results of a group of companies in several non-socialist economies. Specifically, the study evaluated 61 companies in 32 industries from 18 countries that were wholly or partly sold to the public via share offerings over the period 1961 through 1990.

Meggenson *et al.* (1994) report:

> "... strong performance improvements, achieved surprisingly, without sacrificing employment security. Specifically, after being privatized, firms increase real sales, become more profitable, increase their capital investment spending, improve their

---

[14] See Reason Foundation (1995).
[15] *Economic Report of the President* (1989), p. 212.

operating efficiency, and increase their work forces. Furthermore, these companies significantly lower their debt levels and increase dividend payment." (p. 403)

Contrasting the poor performance of government owned enterprises in the U.S. with the success of newly privatized companies abroad, and in light of other evidence consistent with the view that large government sectors impede the creation of wealth (Logue, 1979a), it is indeed difficult to explain the slow pace of asset sales in the U.S.

Vouchers and Grants

In a broad context, Federal provision of Medicare, for example, is akin to a voucher or grant. The government pays for most or all of the service, but the beneficiary is free to choose amongst health providers. Generally, however, vouchers are associated with such uses as educational vouchers wherein parents can send their children to one of many possible schools. Apart from social insurance activities, the Federal government is not heavily involved in voucher programs; whereas states are heavily involved in vouchers and grants, especially with respect to welfare.

It is not clear that vouchers save very much money; the body of relevant literature is comparatively scarce. Indeed, the real benefit of vouchers or grants is not strictly budgetary. By encouraging competition amongst service providers in what had previously been monopolistic situations (e.g. local public schools), service quality should improve.

In principle, contracting out should lead to increased quality. Indeed, the cities of Baltimore and Hartford have contracted out the operation of public schools. However, a major difficulty in the process is developing contract specifications for the performance of complex multi-dimensional tasks, such as education. Accordingly, in instances where contracts are hard to write and enforce, vouchers should provide a superior alternative since each consumer becomes a service quality monitor. This is why it is unlikely that contracting out school services will survive over the long term unless accompanied by a voucher system that would allow for consumer choice and strong competition.

Many communities are also experimenting with "charter schools." These are publicly funded, but competitive to the traditional public school. This introduces competition without true privatization, except to the extent that different groups of charter school organizers can imbue their own educational philosophy into their respective school. Nonetheless, the charter school concept does reduce the power of a monopolistic public school system.

The Pace of Privatization

The late 1970s through the 1980s witnessed rapid growth in privatization activities. Reform minded chairmen at the Civil Aeronautics Board (CAB) Interstate Commerce Commission (ICC) and the Federal Communications Commission (FCC) (Alfred Kahn, Daniel ONeal, and Charles Ferris, respectively), led the charge in the late 1970s. They generated a momentum that lasted well into the next decade. The real excitement in privatization during this period centered around the deregulation of particular industries.

Driving the Success of Privatization

Political scientists Martha Derthick and Paul Quirk (1985) have carefully examined the process of regulatory reform, specifically deregulation, in several agencies. Several factors seem to have been present when meaningful deregulation was achieved.

In the case of passenger airline, freight transportation, and telecommunications, three factors were operative. First, elite opinion converged in support of deregulation. Politicians as well as top level academics and business people came to be convinced that deregulation was appropriate. They finally began to believe the economic analysis – much of which had been around since the 1950s – which showed that deregulation would lower prices and not harm service. The elites came to believe that government withdrawal would be generally beneficial, often over the howls of protests of managers in the regulated industries who would now face stiffened price competition and increased competitive entry.

Second, office holders in positions of leadership took deregulatory initiatives. Surprisingly, one of the staunchest advocates of deregulation was President Ford, who held office after President Nixon's resignation. Perhaps because he had not made too many broad campaign promises, he was free to pursue the national interest. Many of the forces Ford set in motion were sustained by President Carter.

Third, and in their view the most important in the cases they studied, the deregulatory process could begin without Congressional action. The regulatory agencies themselves moved towards deregulation, leading Congress to take a different view of the regulatory process. That is, they were able to demonstrate to Congress that deregulation not only did not raise prices but it caused massive fallout in an industry. The commissions thus got out in front of Congress and dragged the politicians along.

The Slowdown

At the present time, these three conditions do not seem to exist at the Federal level. Not only has the pace of privatization slowed, but privatization activities have been reversed in several areas. One of the chief reasons for these effects is that there is no longer a champion for privatization. That is, the President is not proactively pushing for the withdrawal of government. For example, soon after President Clinton took office he pressed Congress to pass legislation that would re-federalize student loans. Prior to this action, student loans were administered by the Student Loan Marketing Association (Sallie Mae), a private company that itself enjoyed a special relationship with the government because its loans to students were guaranteed by the government. For all intents and purposes, the legislation will result in the eventual dissolution of Sallie May or minimally cause a vast redeployment of its assets. Additional evidence of this Presidentially-led drift back to bigger government is President Clintons health care plan. Irrespective of ones appraisal of its merits, all agree its implementation would have increased the power of the Federal government over the economic actions of individual citizens.

In addition, our nation's elites are no longer unanimous in their views regarding further privatization. Some view it solely in terms of the desirability of reduced government, often failing to note that this would increase personal freedom, including the freedom to be more charitable and humane. Others take a paternalistic view of privatization as simply a budgetary device that could leave many disadvantaged people much worse off than they currently are. There are undoubtedly a few areas where specific activities bring both political as well as economic benefits to privatization. But it is hard to tell what they are. For example, MacAvoy and McIsaac (1995) document the already verified inefficiency of government power companies. As long ago as 1986, the *Economic Report of the President* (1986, p. 186) noted that government operating costs for hydroelectric power generation after adjusting for scale and automation were 20 percent higher than for private firms (p. 186). Yet, there is no obvious widespread support for selling government power generation facilities. It remains unexplained why elites are no longer in broad agreement on privatizing various government power enterprises.

Finally, much of what remains to be done for privatization requires Congressional approval, as is the situation regarding much activity on social regulation as opposed to industry regulation. Where Congressional approval is not required, the regulatory agencies themselves are reasserting their power, as in the case of the Federal Reserve Boards tougher interpretation and enforcement of the Community Reinvestment Act.[16] Further, despite the ideological makeup of the recently elected Congressional majorities, there is no reason to believe that regulatory reform and tougher Congressional oversight of regulatory agencies in lieu of wholesale privatization will result. One example of this is Representative Leach's (R., Iowa) approach to bank regulation which "seems to have dropped out of a time warp" and which is "a complex model of intrusive micromanagement (which) allows bank holding companies to establish securities subsidiaries under the wary eye of the Federal Reserve Board." (Wallison 1995). Of course, a counter example may be offered by positioning out the reduced telecommunications regulatory burden. But this seemed to occur because there was no constituency for the status quo.

Milton Friedman (1995) recently predicted the U.S. will never adopt a flat tax, despite the support of some exceptionally powerful political leaders. The reason, he argued, is a complex tax code gives lobbyists and the politicians they rely upon something to sell. Seemingly, minuscule provisions of a complex set of tax laws can result in millions of dollars changing hands. To the extent a Congressman can get a provision changed for a constituent or, better yet, a major campaign contributor, the Congressman remains valuable. A simple code means the lobbyist has no Congressional access to sell for fees, and the politician has no access time to sell for campaign consideration.

[16] See Scott (1995).

This reveals another reason the U.S. push for privatization has slowed considerably. State owned enterprises and regulated industries make access to politicians more valuable than otherwise. So long as the government can distribute, or rather redistribute, economic benefits via state owned enterprises or regulation, potential major campaign donors will be nearby, trying to influence the outcome of Congressional debate. This leaves us with one more evil we can lay at the doorstep of political campaign financing – the slowed pace of privatization despite the tremendous volume of evidence supporting economists predictions about increased operating efficiency and gains to consumers.

Consider the way regulation gets established and implemented. In the case of most activity regulation and some industry regulation, there is first some sort of crisis or calamity. For example, the 1962 Food and Drug Amendments arose from the thalidomide situation; automobile safety standards were in large measure prompted by Ralph Nader's scare-mongering book, *Unsafe at Any Speed*. Given the prospect of a regulatory response, crises give politicians something about which to wage their political campaigns. Politicians can, through the stroke of a magic wand, save us from some terrible evil that will befall us if we do not regulate an industry or activity. All too often the scare motivating the regulations gets blown out of proportion. Emotional outcomes, not grounded in cost-benefit analysis, result. Years later economists and journalists get to write articles about the fact that the value of a human life implied by a particular regulation is tens of millions of dollars.

Second, bureaucrats implement the regulations. Sometimes the implementation makes the cure worse than the disease. Again, the dead weight costs of the cure may be greater than those associated with the unregulated activity. When the control of an activity is based upon some measure that is correlated with the regulated activity, the control moves to a point where achieving the measurable standard, rather than achieving the initial objective of the regulation, becomes paramount. For example, automobile safety standards could easily lead to engineering cars which are heavier and stronger but certainly not safer; environmental regulations can lead to vast expenditures with no increase in health, safety, or aesthetics. What may be even worse is politicians can then campaign against the insanity of regulation, campaign against the "Inside-the-Beltway" mentality, or minimally help constituents and campaign contributors steer their way around the more absurd regulations.

Politicians can also benefit from straightforward economic regulation. If the regulatory standards can be twisted to benefit one organization but be harmful to another, a good politician can broker the difference, leaving two slightly grateful parties. Or the politician could straightforwardly go for the campaign support – votes or financial contribution – by helping one entity at the expense of the other.

Without onerous, sometimes irrational regulation, citizens and organizations would have less need for access to political leaders. Because political leaders can generally benefit from that which causes their constituents pain by helping to alleviate the pain, it would indeed be surprising to find politicians wholeheartedly supporting legislation which turned significantly more economic and social regulation over to markets, leaving their "good offices" with less to do. They would have less opportunity to interact with campaign contributors.

H. L. Mencken perhaps best captured the true spirit of privatization opponents when he wrote:

> "The government consists of a gang of men exactly like you and me. They have, taking one with another, no special talent for the business of government; they have only a talent for getting and holding office. Their principal device to that end is to search out groups who pant and pine for something they can't get, and to promise to give it to them ... by looting A to satisfy B. In other words, government is a broker in pillage, and every election is a sort of advance auction sale of stolen goods." (*Carnival of Buncombe*)

A low rate of privatization or alternatively a highly regulated economy activity reduces the search costs for politicians seeking groups who need their help.

Conclusion

In the United States at the Federal, state and local levels, there has been much privatization activity since the late 1970s. At the Federal level, privatization has largely taken the form of industry deregulation. At the state and local levels, contracting out and vouchers have been the dominant mode of privatization.

No serious study shows that privatization in general results in welfare losses. Indeed, in all but one area, every extant study showed welfare gains. In the case of deregulated cable TV, prices rose but the number of available television channels also rose significantly. Judging by the growth of cable installations, despite higher prices, even here there was probably a welfare gain. This mountain of evidence is inconsistent with the rate at which activities at the Federal level are being privatized. This rate has slowed considerably since the late 1980s. The question is, why?

Three reasons emerge. The first is that support for privatization is becoming much more selective. Supporters of privatization for efficiency and ideological purposes are few and far between, especially among opinion leaders. Second, evidence shows that the people at the top of the Executive branch of government are more likely to want to regulate than not. Third, the easy deals have already been struck. What remains are possibilities which are more ambitious and therefore require Congressional action. However, unless there is an overwhelming political constituency such as a unified elite pressing them to do so, Congressmen will not scramble to support any activity which will reduce the power of government or make it more difficult for them to raise campaign funds.[17]

[17] It is informative to note that despite the ideological twist of the new Congress and the Republican party's Contract with America, Congress turned down term limits legislation. So all incumbents will still have a reason to raise campaign funds.

At least two things are therefore necessary before the rate of privatization moves forward in high gear. First, broad constituencies for privatization have to be built. And they cannot be built if the proponents of privatization only promote the concept of limited government or budget issues. Airlines, freight transport and communications were deregulated because they became issues of consumer sovereignty. The positive virtues of privatization, *e.g.* better schools, must be the focus of publicity. The elites and the electorate must unite on this just as Ralph Nader and the family wishing to visit Disneyland united on the issue of lower airfares.

Second, campaign financing must be fixed. The politician's benefit of providing political access must be reduced. This will only happen if elected officials do not have to finance their campaigns with substantial contributions from special and single interest groups. It is not clear to me how to reform campaign financing. But if privatization is to have a chance, politicians will have to rely less upon those who want regulatory rules twisted to their advantage, but not abandoned and more on those who seek to limit the size and scope of government.

Only when these kinds of political changes become reality, can we expect some dramatic movement in the privatization arena. The key next step in devising a strategy for privatization is reforming those aspects of our political system which push politicians to "sell" access. Until then, what depoliticization that occurs will be idiosyncratic, not done in accordance with an externally discernible strategy.

Bibliography

Breyer, Stephen (1982) *Regulation and Its Reform*, Cambridge, MA: Harvard University Press.

Cohen, Linda R. and Roger G. Noll (1995), "Privatizing Public Research: The New Competitiveness Strategy," Working Paper.

De Alessi, Louis (1987), "Property Rights and Privatization," in Steve H. Hanke, *ed. Prospects for Privatization*, Academy of Political Science, V. 36, N. 3, pp. 24–35.

Derthick, Martha and Paul J. Quirk (1985), *The Politics of Deregulation*, Washington, DC: The Brookings Institution.

Economic Report of the President, various issues.

Foster, C.D. (1992), *Privatization, Public Ownership and the Regulation of Natural Monopoly*, Cambridge, MA: Blackwell Publishers.

Friedman, Milton (1962), *Capitalism, Freedom and Democracy*, Chicago: University of Chicago Press.

Friedman, Milton (1995), "Commentary", *Wall Street Journal*, March 30 1995, p.-A-14.

Goodman, John B. and Gary W. Loveman (1991), "Does Privatization Serve the Public Interest?" *Harvard Business Review*, (Nov.-Dec. 1991), pp. 26-ff.

Gore, Al (1993), *From Red Tape to Results: Creating a Government that Works Better and Costs Less*, Report of the National Performance Review, (September 1993).

Hanke, Steve *ed.* (1987), *Prospects for Privatization*, New York: Academy of Political Science, 1987.

Henig, Jeffrey R. (1989), "Privatization in the United States: Theory and Practice," *Political Science Quarterly*, V. 104, N. 4, (1989–90), pp. 649–670.

Ippolito, Richard A. (1986), *Pensions, Economics and Public Policy*, Homewood, IL: Dow Jones-Irwin.

Ippolito, Richard A. (1988), "A Study of the Regulatory Effect of the Employee Retirement Income Security Act," *Journal of Law and Economics*, V. 31, N. 1 (April 1988), pp. 85–125.

Logue, Dennis E. (1979a), "Growth of Government and Stock Prices: An Exploratory Study of the International Evidence," *Columbia Journal of World Business*, (Winter 1979), pp. 136–140.

Logue, Dennis E. (1979b), *Legislation Influences on Corporate Pension Plans*, Washington, DC: American Enterprise Institute.

Logue, Dennis E. (1991), *Managing Corporate Pension Plans*, New York: Harper Business.

MacAvoy, Paul (1995), "Twenty Years of Deregulation," this volume.

MacAvoy, Paul W. and George S. McIsaac (1995), "The Current File in the Case for Privatization of the Federal Government Enterprises," this volume.

MacAvoy, Paul W. (1993), "Prices After Deregulation: The United States Experience," *The Hume Papers on Public Policy*, V. 1, N. 3, Autumn 1993, pp. 42–48.

McDonald, Kevin R. (1993), "Why Privatization is Not Enough," *Harvard Business Review* (May–June 1993), pp. 49–59.

Meggenson, William L., Robert C. Nash, and Matthias Van Randenborgh (1994), "The Financial and Operating Performance of Newly Privatized Firms: An International Empirical Analysis," *Journal of Finance*, V. 44, N. 2, June 1994, pp. 403–452.

Mitchell, William C. and Randy T. Simmons (1994), *Beyond Politics: Markets, Welfare and the Failure of Bureaucracy*, Boulder, CO: Westview Press.

Posner, Richard (1971), "Taxation by Regulation," *Bell Journal of Economics*, pp. 22–50.

Quayle, Dan (1992), *The Legacy of Regulatory Reform: Restoring America's Competitiveness*, Washington, DC: U.S. Government Printing Office (September 1992).

Richardson, Craig E. and Geoff C. Ziebart (1995), *Strangled by Red Tape*, Washington, DC: The Heritage Foundation.

Reason Foundation (1994), *Privatization '94*, Los Angeles, 1994.

Report of the President's Commission on Privatization (1988), *Privatization: Toward a More Effective Government*, Washington, DC: Government Printing Office, March 1988.

Samson, Colin (1994), "The Three Faces of Privatization," *Sociology*, V. 28, No. 1 (February 1994), pp. 79–97.

Sclar, Elliot D. (1994), "Public Service Privatization: Ideology or Economics," *Dissent* (Summer 1994), pp. 329–336.

Scott, Hal S. (1995), "The Reinvented Community Reinvestment Act," *The Heritage Lectures*, #516.

Swann, Dennis (1988), *The Retreat of the State*, Ann Arbor: University of Michigan Press.

Smith, Fred L. (1987), "Privatization at the Federal Level," in Steve H. Hanke *ed.*, *Prospects for Privatization*, New York: Academy of Political Science.

Vickers, John and George Yarrow (1991), "Economic Perspectives on Privatization," *Journal of Economic Perspectives*, V. 5, N. 2 (Spring 1991), pp. 111–132.

Wallison, Peter J. (1995), "All Banking Regulation Isn't Equal," *Wall Street Journal*, April 20, 1995, p. A.12.

Winston, Clifford (1993), "Economic Deregulation: Days of Reckoning for Microeconomists," *Journal of Economic Literature*, V. 31, N. 3 (September 1993), pp. 1263–1289.

Winston, Clifford and Robert A. Crandall (1994), "Explaining Regulatory Policy, " *Brookings Papers on Economic Activity: Microeconomics* 1994, pp. 1–49.

The Failure of Postal Reform

Sharon M. Oster

Synopsis

In 1970, after decades of poor performance, the U.S. moved postal operations out of the government bureaucracy and transformed them into a public enterprise. Advocates of the change argued that the restructuring would create a more 'business-like' postal service, able to combine the public goals of postal operations with private-sector efficiency. In fact, the last twenty years have seen little, if any, improvement in postal operations. This paper traces the failure of the 1970 Postal Reform Act and attributes that failure to the governance structure of the Postal Service, in particular to the lack of incentives for enhanced efficiency. The Postal Service's diminished incentives to bargain effectively with its suppliers, and its reduced opportunities to negotiate with customers, are described in the paper. A system for reform is proposed which would couple privatization of long-distance postal operations with regionalization of local operations, following the telecommunications model.

$$* \quad * \quad * \quad *$$

Introduction

For an industrial organization economist working on regulation, the last several decades have been an exciting time for looking at organizational change. In the traditional regulated fields of telecommunications, transportation and even energy we have seen enormous changes. Many of these changes have been stimulated by technological developments which have increased the potential for intramodal competition and reduced the importance of scale economies; other changes have come from the political arena as sentiments have shifted away from command and control towards market incentives. In the face of these changes, the U.S. Post Office has remained largely unmoved. Indeed, George Priest, asked to update his classic 1975 *Journal of Law and Economics* article on the Post Office, opined that "it is not in the slightest degree difficult to bring my article up to date; there has been no change whatsoever in the U.S. postal monopoly." (Priest, 1994, 47). This article examines some of the reasons that statutory and legislative changes made to the U.S. Postal system in the last two decades have failed to substantively change the operations of what Priest has called "the greatest example of socialist enterprise in the United States." (Priest, 1994, 53.) I then follow in the perhaps quixotic footsteps of earlier colleagues in economics to suggest some avenues for reform.

The Eroding Basis for Postal Regulation

Before we turn to look at the failure of postal service reform, it is useful to review the literature on the original basis for postal regulation. Why did government get involved with the postal service in the first place and to what extent are the original reasons for intervention still salient?

A critical look at the legislative history of the postal monopoly suggests that economics played very little role in stimulating government intervention in this market; the principal force behind the granting of the monopoly was the political desire for universal service as a way to support the growth of the democratic state (Priest, 1975). This argument that monopoly – and then regulation of that monopoly – is a vehicle for knitting together the far corners of our nation is, of course, a familiar one to those of us who study regulated industries. Precisely the same argument has been made to justify policy in the fields of transportation – both rail and air – and telecommunications. But, however legitimate or not this motivation for market interference was in the 18th century, it is difficult to take this argument seriously in the modern period. In the current period, Americans are surely more linked together by electronics than by mail and few would argue that democracy rests on as thin a reed as a universally priced stamp or universal home delivery.

A more modern basis for the postal monopoly involves scale economies. Here, too, the story is familiar to students of the other regulated sectors. To the extent that scale economies in mail are substantial, granting a postal monopoly and then subjecting it to regulatory oversight could well be in the public interest. Here, too, however, developments both in technology and in our broader understanding of the possibilities of economic engineering have reduced the salience of this story. As Panzar has recently argued (Panzar, 1994), the economics of the postal service looks remarkably like telecommunications. In particular, Panzar argues that the postal service is a network industry in which the principal economies of scale and scope occur at the local delivery and collection area. To the extent that this is the case, granting a monopoly on the full postal service and then subjecting that service to substantial political oversight is difficult to justify. Indeed, Panzar's suggestion that the postal service follow the lead of telecommunications by opening up most of its services to competition, preserving local monopolies on collection and delivery with appropriate rules on access pricing would seem much superior economic advice.

In sum, the sands on which the postal monopoly rests are rapidly eroding. In other parts of the world, we have begun to see major changes in the organization of postal services. In 1992 and 1993, Singapore and Pakistan led the way in opening private sector postal services, funded through the private equity market and responsible to a group of shareholders. (Xinhua, 1993) The German Bundespost converted in 1994 into a government owned stock corporation with plans to privatize by 1996 (WSJ, 1994). Perhaps the most dramatic example of organizational change has been the Dutch postal service. In 1989, the Dutch PTT became a state-owned corporation. Over the past six years, the Dutch PTT has been simultaneously transforming itself into a private corporation – a move completed in 1994 – and expanding internationally. At present the Dutch have offices in the U.S, Canada, Singapore, Thailand and the U.K. and are competing aggressively for international mail business. (Milbank, 1994). The U.S. postal service, on the other hand, seems to have exhausted its energies in the 1970 reform effort, an effort which I will argue in the next section of this paper reflected a lack of understanding of both governance and incentives.

The Postal Reorganization Act of 1970

In 1970, when the Postal Reorganization Act was passed, the goal of its architects was clear: to make the mail service a more businesslike operation. But while the new structure created did indeed look a good deal more businesslike than the government department it replaced, it was still far from a business in either structure or function. In particular, while the 1970 Act gave the United States Postal Service a number of the managerial instruments of the private sector, it left the Service with a set of incentives and controls more like those found in either the non-profit or public sector. This inconsistency has had substantial costs in terms of the performance of the Service as the paper by MacAvoy and McIsaac contained in this volume so well describes. (MacAvoy and McIsaac, 1995).

Like public agencies and most nonprofits, the Postal Service is designed to serve a public purpose, not a private one. In common with government agencies and nonprofits, the Postal Service has no stockholders and cannot directly redistribute any surpluses earned. Indeed, it is generally believed that the Service, again in common with nonprofits and government agencies, should be setting prices so that it does not earn large surpluses over a sustained period. It serves multiple constituencies with quite different goals.

As a government corporation, however, the Postal Service does share some of the characteristics of the private firm. Most significantly, the Service is intended to cover its costs with revenues generated from commercial activity, without relying on either tax dollars or charitable donations. Indeed, one of the stimuli for transforming postal operations from a government department to a government corporation was to reduce the large deficits that characterized the operation in earlier periods. Finally, in negotiating with its suppliers and work force, the Postal Service is intended to have available the collective bargaining tools typically used by large private corporations.

In short, the Postal Service as created in 1970 is a **horizontal** blend of features of the private, public and nonprofit forms. This is in contrast to a form which we are beginning to see much more in the economic landscape – the vertical blend in which organizations with different governance structures cooperate in the delivery of goods and services by assuming different roles in the production process. For example, the U.S. defense industry delivers its products and services through a process that uses the funding and planning capacity of the public sector with the production process of the private sector. The delivery of much of the social service output in this country comes from funding by various governmental levels to nonprofit organizations. Here, the nonprofit organizes production. These nonprofits, in turn, often produce their fund-raising output with the help of for-profit solicitation firms. In the typical vertical blend, the attempt is to exploit the ability of one sector to be efficient in production, while using the ability of the other to accomplish complex public goals. In the revised Postal Service, on the contrary, the attempt is to try to exploit the comparative advantage of the different sectors all within one blended organization. In part, the poor performance of the Postal Service since its reorganization can be attributed to the contradictions manifest in trying to manage this horizontal blend.

Perhaps the most important change to result from the 1970 Reorganization Act was the change in governance. Before the reorganization, the Postmaster General and most of the remaining top managers of the post office were appointed by the President, with the consent of the Senate. Terms of office of postal managers coincided with terms of the President, making quite clear the political nature of the appointment. Detailed Congressional oversight of the postal service further discouraged attempts by postal managers to think of themselves as running a business. Indeed the politicized nature of postal management was one of the major forces behind the reorganization. The Kappel Commission which was largely responsible for the reorganization were quite explicit about their views of the pre-1970 system:

The legislative process makes most managerial decisions for the postal service; it sets rates and wages, approves postal facilities and decides many other postal matters. This process, however conscientiously and well it is followed, is simply not a substitute for sound business decision making in a business context. (President's Commission on Postal Organization, 1968. 37).

In fact, what actions were taken to help the postal operation move to a more businesslike footing? First, the Post Office Department was abolished, and its functions transferred to the U.S. Postal Service. Thus, the postal operation moved from its status as a public agency to the more mixed government corporation form. The newly created Postal Service is governed by an eleven member Board of Governors. Nine of the governors are appointed by the President, with the consent of the Senate. These nine then appoint the postmaster general and those ten in turn appoint the deputy postmaster. Political patronage in appointments and promotions was also prohibited.

It is interesting to consider the structure and functioning of this Board from the perspective of our current understanding of the governing role of boards in general. Does this board look very much like the typical corporate board which it is at least in part intended to emulate? In the ideal publicly traded corporation, the role of the board can be characterized as follows: The stockholders own the company. They delegate the responsibility for running the company to the board and it, in turn, delegates most of that operating responsibility to the management of the company. The board, however, retains ultimate control over the management. In particular, it typically remains active in overseeing broad policy decisions of the management and in hiring, firing and deciding compensation of the top management. Moreover – and quite importantly here–the board carries on its functions within the context of a market for the ownership rights of the company – the stock market – and consequently within a market in which takeover is possible. This market constrains the actions of the board by providing the stockholder with a "court of the last resort" in the case of board failure. (Fama and Jensen, 1983).

Now consider the governance of the U.S. Postal Service. As a public corporation, the Postal Service is owned by the public. In theory, the Board represents that public. But the differences between this kind of ownership and the ownership that comes to for example a stockholder of General Motors is profound. First, consider the ways in which the public and private stock-holders can make their views known. For the GM stockholder, both of Hirschman's options, exit and voice, are available. Disgruntled stockholders can sell their stock on the one hand, or periodically have the right to vote out directors. To be sure, these control mechanisms are imperfect even in the corporate sector. But in the public corporation, they are virtually non-existent. There is no stock to be sold, nor proxies to be voted. The President appoints the board and thus voters have an indirect, periodic voice in its selection. Even this indirect voice, however, is a muted one. In 1993, a federal court ruled that President Bush did not have the right to remove board members because such removal would violate the independence of the postal service. (Geddes, 1994). In this context, it is difficult to see how the owners of the Postal Service – the public–have any real control over the board.

Moreover even if the public owner had more control over the board, it is not clear that the basis on which one would expect them to exercise that control parallels very well the private sector. The typical owner of G.M. stock has a clear agenda he or she wishes to see the board represent: the shareholder wants G.M. to make money to boost dividends and stock price. What does the typical public owner of the Postal Service want? Most citizens are most intimately connected with the postal service as **consumers.** In all likelihood, they are most interested in low stamp prices and better service. While improving these product characteristics may be the result of a profit maximizing strategy, it is clearly not equivalent to a profit maximizing strategy. In sum, the ostensible owners of the Postal Service themselves have mixed motives in whatever modest control they play.

Thus, it is difficult to see the Postal Board as playing a role closely parallel to that played by the corporate board. Indeed, the fact that board members are called Governors speaks to the continuing political nature of the task. Nonprofit governance shares some of the characteristics we have just de-scribed in the postal service. Most notably, given the absence of stock ownership and an equity market, exit possibilities as a discipline mechanism are muted. But even here, some exit is possible. Most nonprofits generate a substantial fraction of their revenues from donors, and these donors are typically well-represented on those boards. These "owners" of the nonprofit can and do leave boards, taking their money and influence with them. Government – another donor to the nonprofit through the tax exemption – is also typically well represented on the nonprofit board. Finally, many non-profit boards are staffed by clients of the nonprofit. Because funding and use in the typical nonprofit is generally more concentrated than it is for the postal service, boards can use representation as a control mechanism. Board composition in the Postal Service is quite different. The Board of Governors of the Postal Service according to statute is chosen to represent the public interest and members *cannot* be representatives of special interests (USPS, 1985, 4). Most of the board members are business people, and few have any post office experience. (Baxter, 1994).

The board structure created by the 1970 Act to govern the Postal Service yields little control to either the true owners of the organization or the funders of that operation. In this sense, oversight is attenuated relative to either the for-profit or the nonprofit. On the other hand, the reorganization has left intact some of the original political oversight which has historically characterized postal operations. In designing the new Board structure the Kappel Commission intended to reduce the political meddling of Congress. And, there is some evidence that this has indeed occurred. But the intent of the reorganization was only to reduce Congressional interference, and not to eradicate it. Congress retains the power to change policies or powers of the Postal Service and the Service is explicitly accountable to the Congress, the General Accounting Office, the Postal Rate Commission, the President and at least 30 executive agencies. (Baxter, 1994). Selective interference by the Congress in particular has made it difficult to transform the Postal Service into a more business like operation.

The leasing practices of the Postal Service provide an interesting window on to the problems of politics at the postal service. Approximately 28,000 of the 34,000 post offices located throughout the U.S. are leased. (Iudicello, 1991). Many of the leases for these properties are long term leases. To the extent that the postal service operates as a business, one would expect these leases to be negotiated with the financial interests of the postal operation in mind. And, indeed, in many cases the postal service appears to have made quite good deals on its leases. The problem has been the re-negotiation process, once leases were signed. In particular, on several occasions since 1970 the Association of Postal Lessors – representing its 1000 members – has testified before Congress to obtain relief from existing leases. The Postal Service pursued leases which were "too good" from the *ex post* perspective of lessors, resulting in payments on long-term leases which were unfavorable to lessors. The result of political pressure by the lessor lobby was the renegotiation of lease terms, including in many cases the assumption by the Postal Service of both maintenance and tax responsibilities for lessors. (Iudicello, 1991). In other words, on occasions when the postal service uses its private sector instruments too well, it faces political pressure to back down.

In sum, the 1970 Act replaced the overly-meddlesome, highly politicized oversight of the postal organization by Congress with oversight by a board which is under almost no control at all, coupled with sporadic Congressional inquiry when particular interests are threatened! In fact, as Geddes (1994) has argued, the governance change of 1970 may well have exacerbated the agency problems of the postal service. It seems clear that the incentives of the governing board to mimic private sector management are modest at best.

The difficulty of the Postal Service in applying private sector management tools is further manifest in labor management. Between eighty and eighty five percent of the costs of mail delivery consist of wages and benefits. (U.S. Postal Service, 1993, 39). More efficient management of this labor, including the more aggressive use of automation clearly was an important goal of the reorganization. In the 1960's innovations allowing for the expansion of zip code readers as well as the introduction of optical character readers opened up possibilities for work redesign and, indeed, for potentially large reductions in the labor force. It was soon recognized that both the capital infusion and the labor reduction associated with these innovations would be difficult in the highly politicized context of a government agency. (President's Commission, 1968). Thus, one goal of the reorganization was to enable the postal organization to deal more effectively with labor, first by changing the governance structure of the Postal Service and second by replacing the Civil Service structure of the Post Office with private sector labor structure and negotiations. We have already seen some of the ways in which the new governance structure was wanting. We turn now to see how well the Postal Service has done in using the labor negotiation tools to which it has in theory been given access.

Before we look at the results of the reorganization for labor management, it is interesting to do a little historical political economy. How did the various interest groups react to the prospect of postal reorganization in 1970? In February 1969, there were two major postal reform bills being debated in the House of Representatives. House Bill HR4, backed by the postal union, proposed to reform operations within the existing structure. The alternative bill – which was eventfully passed – proposed the establishment of a government corporation. Postal unions were strongly opposed to the formation of a public corporation arguing that the change would reduce worker rights, tilting the balance of power in favor of management. (Baxter, 1994, 86–88).

In fact, many of the concerns of the postal union appear to have been unfounded or at least exaggerated. Several careful empirical studies of postal wages for the decade after the reorganization suggest that the structural changes did little to shift power away from management: postal workers appear to have enjoyed a substantial wage advantage over comparable private sector workers both before and after the reorganization. (Adie, 1980, Smith,1980). Attempts to reduce the labor force to reap the fruits of automation have been particularly slow. Testifying before Congress in 1990, then Postmaster General Anthony Frank reported that with $5.6 billion invested in automated equipment the Postal Service has been able to reduce its work force by 23,000. (Frank, 1990). With a workforce of 700,000, this is clearly just a drop in the bucket! New Zealand's postal operations, on the other hand, managed to reduce their work force by 20% in the first 5 years following reform efforts. (Crutcher, 1990). Indeed, William Mayton, in an interesting history of the postal service, has argued that in the 1990's postal workers are "stronger and better organized than ever." (Mayton, 1994, 107). MacAvoy and McIsaac (1995), in this volume, describe the problems the Postal Service has had in actually implementing the labor reductions anticipated from its capital investments.

Searching for what went wrong leads us again to the matter of incentives and control. While postal management in theory has the instruments to discipline labor, its incentives to do so are quite weak. Here, understanding the financial arrangements in the Postal Service are key. As a public corporation, the Postal Service is intended to cover its costs and thus not be a drain on the Treasury. On the other hand, the possibility of bankruptcy should costs get out of hand seems remote. Indeed, the Postal Service has run deficits consistently since the reorganization and while these deficits have occasioned pressure and wrangling, management jobs have not been on the line. In 1994, for example, the deficit at the Postal Service was $914 million. Financial pressures on the Postal Service are considerably more relaxed than those typically facing either for-profit or nonprofit firms. Nor could the Postal Service gain very much should it control wages sufficiently to run a surplus. As a public corporation, the Postal Service is intended not to run a surplus and it seems clear that any surpluses that accrue from aggressive labor management will go to the Treasury. And, since the Congressional budget cycle and scrutiny is annual, the Postal Service operates like a regulated industry with no regulatory lag. As a result, the Service has attenuated incentives on the up-side as well. Finally, since the government requires of the Postal Service certain services – both universal service and nonprofit mailing – which are deliberately priced below the market, even the meaning of running a balanced budget becomes murky. Under these circumstances, it is no wonder that management has been relatively ineffective against the very cohesive, powerful postal unions.

Indeed, as in the governance area, there are some aspects of the reorganization which may have made the new structure less able to do its job than the old. Under the early Civil Service, postal workers in many ways resembled the typical nonprofit worker, for whom ideology helps to reduce shirking. (Preston, 1989). Removing the Civil Service apparatus may have reduced the ideological appeal of the work without replacing it with a hard-nosed ability to negotiate.

A final ingredient in the Postal Service's ability to perform as a commercial operation is its control over prices. In this aspect of its operations, the Postal Service most closely resembles a regulated firm, where regulatory oversight is provided by a combination of a regulatory commission – the Postal Rate Commission – and Congress. In this area as well, we see the role of politics in frustrating the rationalization process.

Charitable, educational and other nonprofit organizations pay considerably reduced rates for postal service. Under the Reorganization Act, authorizing special rates of postage and deciding who should benefit from them are entrusted to Congress. As a matter of public policy, Congress supports reduced postal rates for nonprofits. Reduced rate carriage is thus a service that the government wishes to procure from the Postal Service business, much like the delivery of a program to help the homeless is a service that local governments wish to buy from the nonprofit sector, or in an earlier example, fighter planes are acquired by the Defense Department from Lockheed. And, in principle at least, Congress is intended to pay for the revenue foregone by the Postal Service in supplying these services by an appropriation from the budget. In theory, this system of financing is supposed to encourage Congress to weigh the benefits of providing reduced rates to particular groups against costs to the taxpayer of so doing. (See, for example, the statement before Congress of Comer Coppie, at the Postal Service, November 12, 1991).

In fact, the current transaction involving the reduced rate for nonprofits is actually quite different from the usual commercial government negotiation. In most government transactions, in either the for-profit or nonprofit arena, the potential seller has the opportunity to reject the government's business should the terms of trade not be agreeable. When the Department of Mental Retardation offers a social service agency a contract to establish a group home, that agency can choose to reject the contract should it be unattractive. The Postal Service, however, has the obligation to carry the reduced rate mail, even if the payment offered by Congress is grossly inadequate. When Congress appropriates less than is required to make up the reduced rate shortfall, the Postal Service is, in effect, forced to "lend" this difference to Congress, rolling the bill into future appropriations requests. In 1992, for example, $89 million was lent in this way. (Coppie, 1991). In this sense, the Postal Service has less bargaining clout than the typical nonprofit or for-profit partner, capable of both setting rates and demanding prompt payment. But Congress also lacks the option of bargaining with a variety of possible vendors, an option we typically see in the kinds of vertical blends of organizations we described earlier. Thus, both parties to the transaction have less flexibility than is usual and the kinds of efficiency enforcement mechanisms normally promoted by arms' length transactions are missing.

The requirement that the Postal Service provide a service – here reduced rate mailing – that would not be provided by the market is, of course, familiar to regulatory economists. In the transportation area, for example, regulators historically required firms to serve low density markets at below market fares. Similar requirements to provide low priced service occur in the telecommunications industry. In those industries, however, the provision of these services has typically been subsidized by higher prices in other products or services provided by the regulated firm, a practice which became increasingly difficult as competition decreased the number of inelastically demanded products which could be so taxed. In the attempt to commercialize the postal operation, it was decided that revenues lost from reduced rate carriage should **not** be compensated for by increasing rates in other products. The model was instead that Congress should act as though it is "buying" this public service. But, as we have just seen, the purchase is by no means an arms' length transaction. Again we have a transaction that appears on the surface to have the "right" form, but without the underlying governance and enforcement structure to make the system work.

The dismal record of Postal reform stands in stark contrast to the picture of the past twenty years of deregulation described by MacAvoy in this volume (MacAvoy, 1995). And yet, postal reform was stimulated by many of the same factors which led to derregulation: poor prior operating performance, increased private-sector competition and technological change. But while – as the papers in this volume suggest – reform of transportation, energy and telecommunications has led us gradually to improvement through an increasing reliance on market mechanisms, the mode of postal reform – adoption of the public enterprise form – has led us to a dead-end. Improvement in this sector will require drastic measures.

What is to be Done?

The U.S. Postal Service has revenues of $50 billion, a labor force of 700,000 located in 34,000 sites, delivering one-third of the world's mail. (Crew and Kleindorfer, 1994). The system is enormous and enormously complex, the management of which would challenge even the most carefully re-engineered structure. The difficulties of the current system operating with a set of incentives at odd with the business goals of the operation are easy to understand.

That the current U.S. system needs to be reformed is uncontroversial; indeed it is difficult to find an economist writing in this area who does not have a proposal for reform. (See Sidak, 1994 for some samples). Even the current Postmaster General, Marvin Runyon, has argued for reform, noting that earlier reform gave the Postal Service "the responsibility but not the authority to act."[1] (Runyon, 1995). Agreeing on the nature of reform is more difficult, and even more difficult is finding anyone who is very optimistic about the prospects of securing reform. Nevertheless it seems unfair to conclude a paper on the failures of earlier reform efforts without offering at least some preliminary ideas on alternative reforms.

The advantages of moving in the direction of privatizing the postal service seem clear. Indeed, substantial improvement seems to be impossible within the current institutional structure. However well meaning reform efforts might be, the current structure of the Postal Service provides too few managerial incentives for any real re-engineering of the organization to occur. In addition to adding my voice to the privatization chorus, I would like to suggest another avenue for re-structuring. Panzar has argued that the principal economies of scale and scope in the postal system reside at the local collection and delivery level. (Panzar, 1994). Based on this proposition, he proposes that the mail system be vertically dismantled, with long distance service opened up to competition and access to local operations available to all comers at appropriately determined prices. (Panzar, 1994). The localized nature of postal scale

---

[1] Notice, however, that Runyon bemoans the lack of 'authority', and not the absence of incentives, a problem this paper has focused on. Postmaster Runyon has not come out in support of privatization.

economies suggests an additional avenue for reform: breaking up the postal monopoly horizontally, creating locally distinct – and locally managed operations – to replace the cumbersome, nationwide system. Rather than having a national, U.S. Postal Service, in which central bureaucrats try to manage a vast network of local operations, the postal operations would be divided into local operations, perhaps organized around the regional bulk collection operations.

Here again telecommunications provides an interesting model for reform. Since the Modified Final Judgment of Judge Green, we may not yet have benefitted from competition among the long distance carriers, but we have realized substantial gains from having independent regional operating companies. Such independent operations have provided yardstick competition both for local regulators and local managers. Opportunities for experimenting with both new technologies and new management styles are enhanced by multiple operations as are opportunities for evaluating those experiments. In telephony, we have seen aggressive regional operating companies move to expand their geographical boundaries, providing in this way direct competition for other companies. Disentangling the national web would seem to offer promise for improved postal operations in this way as well.

Some Final Thoughts

What are the prospects for serious reform of the postal system? An application of traditional models of political economy are not encouraging: On the one side – against reform – are the powerful postal labor unions, with clear and concentrated interests in maintaining as far as possible the postal monopoly. On the other side of the table are the diffuse interests of consumers, most of whom stand to gain very little individually from reform. This alignment of economic interests is unlikely to yield socially optimal reform. Nevertheless, there are some positive signs on the horizon. Some fraction of the Postal Service's operations has been effectively privatized by the actions of United Parcel Service and other private competitors. While the pre-1970 Post Office carried virtually all of our nation's parcel post, by 1990, its share had fallen to 4% (Crutcher, 1990). Similar slippage has occurred in the express mail business. In the long run, the market may well accomplish what legions of well-meaning economic analysts could not.

Bibliography

Adie, Douglas, "How have the postal workers fared since the 1970 Act? in Roger Sherman, ed. *Perspectives on Postal Service Issues.* American Enterprise Institute Press, 1980.

Baxter, Vern, *Labor and Politics in the U.S. Postal Service.* New York Plenum Press, 1994.

Crew, Michael and Paul Kleindorfer, "Pricing, entry, service quality and innovation under commercialized postal service," in Sidak, *Governing the Postal Service,* 1994, 150–169.

Coppie, Comer. "Statement before the subcommittee on Postal Operations and Services House Committee on Post Offices and Civil Services," November 12, 1991.

Crutcher, John. "In New Zeland, free enterprise delivers the mail," *Wall Street Journal,* March 8, 1990, 14.

Frank, Anthony, "Statement before subcommittee on Postal Operations and Services of the House Committee on Post Offices and Civil Service," September 18, 1990.

Geddes, R. Richard, "Agency costs and governance in the United States Postal Service," in Sidak, *Governing the Postal Service,* 1994, 114–239.

Iudicello, Al. "Remarks before the Subcommittee on Postal Operations and Services, vs. House of Representatives," June 25, 1991.

Mayton, William, "The missions and method of Postal Power," in Sidak, *Governing the Postal Service,* 1994, 60–109.

Milbank, Dana, "Marketing: Dustch Service hopes to deliver world's mail," *Wall Street Journal,* July 28, 1994, 1.

National Academy of Public Administration, *Evaluation of the U.S. Postal Service,* July 1, 1982.

Panzar, John. "The Economics of Mail Delivery," in Sidak, *Governing the Postal Service,* 1994, 1–30.

President's Commission on Postal Organization. *Report of the President's Commission on Postal Organization,* Washington, D.C., 1968.

Preston, Anne, "The nonprofit worker in a for-profit world," *Journal of Labor Economics,* Vol. 7, no. 4, 1989.

Priest, George, "Socialism, Eastern Europe and the Question of the Postal Monopoly," in Sidak, *Governing the Postal Service,* 1994, 46-59.

Priest, George, "The History of the Postal Monopoly in the United States," *Journal of Law and Economics,* 33, 1975.

Runyon, Marvin, "Remarks before the National Press Club," January 31, 1995.

Sidak, Gregory, ed., *Governing the Postal Service,* Washington, D.C., AEI Press, 1994.

Smith, Sharon, "Commentary," in Sherman, ed., *Perspectives on Postal Service Issues,* American Enterprise Institute Press, 1980.

U.S. Postal Service, *Annual report of the Postmaster General,* Washington, D.C.: USPS, 1985, 1993.

Xinhua News Agency, "First private post office in Capital starts function," January 27, 1993, 1.

The Current File on the Case For Privatization of The Federal Government Enterprises

Paul W. MacAvoy and George S. McIsaac

Synopsis

Performance of the largest federal public companies has departed from that of comparable private companies in the last fifteen years. The public companies prices have increased more rapidly, based in part on their capital outlays having been much larger. But such intensive capitalization did not prevent relative declines in productivity. That these companies have lost their rationale for public ownership is revealed by this recent record.

*　　　*　　　*　　　*

Introduction

The largest federal companies that provide goods and services throughout the economy have long been established in the American business landscape. Most were founded fifty years ago, at a time when federal programs were being devised to expand the economy's infrastructure so as to increase economic growth. Most now are commercially invisible, while offering the same kilowatts of electricity, transportation, or delivery services as private companies. But they have access to the U.S. Treasury for subsidized loan rates, and the authority of the U.S. Justice Department to prevent entry of others into their markets, so that the case for their public status has to be periodically examined.

This case is subject to reexamination here based on current evidence on the performance of the major federal enterprises compared to private enterprises providing the same or similar goods or services. Where that performance lags behind that of the private companies in efficiency and progress, then the rationale for public status fails.

In fact, the public companies are known in very general terms to have not performed as industry leaders, or as sole sources of indispensable services, so that they have become increasingly visible targets for privatization. The election of 1994 helped focus attention on them even further by putting in place a Congress that questions any justification for public enterprise, as well as one more active in seeking non-tax revenues to balance the Federal Budget – revenues that can be obtained from selling these companies off to private investors.

There are at least fifty major federal enterprises. They employ over 800,000 people, generate annual revenues in excess of $50 billion, and in fiscal year 1993 added to federal receipts net cash flow of $2 billion. They provided more than fifteen percent of the nation's electric power, one hundred percent of the intercity rail passenger service, and more than ninety percent of residential mail delivery. They play a significant role in the provision of credit and finance throughout the economy, with borrowing authority through the Treasury of nearly $50 billion and potential funding capacity of nearly $200 billion in federal loan guarantees.

The rhetoric is that they were developed because private companies had failed to provide necessary or desirable service for consumers in certain important industries. The national postal system began in the eighteenth century because no private company would walk the back roads of rural America to deliver daily mail to every household. The Tennessee Valley Authority (TVA) was intended to foster development of all aspects of manufacturing and trade throughout the valley, by providing low priced electric power and other infrastructure services. The federal government assumed responsibility for railroad passenger service when private railroads were in the bankruptcy process and threatening to exit.

These specific development projects together provide a comprehensive justification for public enterprise. In each the specific goals were put into the record, for example, increasing regional development, restoring services abandoned by private companies, and extending services to rural or low-income consumers. Together, they constituted an expressed political demand for more services at lower prices at least in infrastructure industries.

Even so, after initial stages of development, these public enterprises provided services on terms and conditions not different in kind from those of private companies. Their prices in the last decade increased more rapidly than those of comparable private companies. While their operating costs increased, they have not increased as rapidly as in earlier decades or as rapidly as their prices. Thus public company profit margins ("price-cost margins") have widened relative to increases in these industries. These changes raise the question as to what is "special" about the public enterprises.

Assessing such "public" performance requires a detailed inquiry into the behavior of the important federal enterprises. In the sections that follow, the performance of two sets of these enterprises is set out relative to that of samples of comparable private companies. The first comparison is between public and private companies at the sectoral level of the economy. The second comparison is between price and cost behavior of three large public enterprises – Amtrak, the Tennessee Valley Authority, and the Postal Service – and that of private companies in their industries. A fourth enterprise, Conrail, is also examined because it was first public and then privatized in the last decade, so that its public and then private performance can be compared over time and with other private railroad-freight transportation companies. Both comparisons establish how well the public companies have done in pricing and service growth along the lines called for in the rhetoric accompanying their creation.

At that point in the case file on the public enterprises, the comparisons raise the question whether public management systems and practices justify special status. The three large federal enterprises are examined once again, this time for excellence in management practice; they are found to have in common systems that had to result in poor performance. The prevalence of these systems, associated with these companies being "public", makes the case for privatizing these organizations.

Indices of Public and Private Corporate Performance

The public-sector corporations have been expected to provide more service at less cost to the consumer. But that has not been all that has been expected of them. Whether in providing insurance for bank deposits, or electricity in a rural community, the public corporations still have had to generate revenues to cover all or a targeted portion of operating and capital costs. Only when government enters a market to provide service in which no company can survive is the public goal of covering costs abandoned. Even then, goals have usually been set to hold losses to certain levels. In most cases, then, the tradeoff in "public" services has been towards lower prices and higher sales subject to a zero or limited (prespecified) loss. That is, "public" operations should be marked by lower prices and larger demands for service when compared to those of private companies in similar markets (Funkhauser and MacAvoy 1979). Assuming that demands at the same price level do not differ between private and public companies for the same services, and that conditions of factor supply are not more limited for one than the other, then this comparison should reveal distinctive "public" pricing and service quality strategies.

The first such comparison undertaken here is based on indices for that sector specified as "government enterprise" based on statements of fifteen federal government corporations compiled by the Bureau of Economic Analysis of the Department of Commerce.[1] From 1977 to 1982, a period of high inflation and slow economic expansion, the index for government-enterprise prices increased at almost twice the rate of those for private companies in the transportation and finance industries, but at approximately ten percentage points less than the rate for prices in private electric power

---

[1] These corporations are as follows: The Bonneville Power Administration; The Canteen Service Revolving Fund of the Veterans Administration; The Federal Housing Administration Fund; The Federal Crop Insurance Company; the National Flood Insurance Fund; Military Post Exchange Funds; The Overseas Private Investment Corporation; The United States Postal Service; The Southeast Power Administration; The Southwest Power Administration; The Tennessee Valley Authority; The Upper Colorado River Basin Corporation; The Lower Colorado River Basin Corporation; Western Power Administration Marketing Fund.

TABLE 1   PRICE INDICES, 1978–1992

Year	Government Enterprises	Finance & Insurance	Transportation	Electric & Gas Utilities
1977	40.1	42.7	65.1	42.8
1982	72.5	61.5	94.3	82.9
1987	100.0	100.0	100.0	100.0
1992	131.2	128.0	105.5	110.4

Source: Bureau of Economic Analysis: Department of Commerce.

(see Table One).[2] In 1982–1987, the index for government enterprises increased at a greater rate than two of the three comparable sectors once again. But during 1987–1992, a period in which the economy was in recession for two out of the five years, and in which the inflation rate was lower than in the early 1980's, index prices for government enterprise services increased on average at three times the rate of index prices for private companies in the transportation and electric sectors, and at one hundred twelve percent of the rate realized in the financial sector.

The relatively high rate of public-sector price increases could be explained in a number of ways: profit margins increased more, or costs increased more, with or without relatively more rapid increases in demands for services. But extremely low relative production rates (in Table Two) rule out the possibility that higher prices followed from greater demand growth. The constant dollar gross product of the public enterprises in the index did not increase from 1977 to 1992, although gross product in comparable sectors of the economy experienced substantial expansion over that period, with the electric and gas industries growing twenty-eight percent, and the transportation and financial sectors realizing increases in real terms of fifty percent.

The combination of sharply rising prices with stagnant production in the public enterprises had to be the result of increases in either profit margins or

TABLE 2   GROSS DOMESTIC PRODUCT BY INDUSTRY IN 1987 DOLLARS
(BILLIONS OF DOLLARS)

Year	Government Enterprises	Finance & Insurance	Transportation	Electric & Gas Utilities
1977	37.7	207.5	117.2	123.7
1982	33.8	243.6	115.5	114.3
1987	34.0	288.6	152.8	139.5
1992	36.9	318.4	183.7	157.1

Source: Bureau of Economic Analysis: Department of Commerce.

[2]   Changes in price levels in Table One are defined as changes in the implicit price deflator for that sector of the economy. This deflator is calculated by dividing the annual gross product for the industry in current dollars by the same domestic product in constant dollars (U.S. Department of Commerce 1983). The four industries selected are the same as those in which public corporations reside for those public corporations included in the indices.

TABLE 3   OPERATING INCOME AS A PERCENT OF SALES

Year	Government Enterprises	Finance & Insurance	Transportation	Electric & Gas Utilities
1977	-7.2	30.4	5.1	17.8
1982	7.3	10.0	-0.3	15.6
1987	7.9	13.6	2.8	13.6
1992	8.5	22.9*	0.8	16.4

Source: Bureau of Economic Analysis: Department of Commerce.
*1991

in costs of production. Profit margins, or operating income margins on sales, for the public companies were negative in 1977, a year quite late in the recovery from the 1974 recession, but rose to an average 7.3 percent in 1982 – an increase of a full fourteen percentage points in that five year period. Profit margins increased by 0.1 percent per year in the five years from 1982 to 1987, and again from 1987 to 1992, the same as in transportation and the public utilities but one tenth of that in the private financial sector (see Table Three).

Cost increases were not as important in explaining the increase in prices. Wages and salaries per unit of production were changing at rates in the public companies consistent with those of private firms in comparable sectors (see Table Four). From 1977 to 1982, a period of high inflation, the subject enterprises unit labor costs declined by fourteen cents per dollar of real GDP, whereas unit labor costs increased by seven cents in finance and two cents in transportation for private-sector firms. Since 1982, the government companies on average realized small declines in unit labor costs per dollar of real GDP – the same as for private firms in those sectors (except the financial sector, where the decline was fifteen percent rather than two percent).

That the source of relative price increases in the public companies has not been cost increases is further indicated by growth in productivity in the public, relative to the private, companies (see Table Five). The government enterprises experienced a two percent increase in labor productivity from 1977 to 1992, while private firms in two of the three comparable industry sectors realized growth in labor productivity of approximately minus two to six percent. Stagnant demand for energy kept the utility sector's productivity constant, while increased service quality has probably had the same effect in the finance and insurance sector. The public companies, with two percent labor productivity

TABLE 4   UNIT LABOR COSTS BY INDUSTRY
(LABOR COSTS PER DOLLAR OF REAL GDP)

Year	Government Enterprises	Finance & Insurance	Transportation	Electric & Gas Utilities
1977	1.07	0.61	0.68	0.30
1982	0.93	0.68	0.70	0.30
1987	0.92	0.60	0.64	0.27
1992	0.91	0.58	0.66	0.29

Source: Bureau of Economic Analysis: Department of Commerce.

TABLE 5   LABOR PRODUCTIVITY BY INDUSTRY
(CONSTANT DOLLAR PRODUCT PER HOUR WORKED)

Year	Government Enterprises	Finance & Insurance	Transportation	Electric & Gas Utilities
1977	21.5	28.6	20.4	84.4
1982	20.6	27.4	19.4	66.3
1987	20.2	27.0	22.6	76.8
1992	22.0	29.4	25.4	82.9

Source: Bureau of Economic Analysis: Department of Commerce.

growth over fifteen years, contained cost increases better than in one sector but worse than in two other sectors.

These price, cost, and margin indices lead to a finding contrary to what could be expected from public companies. In the 1980's and early 1990's, the public-sector companies increased their relative prices, and thereby reduced demands for their services. The relative price increases were not justified by rising production costs, but were the result of a concerted program of increasing operating income margins. These public companies increased these margins – termed "profit margins" in private enterprise – to an extraordinary extent.

The Performance of Three Important Public Corporations

Three of the largest public-sector corporations provide case studies of the extent to which these sectoral patterns have been distinctly "public" aspects of performance. In the last ten years these three companies' price and output behavior have been marked by the same pattern of rapidly rising prices relative to private sector companies. More fundamental, this relative price inflation has been justified as necessary to provide returns on federally-financed loans to cover capital outlays in excess of those of private sector companies.

Each of these companies provide services which had previously been established by private companies but were then deemed insufficient. The Tennessee Valley Authority (TVA) was founded in the early 1930's after President Roosevelt called for a new government corporation to use resources made idle by the Depression of 1929-1933 to achieve economic development and agricultural reform.[3] Region-wide coordinated projects were to be undertaken by the new TVA to accomplish what had not been forthcoming from industry throughout the valley. And government expenditures to further economic development in the Tennessee Valley were substantial in the early years. While TVA was the focus for financing this development, its commitment to that

---

[3]   The Tennessee Valley Authority was formed to "improve navigability, provide for flood control, reforestation and the proper use of marginal lands in the Tennessee Valley" (Source: The Tennessee Valley Authority Act of 1933).

objective changed after 1933, and it became no more than a producer of electricity.[4]

The rationale for the establishment of an independent federal corporation to provide postal service was developmental as well. While there had been government postal service for more than 150 years, the provision of "universal and equitable mail service" was newly mandated in the 1960's with the creation of the United States Postal Service (USPS). There was substantial concern in Congress at that time that express companies would undermine the capacity of the then-existing federal cabinet-level department to provide universal service. At the same time, it was understood that political dominance of operations was then preventing the development of efficient service. The step taken to counter these concerns was the creation of an independent public organization to provide mail delivery.

The roots of Amtrak's existence can be traced to the reduction and abandonment of passenger service by several of the largest railroads in the 1960's. A new federal corporation was created by the Rail Passenger Service Act of 1970 (Public Law 91–518) to "restore" domestic rail passenger service, which had declined from 40 billion passenger-miles in 1947 to just over 6 billion in 1970. Whether this meant just to provide limited service, or to bring back 60 million riders, was never made explicit; recovery was the general strategy.

Each of these organizations has, since inception, operated in markets that could have been served by private-sector corporations. TVA is only one of many large electric utilities in the country.[5] While the Authority has a statutory monopoly in the distribution of power in the Tennessee Valley, broadly defined, it is not based on inherent scale advantages in either generation or transmission. In fact this public company is part of a distribution network based on generating stations throughout the South, and could both wheel in and wheel out power with respect to its service area. While Amtrak is the country's sole provider of intercity rail passenger service, there are alternative service providers in airline, bus and automobile transportation. The Postal Service operates under a statutory monopoly in first-class mail and carrier-delivered third-class mail, but it faces competition in the parcel post and express mail markets from a number of private corporations including United

---

[4] The table below shows power-related expenditures from 1936 to 1984, as a percent of total Authority expenditures.

Year	% Power
1936	8.35
1944	61.97
1954	79.99
1964	85.09
1974	96.47
1984	96.11

[5] But unlike most private utilities, only a small amount of TVA's generated electricity is sold directly to commercial and residential consumers. TVA sells most of its electricity to municipalities and cooperatives for resale to final consumers.

TABLE 6   OPERATING INCOME AS A PERCENT OF SALES

Year	Electric Utilities Industry	TVA[a]	Railroads Industry	Conrail[a]	Mail Services Industry	USPS[a]	Passenger Services Industry	Amtrak[a]
1977	23.1	14.1	-0.9	-20.3	8.5	-4.1	4.9	-151.9
1982	26.2	33.8	3.0	-3.7	9.5	-1.0	2.3	-103.0
1987	25.9	36.1	6.6	7.4	11.3	-3.1	3.4	-71.8
1992	23.5	36.9	7.1	10.8	9.6	0.5	0.6	-53.7

Sources: COMPUSTAT Annual Industrial and OTC file, Quarterly Utilities file and annual Research file for Industry data. Various Annual Reports are used for individual companies; Edison Electric Institute Statistical Yearbook (1981-1985) and Association of American Railroads "Railroad Facts" (1986).
Notes: a) Profit margins as a percent of sales is equal to operating revenues minus operating expenses divided by operating revenues.

Parcel Service and Federal Express.[6] Thus none of these enterprises has a unique service, nor does it have unlimited market power across its important service markets.

But in each set of markets, public company behavior has differed substantially from that of counterpart private-sector companies. Their pricing behavior in the last decade departed most significantly from that of other private companies. Prices net of unit operating costs of TVA increased by nine percent but declined by eleven percent in counterpart private companies from 1982 through 1992 (as in Table Six).[7] Postal Service price-cost margins increased slightly over the last ten years, by 1.5 percent, but those of other firms in the same industry declined by almost twenty percentage points in the same period.[8] Amtrak price-cost margins increased by forty-nine percent while those of airlines and bus companies in short-distance intercity service markets were constant from 1982 to 1992.[9]

Even with these increases, however, two of the three public companies did not establish profit margins at levels comparable to the private sector companies. Postal service margins were still negative until 1992, and Amtrak margins

[6]   In heavily populated areas, the Postal Service also faces competition in the delivery of second-, third- and fourth-class mail. Such competitors include large magazine publishers, newspapers, advertisers, book and record clubs, and telemarketers. 1985 market shares for companies in the overnight courier service are: Federal Express – forty-six percent, USPS – nineteen percent, UPS – sixteen percent, Airborne – eight percent, Purolator – six percent, Emery – five percent (U.S. Postal Service 1984).
[7]   The TVA's rates of investment grew relative to private industry utilities between 1977–1984, which forced a significant increase in prices due to increased cost of debt service. Prior to 1975, TVA's rates for electricity were fifty percent of the national average; in 1985, TVA rates were only seventeen percent lower than the average for U.S. investor-owned utilities (U.S. Senate 1985a).
[8]   Postal Service prices for "same day/next day" mail (and other classes) do not necessarily reflect the cost of provision. The Postal Service costing mechanism permits charging a disproportionately high share of institutional costs to first class mail. However, this anomaly should not affect the time-series behavior of prices of individual classes of USPS mail.
[9]   While these increases raised prices relative to costs, they did not result in positive price-cost margins. Amtrak started and ended the period with negative operating margins.

TABLE 7   TOTAL PRODUCTION BY INDUSTRY AND COMPANY (1987 = 100)

Year	Electric Utilities[a] Industry	TVA	Railroads[b] Industry	Conrail	Mail Services[c] Industry	USPS	Passenger Services[d] Industry	Amtrak
1977	70.9	112.4	94.5	116.6	83.6	59.9	53.6	91.9
1982	81.2	100.4	87.2	83.9	79.1	74.1	68.3	79.9
1987	100.0	100.0	100.0	100.0	100.0	100.0	100.0	100.0
1992	114.7	110.7	115.9	103.9	123.3	108.1	107.3	116.7

Sources: COMPUSTAT Annual Industrial and OTC file, Quarterly Utilities file and annual Research file for Industrial data. Various "Annual Reports" of individual companies.
Notes: a) Megawatt hours; b) Revenue ton miles; c) Millions of individual packages or other pieces equivalent to mail; d) Millions of passenger miles.

rose from -151.9 percent only to a still negative -53.7 percent over the ten years, against positive margins in comparable private companies. But TVA had higher margins than comparable private companies. Its margin for prices over direct costs was positive throughout the period, at thirty-seven percent, while the average for comparable private utilities was twenty-four percent. The difference in good part was due to TVA's relatively low fuel costs and its use of more hydro and nuclear capacity with higher capital/fuel ratios.[10]

Even so, more rapid rates of public-company price increase in all three public companies adversely impacted relative production growth for those companies in the 1980's. Annual production increases for 1977 – 1992 for the three public enterprises were in the range of zero to three percent, while private-sector firms in their industries had twice that rate of growth (see Table Seven). TVA, USPS, and Amtrak had lower rates of growth in their deliveries for any number of reasons, but these lower rates were responsive to price sensitivities in demands in their at least partially competitive markets.

Conrail and the rail transport industry provide another public- versus private-sector comparison that confirms these findings. Conrail's margins rose rapidly in its pre-privatization years, before 1982 and at average industry rates of increase thereafter. Conrail's traffic levels decreased relative to the industry's until privatization but increased, even if at slightly lower levels than the industry, in the 1980's.

As public enterprises, then, these three "key" corporations raised their prices more than did comparable private-sector enterprises.[11] While doing so, however, they did not succeed in raising profit margins to comparability with

[10]   As discussed below, TVA had invested extensively in nuclear plants that proved to be too costly to operate; this public company then embarked on a campaign to generate cash flow from price increases to pay the bonded indebtedness on the "cold" plants. This was extensive: "as of December 1993 TVA's investment in cold or incomplete reactors and associated fuel stood at almost $15 billion compared to a total of $13 billion in capital assets generating [power] revenue." Cf. Allan Pulsipher, "TVA's Debt Limit", *Public Utilities Fortnightly*, March 1, 1995, p. 41.
[11]   The major source of increased costs for TVA were interest costs resulting from their aggressive expansion program and nuclear fuel inventory costs which were nearly ten times those of the private utilities.

those of the private companies. To be sure, each of them faced limited competition in its markets and to some extent that competition had the potential of holding down relative price increases. TVA has had to operate in wholesale markets against increased competition as energy-intensive industry in its service region has shopped more widely for low-priced electricity.[12] Amtrak has had less price-setting power recently than at its inception given the growth of commuter airline service and the return to financial health of the interstate bus service companies (U.S. Congressional Budget Office 1982a). The Postal Service has been faced with more competition in express mail and from self-delivery of bulk advertising in the past decade.[13]

But these price increases have been ameliorated by disparities in the extent of regulation between private- and public-sector companies. TVA has been unencumbered by the regulatory process since it does not have to seek approval for price increases before state or federal utility commissions.[14] When regulatory price caps on private companies were most stringent, in the first half of the 1980's, the relative price increases in TVA were greatest.[15] To allow Amtrak maximum pricing flexibility, the Rail Passenger Services Act exempted it from Interstate Commerce Commission jurisdiction over charges and service offerings. Amtrak was also granted exemption from state laws applying to passenger rail operations, which provided it with the opportunity to test markets with selective fare increases for short distance rail passenger service. Similarly, although the Postal Rate Commission sets prices based on USPS requests for increased revenues on all system services, its finding can be rejected by the Postal Service's Board of Governors (so that whether this

[12] As is the case with other U.S. utilities, TVA has faced indirect competition from large buyers moving plants from one region to another. It has not faced a new threat of entry, however, from municipalities and cooperatives terminating their franchises with TVA to wheel power in from outside the region, because of TVA's statutory monopoly.

[13] The growth of courier services over the last decade and the development of self provided delivery of bulk advertising at the local level has been obviously extensive even though concrete estimates of volumes have not been available.

[14] In the TVA enabling legislation, a three-person board of directors was given total autonomy over management and was immunized from any regulatory body. President Roosevelt took the position that by putting the operation of TVA in the hands of a technocracy, management problems could be solved on ostensibly "non-political" grounds by using scientific, engineering and administrative expertise without the constraints of regulatory intervention. As Roosevelt desired, this management structure allowed TVA to "be clothed with the power of government yet enjoy the flexibility and initiative of private enterprise" (Sources: The Tennessee Valley Act of 1933 and U.S. Senate 1985a).

[15] The rates of growth in electricity rates in the first half of the 1980's for TVA versus the U.S. average for electric utilities were as follows (U.S. Senate 1985a):

Year	TVA	U.S. Average
1977	-3%	4%
1978	8%	-1%
1979	2%	-1%
1980	1%	4%
1981	15%	4%
1982	11%	3%
1983	22%	4%
1984	9%	5%

constitutes regulation is doubtful). There was less constraint on pricing and thus more opportunity for relative price increases in public-sector companies.

Even so, it is still necessary to look within the public corporation itself for the source of a rationale for this deviant performance on pricing and growth in services. There are two potential sources. The first is that set of policies which determine the rates of investment in plant and equipment. The second is the management structure and practices of these organizations.[16]

Investment policies have been unique. The public enterprises have had special access to capital through the Federal Financing Bank (FFB) which guarantees public bonds at interest charges less than market rates for private companies of comparable risk. Both TVA and USPS financed their placements of debt with the FFB at a 12.5 basis-point premium above Treasury bond rates. This rate was lower than on bonds of companies with comparable financial performance. For example, the price spread between TVA and Treasury bonds was generally less than that between comparable private utilities and Treasury bonds by more than 60 basis points.[17] Amtrak not only issued bonds for more than $900 million, but received direct capital grants, so that its whole package of financing was at rates far below market rates.[18] If these organizations had not had access to FFB financing, the additional interest charges which they would have incurred probably would have exceeded $5 billion over the first half of the 1980's.[19]

TVA's capital accumulation rate exceeded that of the thirteen company industry sample in the late 1970's and again in the late 1980's (as in Table Eight). The early high rate can be associated with misforecast of growth in demand for power by the federal Uranium Enrichment Program; the later high rate was not more than a continuation of the same plan, which was to put in place more baseload nuclear generating capacity than any private company. Amtrak had two extended surges in capital growth, as well. In the late 1970's the public company outlays were twice those of other surface transportation companies and were system-wide; after some reduction in this rate in the mid-1980's, it increased again in the late 1980's with a building program confined to its eastern corridor commuter and shuttle service where the

---

[16] Both TVA and Amtrak have gone to the capital markets for financing to a very limited extent. TVA's publicly traded bonds represent ten percent of its total capitalization. The Postal Service's bonds sold on the market account for eight percent of long term debt. (Source: Annual Reports of TVA and USPS.)

[17] Based on a time series (a sample of monthly data from 1/75 to 12/86) comparing the yields of publicly traded TVA bonds and comparable Treasury bonds, it was found that the yield on TVA bonds is on average 77.21 basis points higher than Treasury bond yields.

[18] Federal assistance to Amtrak (in millions of dollars):

Amtrak Operating Grants	Loans	Amtrak Capital Grants	Northeast Corridor Program	Total Federal Assistance
$4083	$930	$882	$1957	$7853

(Source U.S. Congressional Budget Office 1982a)

[19] From the Budget of the United States Government, 1975–1985, and Standard and Poor's Bond Guide, 1975–1985.

TABLE 8   INDUSTRY AND PUBLIC COMPANY RATES OF CAPITAL ACCUMULATION
(1987 = 100)

Year	Electric Utilities Industry	TVA	Mail Services Industry	USPS	Passenger Services Industry	Amtrak
1977	48.9	40.8	11.1	46.9	50.9	27.8
1982	67.9	72.9	32.8	56.8	56.7	82.4
1987	100.0	100.0	100.0	100.0	100.0	100.0
1992	116.2	126.1	132.7	176.2	113.3	119.8

Source: Company Reports; the sample of private companies is the same as in
previous tables.

revenue increases were taking place. The postal service had the lowest relative
rate of investment growth in the pre-1987 period and the highest thereafter.
To an important extent this is misleading and understates the extent to which
capital growth at USPS exceeded that elsewhere, because investment growth
in private-sector delivery firms was dominated by Federal Express outlays on
airframe capacity (for a service not directly comparable to the full range of
postal services). USPS, as with the other two public enterprises, went on a
campaign of capital funding at the Federal Financing Bank that was extraordinary in scope relative to both its markets and to most other companies in
similar markets.

The effects of these differences were apparent. The accumulation of assets
by TVA and the Postal Service was extremely large in comparison to private
firms in industries. (See Table Nine). The 3.5 fold enlargement of capital in
TVA was more than one hundred and fifty percent that of the industry,[20] and
the four-fold enlargement of Postal Service capital was also twice that of the
mail services industry. Only Amtrak, with its fourfold capital increase, fell

TABLE 9   INDUSTRY AND PUBLIC COMPANY ASSETS (BILLION CURRENT $)

Year	Electric Utilities Industry	TVA	Railroads Industry	Conrail	Mail Services Industry	USPS	Passenger Services Industry	Amtrak
1977	59.2	9.1	38.4	3.2	6.1*	12.3	6.4*	1.0
1982	86.4	19.0	48.1	5.5	8.1	19.8	11.5	3.1
1987	132.7	25.6	55.6	6.8	18.3	32.1	31.6	3.8
1992	151.2	30.5	58.4	7.3	30.1	47.7	40.8	4.3

Sources: COMPUSTAT Annual Industrial and OTC file, Quarterly Utilities file and
annual Research file for Industrial data. Various "Annual Reports" of individual
companies. The "industry" estimates are the levels of assets for the counterpart
private sector firms.
* = 1980; 1978 not available

[20]   In the middle to late 1970's, TVA's forecast of annual growth of electricity demand justified
a plan to extend capacity. From 1977 to 1984 net utility plant investment actually increased
by forty-seven percent. Because of TVA's favorable financing relationship with the Federal
Financing Bank, they were able to accumulate this amount of debt without increased rates or
a financing limit.

short of the six times increase of the local service airlines that made up the counterpart private companies.

While public company labor costs were high relative to levels in private companies throughout the last fifteen years, they did not increase rapidly. Labor costs as a percent of sales did not increase more rapidly in the Postal Service than in private mail-type services, even though they were considerably greater as a percent of sales (see Table Ten). Amtrak's labor costs as a percent of sales were more than twice those of the airlines and bus companies offering comparable service; and on a passenger-mile basis, they were more than twice as much as the airlines and more than triple those of the bus companies. But as a percent of sales they declined over the 1977-1992 period. The Postal Service continued to realize declines in employee costs per dollar of revenues at levels sufficient to match those of the private carriers. This improvement in revenues generated per employee was the result of the capital outlay program on "automation" and of reductions in the rate of growth of employment. All three also experienced increases in output per employee (see Table Eleven), based on large capital outlays and reduced employment growth. Indeed, TVA matched the performance of private companies while Amtrak reached levels one-fourth rather than one-fifth that of the private transportation companies by 1992.

Altogether the three public companies set out on similar strategies in investment and in pricing. They invested at a prodigious rate, and covered part of those higher costs with cash flow from price increases. The low rates of sales growth consequent from the large price increases placed the public enterprises in the position of relative stagnation, a position not associated with this "public" status. The contrast raises questions about their basic management plans and practices.

Management Practices In The Three Public Corporations

Were there procedures in the workings of the corporations that caused such results? In fact, their management systems do not require them to respond to changes in financial condition, unless such changes bring about withdrawal of

TABLE 10   LABOR COST AS A PERCENT OF SALES (ANNUAL PERCENT)

Year	Electric Utilities Industry	TVA	Railroads Industry	Conrail	Mail Services Industry	USPS	Passenger Services Industry	Amtrak
1977	17.4	16.8*	38.6	53.2*	44.4	89.2	34.5*	261.9
1982	18.4	13.3	36.6	54.2	47.2	81.9	37.7	203.0
1987	17.0	6.1	31.5	44.2	48.7	85.7	34.2	171.8
1992	19.8	7.0	14.9	38.6	48.3	82.2	36.4	153.7

Sources: COMPUSTAT Annual Industrial and OTC file, Quarterly Utilities file and annual Research file for Industrial data. Various "Annual Reports" of individual companies.
* = 1980

TABLE 11   SALES PER EMPLOYEE (THOUSAND DOLLARS PER ANNUM)

Year	Electric Utilities Industry	TVA	Railroads Industry	Conrail	Mail Services Industry	USPS	Passenger Services Industry	Amtrak
1977	120	95	42	36	46*	28*	90	17
1982	184	228	72	55	55	37	134	34
1987	233	229	107	107	57	39	122	53
1992	291	273	144	130	70	56	142	154**

Sources: COMPUSTAT Annual Industrial and OTC file, Quarterly Utilities file and annual Research file for Industrial data. Various "Annual Reports" are used for individual companies; Edison Electric Institute Statistical Yearbook (1981–1985) and Association of American Railroads "Railroad Facts:" (1986).
* = 1980   ** = 1990

federal budget support. When that takes place then their conditioned response takes the form of replacing funds lost by reduced subsidy with those from increased prices or from reduced operating costs to be achieved by adding to high rates of capitalization. Management also responds to changes in the nature of the subsidy, particularly when the subsidy provides for services that are "public" with consumers and voters.

These behaviors follow from structural conditions that are specific to the public company. They include: (1) the relationship of governing boards to management; (2) the nature of responsibility and accountability of the chief executive officer; (3) the independence of subordinate managers; (4) the decision process on capital expenditures and pricing.

Governing Boards

At the highest level, the boards of public corporations have not monitored the performance of management in ways comparable to private company boards elected by beneficial owners.[21] The boards of Amtrak, Conrail, TVA, and the Postal Service have been appointed for diverse purposes. Members have been affiliated with such constituencies as the employees, the business community, or directly-related consumer groups such as railroad passenger associations,

---

[21]   Consider the following remarks of Rep. William D. Ford, Chairman of the House Committee on Postal Service and Civil Service: "The Board of Governors, which Congress created in the Postal Reorganization Act of 1970, was supposed to be akin to a corporate board of directors in the private sector. Our idea worked for a while, but during the last few years we have seen our creation turn into something which isn't remotely similar to a corporate board. Individuals (board members) have interfered unduly with collective bargaining, with financial planning, with service modernization, with procurement, and with direct intervention in personnel matters. During the last 18 months, we have had three Postmasters General – and it will be four with the imminent departure of Albert Casey. All have found it impossible to do the job because of the board's meddlings. We are here today in response to a series of incidents which have caused the members of this committee to question the ability of top management of the U.S. Postal Service to govern effectively." (U.S. House of Representatives 1986a, pp. 2–3).

large Postal Service users, or large industrial consumers of electric power.[22] Still other members have been elected to represent the body politic – the "public interest" – having been chosen as a reward for political service.

In each of the processes of board supervision in these three public corporations, management performance evaluation has been based on concerns such as ensuring levels of employment and maintaining service to certain constituencies.[23] Resolving the resulting differences among board members as to which constituencies can be difficult and prolonged. In effect, most board activity has been directed at reaching compromises among competing interests of constituencies.

The most egregious record on management evaluation has been provided by Amtrak's board and Chief Executive in the 1990's: "Amtrak was distracted by infighting on its board over Mr. [Graham] Claytor's leadership. Mr. Gingrich says he tried to line up fellow board members in 1992 to oust Mr. Claytor but failed to get enough votes. . . even when Mr. Claytor indicated a desire to step down he didn't seem to be in a hurry. 'He just felt he was indispensable because of his contacts [in Congress],' says Donald Walker of Korn/Ferry International." This had adverse effects on current operations: "Because of the delay in finding a new chairman, decision-making atrophy set in and 'all issues that suggest change weren't dealt with' says Amtrak director Robert Kiley almost half a decade was lost".[24]

The Postal System board responds to its 1970 statute mandate to (1) deliver mail to everyone promptly and courteously (2) advance the interests of its employees (3) meet the demands of special mailers for both prompt and low cost service (4) operate so that its revenues cover all costs. Members of the board have come from all parts of the country with varying experience and abilities to deal with delivery issues, work force collective bargaining, and financial problems. They have had differing degrees of attachment to these four goals.[25] Overall the governing boards have operated as political bodies, making tradeoffs among policies. They have not been monitors of senior management.

---

[22] Zeckhauser and Horn maintain that special groups are rewarded when there is an "available pot". An "available pot" is the surplus that could be generated from resources given to the SOE (State-Owned Enterprise) if it were run as a private, for-profit firm (MacAvoy, Stanbury, Yarrow and Zeckhauser, *Privatization and State-Owned Enterprises: Lessons from the United States, Great Britain and Canada*, Chapter 1, p. 14). The larger the surplus, the more benefits will be redistributed to "powerful consumers and employees" (Ibid., Chapter 1, p. 42).

[23] The Amtrak board centers its activities on route decisions. As stated by the Government Accounting Office, "Amtrak has the authority to add or discontinue routes using Congressionally approved procedures that consider economic, social, and environmental factors; however, it has not used these procedures effectively to discontinue its most unprofitable routes. Accordingly, a key provision of the Amtrak Improvement Act of 1975 gave Amtrak's board of directors responsibility for changing Amtrak's routes and services. The act also specified, however, that the Board must publicly describe the procedures it would use in making its route decisions" (U.S. General Accounting Office 1978a).

[24] "How Amtrak Derailed Just Five Years After Its Touted Comeback." *The Wall Street Journal*, April 6, 1995, p. 1.

[25] Cf. W.T. Mayton, "Missions and Methods of the Postal Power," in J.G. Sidak, Governing the Postal Service (The AEI Press, Washington, D.C., 1994) Chapter Four, pp. 96–107.

The Chief Executive

Without a board directed to monitoring performance according to a corporate plan, the chief executive of the public enterprise has had relatively greater freedom to set her/his agenda. Since the governing body does not specify where, across the spectrum of potential results, emphasis should be placed, the chief executive has been able to choose that combination which would best sustain her/his current administration. At the least, given that almost all appointees have demonstrable skill at reaching compromises, the stage has been set for maintaining the support of the various constituencies that could adversely affect continuity. At the most, in the last decade, there has been a lack of accountability for performance measured in terms of providing service at lower prices and in greater volume.[26] Management structures instead permitted a forging of broader interests, in the words of the Amtrak chairman, ". . .we are definitely on the road to our announced goal of covering all of our operating costs with our own revenue. . . (but) only if we get the necessary additional capital".[27]

Again, this state of affairs follows from the limits on boards that prevent them from rewarding or penalizing executive performance.[28] But the constraint has been tightened by that authority having been subsumed in the appointments and dismissals process of the White House staff and Congress.

[26] This is not to say that management has been without constraint. To a great extent, Congressional committees have usurped management foundations. By shaping Amtrak's route structure to fit Congressional, as opposed to market, demands for service, the legislative branch affected operating efficiency. In 1971, when Amtrak proposed its routes, three trains were to stop in Indianapolis, but none in Cleveland. Indiana's Congressional delegation projected a strong interest in national transportation policy. Ohio's did not. Only after the Ohio Congressmen protested was Cleveland restored to the intercity system. The "Harley Staggers Special", nicknamed for the Congressional leader, ran through the state of West Virginia at twenty-two percent of capacity in 1975. Discontinuance of the route was not considered. In 1977, "Senator Mansfield's Train", which ran across southern Montana, suffered a deficit of almost $25 million. That train, too, continued operation. In a typical Amtrak budget dispute, Secretary of Transportation Brock Adams called for route cuts in 1979, but Congress fought off the proposal by citing among other things a need for "regional balance:. Such interference exemplified the difficulty of trying to please legislators in control of Federal purse strings (Itzkoff 1985, p. 126). This pattern has extended into the 1980's up to the middle 1990's. The House in August, 1994 received from Representative John Dingell the proposed Amtrak Investment Act of 1994, a proposal to undertake the first stages of a program to expand station facilities for the Burbank-Glendale-Pasadena routes of Amtrak. Cf. *Amtrak Investment Act of 1994*, Report to the Committee of the whole House to accompany H.R. 4111, p. 16.

[27] *Amtrak Reauthorization*, hearing before the subcommittee on transportation and hazardous materials of the Committee On Energy and Commerce, House of Representatives, 102nd Congress, Second Sess. On H.R. 5, a bill to authorize appropriations for the National Railroad Passenger Corporation, February 20, 1992, testimony of Graham Claytor, p. 45.

[28] Conversely, the boards of directors for private enterprises are theoretically chosen for their reputation and ability to direct and manage a company profitably for the shareholders. Since there is income to be gained by being a board director, there is an incentive for board members of private enterprises to execute their duties appropriately or else be removed by management or in an unfriendly tender offer (Fama 1980, p. 288–307; Jensen and Ruback 1983, pp. 5–50,; Hermalin and Weisbach 1987).

The Presidential Appointments Office designates the individual to be appointed the senior executive in TVA and the Postal Service. In a number of instances in the 1980's, that individual had limited qualifications to manage a complex and large-scale organization in ways that would result in improved performance, even though he brought to the position an impressive record in national politics. In other instances particular legislators involved in that company's operations determined the appointment. Only in the extreme case (e.g. the appointment of Albert Casey as Postmaster General)[29] had the price and cost performance of the public company deteriorated to a point where someone of widely recognized managerial talent and energy had to be brought in to clean up the "mess". But Casey left after nine months,[30] a departure which reflected the continuing problem in public enterprise of concern for performance at the highest level of management.

Subordinate Management

There has been a structural problem with management schemes for achieving goals through improved performance at the middle levels of these organizations. The mechanisms for rewarding achievement in reaching objectives do not exist, at least not comparable with those in private-sector organizations. And, even where such mechanisms have been in existence, the performance standards, particularly in cost control and productivity improvement, have not been comparable to those in counterpart private-sector enterprises.[32]

Further, there has been a unique relationship of second- and third-level executives to outside constituent groups.[33] These managers respond directly

[29] Another example where industry experience improved results was the appointment of W. Graham Claytor, Jr., a former president of Southern Railway, who became Amtrak's president in 1982. Within his first year, he met the Reagan Administration's mandate of covering one half of all operating costs from revenue (Itzkoff 1985), and he managed an important labor agreement covering most of Amtrak's 18,000 workers. He effected a twenty-five percent reduction in headquarter staff ("Amtrak Gets on Right Track", *Business Week*, June 21, 1982, p. 99). But he stayed too long, as noted above, holding back further improvements in performance in the late 1980's and early 1990's.

[30] Terms of Postmasters General in the 1980's included as follows: William F. Bolger, 1978 to 12/84 (retired); Paul N. Carlin, 1/85 to 1/86 (ousted); Albert V. Casey, 1/86 to 8/86 (short term appointment); Preston R. Tisch, 8/86 to 1/88 (resigned).

[31] For example, in the USPS, performance rewards (through merit-based salary increases, bonuses and promotions) are limited due to the statutory cap on top postal executive pay, an administratively set pool of funds available for management pay increases, and salary compression within and among pay grades (U.S. Postal Service 1986, p. 12).

[32] In its study of federal organizational productivity, McKinsey & Co. identified a number of factors that acted as barriers. Among these are: productivity improvement is not regarded as having a major payoff; a continuous "higher level" interest in productivity is thought to be lacking; motivation suffers from a lack of incentives; personnel management constraints limit managerial initiative, and productivity suffers from appointees' lack of experience (McKinsey & Company Inc. 1977).

[33] Although not directly related to the four subject public enterprises, an example of this phenomenon at work occurred when the Western Area Power Administration was formed in 1978 as part of the structure of the Department of Energy. Congressional pressures from both sides of the aisle were brought to bear to add about two hundred employees (or ten percent of the work force) to the staffing tables of that organization. These additional positions were

to specific constituencies. As one example, the rate-setting mechanisms in the Postal Service arguably favor second- and third-class mail users. Given their depth of knowledge, they have been advantageously positioned to assist middle management in determining cost allocations which justify rate levels by class. The countervailing forces of household mail users – largely an appeal to consumer benefits – have been rendered less effective because second- and third-level postal system management have been largely responsive to immediate pressures from these bulk mailers.[34] Moreover, postal workers' unions working through Congressional delegations have established in bargaining procedures with management certain operating practices that otherwise would be determined by middle management (as have rail workers' unions in Amtrak operations).[35] In the 1994 oversight hearings on the Postal Service, Congressman McCloskey "shared concern" with executive vice president Francis J. Conners of the National Association of Letter Carriers that "we are losing a

[33] *continued* sought by a coalition of the new Power Administration's managers and various public constituencies. The resistance of the Assistant Secretary of Energy, who exercised responsibility for these activities, and the Office of Management and Budget, was eroded through several Congressional hearings wherein that particular Assistant Secretary was reminded over and over again that other important items on his and the Administration's agenda would be compromised if his resistance continued. The positions, about half of which were not needed, according to that Assistant Secretary, were added (U.S. Senate 1978a).

[34] The Postal Service Board of Governors proposes new postal rates based on information supplied by Postal Service management. To do so, management must first determine the cost of each class of mail. Each mail class must bear all of its directly attributable costs, as well as a portion of institutional postal costs (those not attributable to specific mail classes). The nine rate-making criteria in the Postal Reorganization Act are sufficiently diverse to allow management considerable latitude as to their methodology of allocating these institutional costs (which usually range between forty and fifty percent of total postal costs). Management has taken the position that assignment of these costs should reflect the estimated demand elasticity of each class of mail. As one example, the Postal Service's billion-dollar National Bulk Mail System, built between 1971 and 1976, handles bulk third- and fourth-class mail, and some second-class mail. Because of their costing methodology, the Postal Service was able to charge fifty-eight percent of the bulk mail system's costs to first-class mail (Tierney 1981, p. 125).

[35] Certain features of railroad union agreements contributed to Amtrak's labor intensiveness. A rail engine crew typically receives a full day's pay for a 100-mile trip. So, at an average speed of forty miles per hour, a two-man crew costs two days' pay for a two-and-a-half-hour run. Similar agreements increase the cost of train crews. For example, a 1978 study by the General Accounting Office examined the costs of Amtrak train number 355 from Detroit to Chicago (U.S. General Accounting Office 1978b, p. 20). For a five-hour trip, the two, two-man engine crews altogether received 5.6 days' pay (an average of 1.4 days' pay per crew member), and the two-man crew each received just under two days' pay. The on-board service crew of three employees was paid on an hourly basis with a guaranteed 180 hours of pay per month. All in all, a trip that required less than forty labor-hours cost Amtrak more than sixty-six labor hours in pay. Not all Amtrak employees work under such costly contract provisions, of course, since labor contracts vary among the operating railroads and the crafts. But such arrangements do pervade the system, and they are very costly to Amtrak (U.S. Congressional Budget Office 1982b). There were reversals of these conditions in the late 1980's, as Amtrak embarked on a new program to contain costs so as to eliminate operating losses by the year 2000. But "Amtrak's labor productivity improvements, brisk in the 1980's, have slackened. Amtrak estimates union work rules and manning levels cost it an extra $60 million a year. Just attaching a passenger car to a locomotive requires a conductor to open the coupler, a car man to connect air hoses and an electrician to plug in electric cables." ("How Amtrak Derailed", op cit. p A 10).

lot of the delivery of magazines and some third-class mail through the alternate delivery firms . . . we are working through the Postal Service to see if we can do something about it."

Subordinate managers, with compensation systems scaled to mail volume and employment, increased utilization of the system no matter how inefficient that may be.[36] The resulting separation of operations from plans has been apparent but the public corporations have not been accountable for the results.[37] This condition has become even more prominent in the 1990's. As explained by R. Handleman, President of the National Association of Postal Supervisors, "While the top echelon in the Postal System would like to see every division implement some of these (automation) processes, it is not done. If a division manager doesn't want to implement, he just says we are not implementing and that is it".[38] What incentive systems there are have been lacking in focus. Upper level managers have not set rewards for middle level managers for performance in accordance with either the "public" or even the "private" objectives of an enterprise.[39] Most pay scales have replicated civil-service standards, based on experience, job scope (including "sizing" factors) and promotion, which work well only when the organization expands.[40] Systems which would have measured performance related to

---

[36] On this matter of what management actually does, John H. Riley, the Administrator of the Federal Railroad Administration, spoke of the lack of supervision: "Is it not true that today in many cases the conductor, the main man in charge or the woman in charge of that particular train, never sees the engineer or the fireman or the brakeman, neither before they go out of that station, nor on the entire run, because they essentially use radio communication? And if that is true, might it not be a good idea for management of the railroads and the railroad unions to get together to begin to affix responsibility by having someone who is in charge take a look at these people who are taking these trains out of the stations?"

[37] David M. Boodman, vice president at Arthur D. Little, testifying to Congress in 1982 as a consultant to the USPS: "One must recognize the differences in the avenues to efficiency available to the Postal Service as compared with a private corporation. Few private investors would consider placing funds in an enterprise required to provide so uniform a service at so uniform a price when the costs of serving different segments of the market vary so widely, and when the degree of variation inevitably will increase as the costs of transportation and labor increase" (U.S. Congress, Joint Economic Committee 1982, pp. 313–14).

[38] Testimony of Rubin Handleman, Committee On Post Office and Civil Service, "Oversight Hearing On The U.S. Postal Service," May 12 – September 30, 1992 # 102–51 (Washington: U.S. Government Printing Office, 1992) p. 381.

[39] From a statement submitted by Congressman John J. Duncan: "TVA's salary structure needs an overhaul. Top-level executives who manage $5 billion in assets with another $12 billion in construction need to be compensated accordingly. Nor can TVA pay the chief engineer and chief construction manager at a nuclear construction site only $40,000 when such individuals would receive at least $80,000 elsewhere. TVA's salaries are generally too low at the top, about right in the middle range, and too high at the entry level for non-engineering skills. This highly skewed pay scale is extremely dangerous, considering TVA's high degree of employment in the middle and lower levels" (U.S. Senate 1981, p. 366).

[40] The Postal Reorganization Act itself limited the compensation of any postal employee to that of Executive Level I in the federal service. As a result, the USPS has experienced salary compression within the Postal Career Executive System (PCES) I salary schedule. Annual increases were limited to executives in the lower levels to reduce overlap between the salaries of mid-level Postal Service executives and those of mid-level managers in the Executive and Administrative Schedule (EAS). However, this further compressed the PCES I Schedule. (U.S. Postal Service 1986, p. 12).

executive responsibility have been absent not only because of the politics of leveling government pay, but also because the information required to do so has been lacking.[41]

Investment and Pricing Decisions

Accumulating capital has become the dominant strategic activity of these three corporations in the last decade. As operating subsidies have become more remote as the source of cash flow to supplement sales revenues, then they have turned to building capital. The recent history of the Postal Service has been marked particularly by decisions on major capital investments with questionable returns.[42] TVA's timing and pace of investment in new generating capacity

---

[41] The McKinsey study found that there is a dearth of useful management information – including information to measure results of activities carried out, and reports that would help federal managers initiate and oversee productivity improvement efforts. One interviewee pointed out that "if we can get smart about designing a limited array of productivity-related information needs, we will find that eighty percent of it is already in existence" (McKinsey & Co. Inc. 1977).

[42] In efforts to win support for large-scale Postal Service projects, management has consistently overestimated the volume of new or increased services due to new projects. Their volume projections often fail to take into account the "debugging" problems associated with new technology, the attractiveness of the new service, or the actual costs to mailers. For example: a) A 1976 study of the General Accounting Office examined the (then) recently completed, one billion dollar National Bulk Mail System. The report documented several major problems of the system, and concluded that the system might not generate savings high enough to justify the investment if the problems were uncorrected. Among the problems were: overestimation of capacity; significant underestimation of the volume of mail that could not be processed by machine; high rates of misdirected mail; high incidence of parcel damage (due primarily to faulty system design); inability to meet delivery standards; and higher rates of accidents and injuries than in the Postal Service as a whole. Estimates of annual cost savings from the system by the Postal Service and its consultants were based largely on significant increases in parcel post volume. The estimates on eventual annual savings ranged from $500 million in 1972 to $138 million in 1975, on expected parcel volume of 400 million pieces (U.S. General Accounting Office 1976). By 1981, the Postal Service had a parcel volume of 200 million, versus United Parcel Service's volume of one billion parcels (U.S. House of Representatives 1981, p. 214).
b) The Postal Services's 1982 venture into computerized electronic mail service (E-Com) ended in 1984 after outlays of millions of dollars. In 1983, about fifteen million letters were handled, compared with fifty million first projected by the Postal Service. The service was criticized for being too slow and lacking "the pizazz" to attract business mailers. In addition, the U.S. Justice Department and Federal Trade Commission had charged that the Postal Service improperly subsidized E-Com with monopoly revenue from first-class mail, and the Postal Rate Commission had recommended that E-Com's rates be more than doubled (*Washington Post*, February 25, 1984, p. 12).
c) The Postal Service's projections of nine-digit zip code (Zip + 4) adoption by business mailers, which was necessary to support its automated letter-sorting program, have been overestimated. The USPS had predicted 1985 Zip + 4 volume at twenty-one billion pieces, but the GAO estimated (in October, 1985) the actual volume to be $6.5 billion (U.S. House of Representatives 1985, p. 194). Critics charged that the volume was so low because the Postal Service neglected to consider the costs to mailers of converting address directories, despite the Service's promotion of the system with tens of millions of dollars of advertisements and discounts. Charges were also made to the effect that the overestimation of Zip + 4 usage coincided with inflated return on investment projections in order to justify the program ("Return Zip Code + 4 to the Sender," *Wall Street Journal*, December 10, 1985).

– particularly nuclear power capacity[43] – has led to twice the rate of capitalization as in other power companies. While Amtrak investment rates were cut off by limits on federal capital grants in the newly constrained federal budget process of the 1990's, the company reallocated its more limited funds to projects extending national coverage of its system instead of to those in the Northeast corridor where traffic growth was largest. Given this focus, they then had to come back for further grants to sustain passenger growth in the Northeast. There has been basic and persistent questioning by academics, public interest groups, and competitors of the procedures used to make these decisions. Federal enterprise has not been as purposeful and consistent[44] in adhering to a decision-making discipline based on assessed returns on investment.[45] Perhaps even more significant, once a capital investment decision has

---

[42] *continued* d) In the first half of the 1990's, the large scale capital investment program of the Postal Service was focused on further extensive automation of the sorting process. Although automation was the "key to future productivity improvement, the Postal Service has not yet determined what its expected contribution to productivity specifically is. They have told us that it is not possible to come up with a reliable rule of thumb of how many work hours could be saved by how much automation" [Testimony of L. Nye Stevens, General Accounting Office, Committee on Post Office and Civil Service, House of Representatives, "Oversight Hearings On The U.S. Postal Service", March 5 # 102–3 (Washington, U.S. General Printing Office, 1991) p. 5].

[43] Dialogue between Ms. Katherine Eickhoff, Associate Director of the Office of Management and Budget, and Senator Gordon Humphrey at a TVA oversight hearing (U.S. Senate 1985a, pp. 614–27):

Senator Humphrey: "... you say that there has been insufficient oversight of the TVA power program. Insufficient oversight by whom, in the eyes of OMB?

Ms. Eickhoff: "Almost by anyone. The mechanism really doesn't seem to quite exist. There is an internal audit function, but that doesn't quite have the same sort of outside look at the agency that you would really think of as oversight. FFB asks no questions whatsoever. If you got the authority to borrow, they write the checks."

From further dialogue between Ms. Eickhoff and Senator Humphrey:

Senator Humphrey: "... the concern here with respect to TVA is that they can come and borrow money when they want it in whatever amount they want up to the cap, and they are far from bumping into that constraint. There is a huge line of credit. They can borrow whatever they want whenever they want in whatever amount they want for whatever [purpose] they want, and nobody examines the proposal. That gives the management of TVA enormous flexibility [and] enormous power for which they are accountable to no one, really, in any practical sense."

[44] "The effect of new equipment purchases on operating costs is not clearly explained in the plan. One of Amtrak's justifications in early five-year plans for new equipment was reduced maintenance costs. Rather than decreasing as more and more new equipment is delivered, the maintenance costs for equipment are increasing. Amtrak's plan showed a $1.3 million decrease in equipment maintenance costs – in 1980 only. In the other four years, the maintenance cost will increase by a total of $14.6 million over the 1977 level. Reasons for the increases are not given in the plan" (U.S. General Accounting Office 1977).

[45] From an OMB report at the same hearing as mentioned in footnote 43, (Ibid., pp. 677–8): "The reasons behind TVA's performance are no doubt due to a number of factors. However, it appears the lack of oversight has contributed to this situation. For example, more vigorous oversight might have prompted TVA to respond more quickly to changes in the marketplace. Miscalculations of electricity demand growth have resulted in the cancellation of eight of the seventeen nuclear generating units originally planned by TVA. While this general problem occurred in a number of utilities, some critics have argued that TVA did not move fast enough or as far as it should have to rein in its nuclear construction program. Stronger oversight might have helped TVA to respond faster".

been made, project management systems have not been disciplined in putting in place the systems to make the equipment generate lower costs and larger net cash flow. Control mechanisms used to ensure achievement of on-stream performance by certain dates have not functioned.[46] The result has been that productivity gains, despite the ability of the government enterprise to raise money at advantageous interest rates, have not been substantial and the returns to these investments have been limited.

Pricing decisions have been reactive to these large scale investment programs of the three companies. As a matter of course, pricing decisions are among the most strategic that any management can make. They set the terms of competition relative to an existing customer base. More central, in these companies they have become the means to generate that return on capital sufficient to ensure that capacity will be available in the future to serve that customer base. To the extent that political concerns impinged on these decisions, the strategic positioning of the public corporation became disoriented from efficiency and competitiveness norms.

In fact, each of these organizations made price changes that favored certain consumer groups while pushing back demands in Congress that they become free of federal budget subsidy. Since TVA has been protected from competition, the USPS with its semi-independent rate commission has been free from direct interference in pricing, and Amtrak has been limited only by intermodel competition, each has been able to increase prices more rapidly than regulated private companies or unregulated competitive companies. And when the 1990's brought increasing Congressional pressure on all three enterprises to reduce annual operating deficits, their responses were much the same – to accelerate the rate of price increase. The increases included those on classes of consumers with price-elastic demands, so that they resulted in reductions in system sales, and affected service to the home consumer of electricity, to the first-class mailer, and to the tourist-class Amtrak passenger. They, for the most part, negated the strategic purpose of these enterprises in providing extended service.

Their programs towards deficit reduction in operations have differed sharply from those in either regulated or unregulated private companies. They increased prices the most for groups that had least recourse to the Congressional oversight or the federal appointments process. They used higher prices to recover outlays for failed investment programs. Private, unregulated companies have not had recourse to higher prices to generate funds to pay for imprudent investments; and regulated companies have had requests for rate increases rejected in most important cases in which the reported cost increases were based on imprudent investments. In contrast, TVA has increased prices

---

[46] As one example, a 1981 GAO report recommended that Amtrak should try to continue to improve its trackage contracts (U.S. General Accounting Office 1981). A similar GAO report in 1977 had described how the incentive contracts with other railroads were costing money (U.S. General Accounting Office 1977). Still, in 1982 $305 million was spent for these services, equal to twenty-five percent of Amtrak's total operating expenses, and seventy percent of its operating income. By 1989 Amtrak had made partially revised agreements with fourteen railroads but continued to operate under the original agreements with five (Conrail; ICG Railroad; Atchison, Topeka & Santa Fe; Baltimore & Ohio; and Chesapeake & Ohio).

rapidly in order to return interest and capital on nuclear plants never put into operation, Amtrak has increased rates to pay for new or refurbished empty long distance trains, and the Postal System has increased its rates to recover investments in automation from which only very limited gains in productivity have been forthcoming. These companies have not only been able, but willing, to increase prices to cover costs for uneconomic as well as economic investments.

Concluding Remarks

Given their financial performance and the workings of their management systems, the three most important public corporations have operated at an extremely low degree of effectiveness. Table Twelve states this position. All three were inferior on the five categories of structure and process in terms of their performance as organizations dedicated to achieving their "public" mandates. The Postal Service was the worst, but only if TVA's recovery of $10-16 billion of mistaken nuclear plant investment is treated as bygones. This ranking is in agreement with a listing from worst to best in price performance – Postal Service and Amtrak had the largest hikes, and TVA the smallest price increases. Poor management practice has been associated with the extent of failure to achieve the mandate for more and better service from the public enterprises.

There are reasons why these public-sector organizations have had more of

TABLE 12   THE STRUCTURE AND STRATEGIES OF THREE PUBLIC CORPORATIONS (RELATIVE TO PRIVATE NORMS FOR EFFECTIVENESS)

	USPS	AMTRAK	TVA	CONRAIL*
Board Authority to Govern	less	same	less	less/similar
Chief Executive Authority	less	same	same	less/similar
Subordinate Management Responsiveness	less	less	less	less/similar
Capital Investment Planning	unfocused	focussed late on revenue generating markets	focussed on nuclear dominance	constrained/ similar
Price Policies	reactive and arbitrary	reactive	reactive and arbitrary	reactive/ similar

Source: See the Text
* Split before and after *The Northeast Rail Services Act of 1981* privatizing Conrail.

a management system problem than comparable private-sector organizations. Public-sector organizations have not been driven by concern for internal effectiveness in operations but rather by serving the "public interest". But "public interest" has been difficult to define, except in terms provided by specific constituencies, and has been interpreted differently at each level of the company administration. Between elections, the public company board and the managers of the public enterprises have engaged in seeking that definition as it pertains to their own interests. This process has worked out to protect groups of employees, specific classes of customers, and management. Most important, it has "protected" very large capital investment, in marginal or irrelevant projects, by providing very large price increases. As a consequence, the managers have operated with only limited concern for the interests of the nominal owner – the consuming public – that would have them keep prices down and sales growing at faster rates than in the private companies.

These were the results because management has had greater discretion, which when applied has led to forms of behavior detrimental to the basic "public" purposes of the organization. Strategic decisions on service offerings, on the level of investment, and on the matching of labor supply to service demand have all proceeded without review and appraisal for effectiveness from any source except the Congressional subcommittee on annual funding authorizations. The mechanism used to substitute for internal discipline to achieve strategic goals – political oversight and inspection – has not worked.[47]

The quarrel is not with de facto subsidization of third-class mail or TVA programs for augmenting its power plant capacity. Nor is it with the original purposes which the Congress pursued in establishing these structured organizations. It is with whether these organizations should continue in a structural mode proven to lack effectiveness on the very "public interest" terms which govern th1e debate on relative merits of private versus public ownership. This is central because their managerial systems have operated so as to achieve neither public nor private goals. With such fault in the public corporate structure, then eliminating government ownership appears to be the only possible means for correction in the long run.[48]

---

[47] Senator Gordon J. Humphrey, Chairman of the Subcommittee on Water Resources, at a TVA oversight hearing stated that "TVA is not accountable to its customers in any meaningful way. It is not accountable to the Governors of the TVA states. I would observe that it is not accountable in any meaningful way to the public utilities commissions, to the state legislatures, nor is it accountable to the market-place, in as much as it can borrow from the Federal Government pretty much when it wants, for whatever purpose it wants, providing it does not exceed its cap line of credit. Nor is it accountable to Congress in a practical sense, because we in Congress are charged to oversee the entire Federal Government, a task which is, frankly, impossible. So, as a practical matter, TVA gets superficial scrutiny once in a while, every several years, and as a practical matter, therefore, in my opinion, TVA is not even accountable to Congress" (U.S. Senate 1985a, p. 611).

[48] The research for this report on industry behavior has been funded by the John M. Olin Foundation Research Program for the Study of Markets and Regulatory Behavior at the Yale School of Management. The assistance of Olin Fellows Paul Coggin, Thanak DeLopez, Lisa Hartmann, Ivailo Izvorski, Eugenio Vega, John Wakiumu, and Sharon Winer is gratefully acknowledged.

Bibliography

Atkinson, S. and R. Halvorsen, 1986. The Relative Efficiency of Public and Private Firms in a Regulated Environment: The case of U.S. electric utilities. *Journal of Public Economics* 29 (April); 281–94.

Borcherding, Thomas E., 1978. Competition, Exclusion and the Optimal Supply of Public Goods. Journal *of Law and Economics* 21:III–32.

Butler, Stuart M., 1985. *Privatizing Federal Spending: A strategy to reduce the deficit.* New York: Universe Books, 136-48.

Conrail, 1981. *Options for Conrail: Conrail's response to Sec. 703 (c) of the Staggers Rail Act of 1980.* Philadelphia.

Fama, E.F., 1980. Agency Problems and the Theory of the Firm. *Journal of Political Economy* 89 (5); 288–307.

Fama, E.F. and M.C. Jensen, 1983. Separation of Ownership and Control, *Journal of Law and Economics* 26 (June); 301–26.

Fama, E.F. and M.C. Jensen, 1983. Agency Problems and Residual Claims. *Journal of Law and Economics* 26 (June); 327–50.

Funkhauser, R. N. and P.W. MacAvoy, 1979. A Sample of Observations on the Comparative Prices in Public and Private Enterprises, *Journal of Public Economics* 11 (June).

MacAvoy, P.W., W. T. Stanbury, G. Yarrow, and R.J. Zeckhauser,1988. *Privatization and State-Owned Enterprises: Lessons from the United States, Great Britain and Canada.* Boston, MA: Kluwer Academic Publishers.

Machalaba, D., 1995. How Amtrak Derailed Just Five Years After Its Touted Comeback, *Wall Street Journal,* April 6, 1.

Mayton, W.T., 1994. Missions and Methods of the Postal Power in *Governing the Postal Service,* edited by J. G. Sidak, AEI Press, Washington, D.C. 4:96–107.

McKinsey & Company, Inc., 1977. *Determining a Strategy for Improving Federal Government Productivity.* (no publisher, no location)

Moore, T., 1970. The effectiveness of Regulation of Electric Utility Prices, *Southern Economic Journal* 36:365–75.

National Academy of Public Administration, 1981. *An Administrative History of the United States Railway Association,* Washington, D.C.

National Academy of Public Administration, 1982. *Evaluation of the United States Postal Service,* Washington, D.C.

National Transportation Policy Study Commission, 1978. *Amtrak: An Experiment in Rail Service,* Special Report No. 2.

Peltzman, S., 1971. Pricing in Public and Private Enterprises: Electric utilities in the United States, *Journal of Law and Economics* 14:109–47.

Peltzman, S., 1976. Toward a More General Theory of Regulation, *Journal of Law and Economics* 19:211–40.

Priest, G., 1975. The History of Postal Monopoly In the United States, *Journal of Law and Economics* 18:33–80.

Pryke, Richard, 1983. *The Nationalized Industries.* Oxford: Martin Robertson.

Pulsipher, A., 1995. TVA's Debt Limit, *Public Utilities Fortnightly,* March 1, 41.

Shleifer, A., 1985. A Theory of Yardstick Competition. *Rand Journal of Economics* 16:319–27.

Spann, R., 1977. Public versus Private Provision of Governmental Services In *Budgets and Bureaucrats: The Sources of Government Growth,* ed. By T. Borcherding, 71-89. Durham, NC: Duke University Press.

Stigler, G., 1971. The Theory of Economic Regulation, *Bell Journal of Economics and Management Science* 2:3–21.

Tierney, John T., 1981. *Postal Reorganization: Managing the Public's Business*. Boston, MA: Auburn House.

Tierney, John T., 1984. Government Corporations and Managing the Public's Business. *Political Science Quarterly* 99:(1):73–92.

U.S. Congressional Budget Office, 1982a. *Federal Assistance to Rail Passenger Service*, Washington, D.C.: GPO.

U.S. Congressional Budget Office, 1982b. *Federal Subsidies for Rail Passenger Service: An Assessment of Amtrak*, Washington, D.C.: GPO.

U.S. Department of Commerce, 1983. Bureau of Economic Analysis, *The National Income and Product Accounts of the United States, 1929–82; Survey of Current Business*. Washington, D.C.: GPO.

U.S. General Accounting Office, 1976. *Problems of the New National Bulk Mail System*. Report No. GGD-76-100. Washington, D.C.: GPO.

U. S. General Accounting Office, 1977. *Analysis of Amtrak's Five Year Plan*. Washington, D.C.: GPO.

U.S. General Accounting Office, 1978a. *Should Amtrak's Highly Unprofitable Routes Be Discontinued?* Washington, D.C.: GPO.

U.S. General Accounting Office, 1978b. *Should Amtrak Develop High-Speed Corridor Service Outside the Northeast?* Report No. CED-78-67. Washington, D.C.: GPO.

U.S. General Accounting Office, 1978c. *Grim Outlook for the USPS's National Bulk Mail System*. Report GGD-78-59. Washington, D.C.: GPO.

U.S. General Accounting Office, 1981a. *Amtrak's Productivity on Track Rehabilitation is Lower than Other Railroads' – Precise Comparison Not Feasible*. Washington, D.C.: GPO.

U. S. General Accounting Office, 1981b. *Further Improvements are Needed in Amtrak's Passenger Service Contracts, But They Wont' Come Easily*. Washington, D.C.: GPO.

U.S. General Accounting Office, 1982. *Replacing Post Offices with Alternative Services*. Report No. GGD-82-89. Washington, D.C.: GPO.

U.S. General Accounting Office, 1983. *Postal Service Needs to Strengthen Controls over Employee Overtime*. Report No. GGD-83-36. Washington, D.C.: GPO.

U.S. House of Representatives, 1976. Subcommittee on Transportation and Commerce, *Amtrak's Criteria and Procedures for Making Route and Service Decisions*. 94th Cong., 2d sess., February 3, 4, and 6.

U.S. House of Representatives, 1980a. Subcommittee on Transportation and Commerce. *Future Funding for Conrail*. 96th Cong., 2d sess., April 15.

U.S. House of Representatives, 1980b. Subcommittee on Transportation and Commerce. *Reauthorization for U.S. Railway Association for FY 1981*. 96th Cong., 2d sess., March.

U.S. House of Representatives, 1981. Committee on Post Office and Civil Service. *Effectiveness of Postal Reorganization Act of 1970, Part I*. 97th Cong., 1st sess., December 10.

U. S. House of Representatives, 1982. Committee on Public Works of Transportation. Subcommittee on Water resources. *The Effect of the TVA Rates on Homeowners, Business and Industrial Activities and the TVA Board Structure and Functions*. 97th Cong., 2d sess., April 30.

U.S. House of Representatives, 1985. Committee on Post Office and Civic service. *Oversight on Operation of U.S. Postal Service*. 99th Cong., 1st sess., Serial No. 99–34.

U.S. House of Representatives, 1986a. Committee on Post Office and Civil Service. *Oversight Hearing on U.S. Postal Service Board of Governors*. 99th Cong., 2d sess., June 25, Serial No. 99-61.

U.S. House of Representatives, 1986b. Committee on Post Office and Civil Service.

Oversight on Reorganization of Postal Service. 99th Cong., 2d sess., Serial No. 99–78.

U. S. House of Representatives, 1987. Committee on Post Office and Civil Service. *Oversight on Operations of U.S. Postal Service.* Excerpts from U.S. Attorney's "Conspiracy Investigation". 100th Cong., 1st sess., July.

U.S. House of Representatives, 1992. Committee on Energy and Commerce. Subcommittee on Transportation and Hazardous Materials. *Amtrak Reauthorization Hearing.* 102nd Cong., 2d sess., February 20.

U.S. House of Representatives, 1992. Committee on Post Office and Civil Service. *Oversight Hearing on the U.S. Postal Service.* 102nd Cong., 2d sess., May 12 – September 30.

U.S. House of Representatives, 1992. Committee on Post Office and Civil Service. *Oversight Hearing on the U.S. Postal Service.* 102nd Cong., 2d sess., March 5.

U.S. Postal Service, 1984. *Competitors and Competition of the U.S. Postal Service.* Washington, D.C.

U. S. Postal Service, 1986. *Comprehensive Statement on Postal Operations.* Washington, D.C.

U.S. Railway Association., 1978. *1978 Report to Congress on Conrail Performance.*

U.S. Railway Association, 1981. *Conrail at the Crossroads: The future of rail service in the northeast.* April.

U.S. Railway Association, 1986. *The Revitalization of Rail Service in the Northeast.*

U.S. Senate, 1978b. Subcommittee on Surface Transportation. *Authorization for the United States Railway Association.* 95th Cong., 2d sess., Serial No. 95–83.

U.S. Senate, 1981. Committee on Environment and Public Works. *Tennessee Valley Authority Oversight.* 97th Cong., 1st sess., March 16, Serial No. 97–H9.

U.S. Senate, 1982. Committee on Commerce, Science and Transportation. *Nomination of Charles Luna to the Board of Directors, National Railroad Passenger Corporation.* 97th Cong., 2d sess., April 13.

U.S. Senate, 1984. Subcommittee on Commerce, Science and Transportation. *Amtrak Safety.* 98th Cong., 2d sess., July 26.

U.S. Senate, 1985a. Committee on environment and Public Works. Subcommittee on Regional and Community Development. *Tennessee Valley Authority Oversight.* 99th Cong., 1st sess., July 16 and 30. S. Hrg. 99–239.

U.S. Senate, 1985b. Committee on Commerce, Science and Transportation. *Sale of Conrail.* 99th Cong., 1st sess., February 28.

U.S. Senate, 1985c. Committee on Commerce, Science and Transportation. *Morgan Stanley Proposal to Purchase Conrail.* Report No. 99–227. July 12.

Wilson, J.Q., 1980. *The Politics of Regulation,* ed. By J. Q. Wilson. New York, NY: Basic Books, 357–94.

Privatization and Regulation in the USA and the UK: Some Comparisons and Contrasts

John Burton

Introduction

Privatization and deregulation have been at the forefront of much economic discussion across the world generally over the past decade. Whilst these developments were to gain enormous impetus from the economic and political rearrangements across Central and Eastern Europe following the dismantling of the Berlin Wall in 1989, the two Western countries that are generally viewed as having been in the lead on these policy developments are the USA and the UK.

As we shall review below, however, the experience of America and Britain in respect of these two developments is somewhat different – if not divergent. The purpose of this short tailpiece essay is to illuminate these matters pithily, and to consider their lessons.

Privatization and Deregulation Defined

An initial stumbling block in the way of such comparisons is that the very terms "privatization and "deregulation are utilized by different authorities in different ways.

Some analysts – such as Logue (1995) in this volume and also the arch-apostle of privatization in the UK, Dr Madsen Pirie of the Adam Smith Institute (Pirie, 1985) – utilize the term privatization in a broad manner to incorporate within it not only transformation of government's stakeholder ownership of a corporation but also both deregulation and contracting-out, whereby government continues to finance provision but opts for private suppliers instead of government-owned enterprises (GOEs hereinafter).

Yet other authors, however, deploy the term privatization in a much narrower fashion, to embrace only those techniques of government down-sizing that involve "transfers from the public to the private sector of entitlements to the residual profits from operating an enterprise" (Vickers and Yarrow, 1988: p.7); or – even more restrictively – cases where the *predominant* share of assets of a concern is transferred by sale to private shareholders (Peacock, 1984: p.3). This latter approach, in contrast to the broad definition of privatization, thus relates only to those techniques of de-politicizing enterprises which involve a fundamental change in ownership rights (from government to individuals).

As Sir Karl Popper (1976) long argued, it is entirely pointless to get bogged down in sterile arguments about the "true meaning" of technical terms. It is equally important, however, to be clear about the way in which terms are used. This essay will therefore explicitly follow the convention of referring to privatization only in the narrow sense, in order to distinguish it from the policy of economic deregulation. This distinction, as we shall see below, is useful for our present purposes of comparing developments in the UK and USA on these two fronts.

Historical Background on GOEs and Regulation: the US and UK

Whilst GOEs are not absent from the American scene – as detailed by MacAvoy and McIsaac (1995) in their essay in this volume – they were never to rise to such economic prominence in the US as in the UK. The estimate of the US Federal Government in 1979, for example, is that in that year GOEs accounted for 1.5% of US national income (US Bureau of Census, 1981: p.245).

The UK's experience with GOEs has deeper historical roots than in the US, and it witnessed – after World War II – a more extensive flowering of this form of economic organisation.

Between 1820 and 1860 the railways, telegraph, gas and water supply industries in the UK emerged and grew, primarily, in private ownership settings. Between the latter date and World War I, however, telegraphy was nationalized (and added to the Post Office – for long a GOE), whilst large local government units variously acquired some 40% of gas businesses, (approximately) 60% of enterprises involved in electricity supply (and also trams), and 80% of water supply concerns (Foreman-Peck and Millward, 1994: p.4).

A second, sharper and more extensive wave of the extension of government ownership occurred in the UK after World War II under the Attlee government, with the bringing under (central) government ownership of the coal, railway, civil aviation, steel, gas and electricity industries, and the Bank of England. Nevertheless, with some exceptions such as steel (subsequently denationalized in 1951 and renationalized in the 1960s; likewise, road transport); coal; shipbuilding and aero-space (nationalized in the mid-1970s); and Roll-Royce – nationalized by a Conservative Government in 1971 as a panic reaction to the company's impending bankruptcy (likewise with British Leyland in 1975 under a Labour Government) – the sphere of GOEs in the UK remained subsequently confined mainly to what is variously described as the utility, "network" or infrastructure industries.[1]

---

[1] The Labour Government of 1974–9 also created the National Enterprise Board to actively expand state investment in industry. This took positions in over 50 companies (in whole or in part), but these were mostly small – with some notable exceptions such as the computer firm ICL, Ferranti (electronics) and Herbert (machine tools). They also established the British National Oil Corporation to handle state investment in offshore oil and gas supplies.

Nevertheless, this was a significant component of the UK economy. By 1976, it is estimated that the British Public Corporations (the major form of UK GOEs), accounted for 11% of UK GDP, and 8% of employment in the country (NEDO, 1976). This is many orders of magnitude larger than the 1979 figure for GOEs in the USA quoted above.

Perhaps because of the relatively lower profile of government ownership in America, the US has been led historically to place greater reliance upon the institution of economic regulation of its utility industries than has been the case in the UK.

American utility regulation has its origins in the nineteenth century, and the sphere of Federal economic regulation was further advanced in the USA in the 1930s in the wake of the Depression, under the Roosevelt Administration. MacAvoy's (1995) estimates in this volume indicate that by the 1970s the economically regulated sector in the US had extended to some 15% of US GDP.

The format for economic regulation that emerged from this long historical development in America is now referred to as the "US model of utility regulation". Although this varies in detail from state to state, it involves the following general features:

* Economic regulation is conducted by state public utility commissions, which have powers of control over the price and non-price (e.g. entry) conditions in the industry.[2]

* In most cases, utilities are owned by private shareholders, and operate as franchised monopolists in legally-defined areas.

* Most of these privately-owned utility businesses are subject to rate-of-return regulation by the regulatory commission. Utilities are typically allowed to charge prices that (supposedly) reflect the "cost of service" and which include a component for a "fair" rate of return as stipulated by the relevant commission.

Historically, economic regulation in the UK was "altogether much less extensive" in the UK than in the US (Swann, 1988: p.28). This, however, was to change radically during the years of the Thatcher government in the 1980s as we shall review below.

Developments in the US and UK on Privatization and Economic Regulation/Deregulation

As noted by Logue (1995) in this volume, privatization in the *narrow* sense was – despite an ostensible commitment to such a policy during the Reagan Administrations of 1980–1988 – to proceed "excruciatingly slowly" in the US.

---

[2] Federal regulatory authorities also exist, particularly to regulate interstate business – e.g. the Federal Regulatory Commission (FERC) which, amongst other things, regulates wholesale electricity supply in the US.

As also detailed by Logue, however, the USA has experienced a certain wave of deregulation since the 1970s; MacAvoy's (1995) estimates here suggest that the economically-regulated sector had fallen to around 11% of US GDP by the 1990s.

In strong contrast, the hallmark of Conservative industrial strategy in the UK under the Prime Ministerships of both Mrs Margaret Thatcher (1979-89) and Mr John Major (1989-?) has, since 1984 (with the successful privatization of British Telecom) been that of privatization. By 1995, this policy had resulted in the domain of GOEs in the UK economy falling to but a mere shadow of that which had obtained in the 1970s, with only British Rail (currently being privatised) and the Post Office remaining as large public corporations.

In equally strong contrast with the trend of US developments, however, this wave of British privatizations was accompanied by a major *extension* of economic regulation, in the form of what has come to be known as "the UK model of utility regulation.

The UK and US Models of Utility Regulation

The general features of the model of utility regulation that was to emerge over the 1980s with the successive privatizations of major British utilities was to diverge substantively from the well-known US model. This was *by design*: the UK model was formulated deliberately with a view to avoiding what were thought to be the inherent flaws – as revealed by both experience and economic analysis – of the American model. Its key features were originally prescribed in two highly influential reports for the British government penned by my erstwhile Departmental colleague, Professor Stephen Littlechild (1983, 1986)[3]. Its main aspects are:

* Economic regulation – which is national in scope – is conducted by an independent regulatory agency (eg, OFTEL in the case of UK telecoms), led by a Director General (DG), who is also referred to as the Regulator.

* US-style rate-of-return regulation is rejected in favour of price cap regulation. In this UK model, the Regulator sets a cap on (certain) prices of the regulated enterprise according to the formula RPI – X, where RPI is the percentage rate of change in the retail price index, and X stands for an adjustment factor formulated with respect to the presumed movement of productivity in the industry concerned (and perhaps other factors). In short, the formula prescribes that the *real* price of the regulated service must fall by X% per annum over a specified period (typically 4 or 5 years, according to the industry). Towards the end of this review period, X is then reset for the forthcoming period.[4]

---

[3] Professor Littlechild was to become a Regulator himself in 1990 – the DG of OFFER (the Office of Electricity Regulation).

[4] Note that different Xs may be – and often are – specified for different services; and that also the regulator may modify the cap in an interim review before the end of the review period.

* According to the original Littlechild specification, the central task of the relevant regulatory agency post-privatization was to be the *promotion of competition*, rather than regulation *per se*.

In his own words:

> Regulation is essentially a means of preventing the worst excesses of monopoly; it is not a substitute for competition. It is a means of "holding the fort" until the competition arrives. Consequently, the main focus of attention has to be on securing the most promising conditions for competition to emerge, and protecting competition from abuse. It is important that regulation in general ... does not prejudice the achievement of this overall strategy (Littlechild, 1983: para. 4.11).

Thus, according to the Littlechild Doctrine, the promotion of competition should be the *primary* element on the regulatory agenda, rather than the price cap element – which he anticipated would wither away, except in cases of intractable natural monopoly. In other words, the explicit assumption of the chief architect of the UK model was that after an *initial* extension of economic regulation to newly-privatized utilities, the British experiment would quickly track (if not overtake) the ongoing US trend towards economic deregulation in the utility area.

There is not the space available in this short tailpiece essay to review adequately how the UK model of utility regulation has worked out in practice; compare the US model. Suffice it to say that the general experience of privatized British utility industries is that:

* Price cap regulation has tended to intensify over time – both in terms of the severity of the X deduction factor, and the complexity of the administration of this supposedly "simple" regulatory approach (Helm, 1994).

* The introduction of competition has generally occurred at a much slower pace than that initially hoped for by Littlechild, and has involved extensive regulatory interventions – often resulting in a very fractured and byzantine competitive playing field. The result has been not that of the rule of the "competitive order" (where feasible) as originally envisioned by Littlechild as a rather swift outcome, but rather one of "ordered competition" (Burton, 1995).

The central problem with the operation of the Littlechild Doctrine of utility regulation – deliberately devised as a "superior", breakaway model to that of the model that has evolved historically in the USA – is that it has been beset by the inevitable problems of partial and gradual deregulation/promotion of competition. In the USA, as the essays in this volume make clear, economic deregulation has not been typically wholesale but, rather, partial – resulting, as one of the eminences of American economic thought in the field of regulation/deregulation, Alfred Kahn (1990: p.483), has put it aptly, in a "host of asymmetries and distortions". The same problems have arisen in the UK.

Prospects for the Future

The forecasting of future political developments is always difficult. Nevertheless, it would seem that currently there are mounting political pressures in the UK to abandon the Littlechild Doctrine – and to turn to some variant of the US model in the area of economic regulation, essentially involving some concept of a "fair"/stipulated rate of return in the utility industries.

The alternative to reregulation is further liberalization – to remove the anomalies and distortions created by partial deregulation. This is the route – if MacAvoy's (1995) diagnosis in this volume is correct – that the USA seems likely to take.

The liberalization route is not without its problems – witness the "stranded costs" problem in the US electricity supply industry dissected by Doane and Williams (1995) in this collection of essays. Liberalization means definitively changing the industry environment in order to unleash competitive forces – a scenario that incumbent enterprises may not have fully prepared themselves for.

Moreover, there are some elements of intractable natural monopoly in some of network/utility industries – although it is increasingly apparent that this element is much less than formerly thought, and may well become even less so over time due to new technological possibilities (e.g. in telecommunications particularly).

The maxim for economic policy that needs to be adopted by any government of a free, democratic society is that of "competition where feasible; regulation only where not". Moreover, where regulation is unavoidably necessary, this needs to be based upon relevant principles of economics, as argued by Baumol and Sidak (1995) in this volume, and elsewhere (Baumol and Sidak, 1994). It seems from the evidence (Bailey and Baumol, 1984) that this is the route – if somewhat haltingly – that developments in the USA have been taking. The collection of essays in this volume charts and examines that course to date – and provides enormous food for thought for policy-makers and analysts in other countries as well as the UK.

References

Bailey, E.C. and Baumol, W.J. (1984). Deregulation and the Theory of Contestable Markets. *Yale Journal on Regulation*, 1 : III.

Baumol, W.J. and Sidak, J.G. (1994). *Toward Competition in Local Telephony*, Cambridge, Mass: MIT Press.

Burton, J. (1995). The Competitive Order or Ordered Competition?: The UK Model of Utility Regulation in Theory and Practice. *Public Administration*, forthcoming.

Foreman-Peck, J. and Millward, R. (1994). *Public and Private Ownership of British Industry 1820-1990*, Oxford: Clarendon Press.

Helm, D. (1994). British Utility Regulation: Theory, Practice and Reform. *Oxford Review of Economic Policy*, 10, 3 : 17.

Kahn, A.E. (1990). Deregulation: Looking Backward and Looking Forward, *Yale Journal on Regulation*, 7, 325.

Littlechild, S.C. (1983). *Regulation of British Telecommunications' Profitability*, London: Department of Industry.

Littlechild, S.C. (1986). *Economic Regulation of Privatised Water Authorities*, London: HMSO.

NEDO (1976). *A Study of UK Nationalised Industries*, National Economic Development Office.

Peacock, A. (1994). Privatisation in Perspective. *Three Banks Review*, No 144.

Pirie, M. (1985). *Dismantling the State: The Theory and Practice of Privatization*, Dallas: National Center for Policy Analysis.

Popper, K.R. (1994). *Unended Quest: An Intellectual Autobiography*, London: Fontana/ Collins.

Swann, D. (1988). *The Retreat of the State: Deregulation and Privatisation in the UK and US*, London: Harvester-Wheatsheaf.

US Bureau of Census (1981). *Statistical Abstract of the United States*, Washington, D.C.: Government Printing Office.

Vickers, J. and Yarrow, G. (1988). *Privatisation: An Economic Analysis*, Cambridge, Mass: MIT Press.